POLITICAL SCIENCE: AN ISLAMIC PERSPECTIVE

Also by Abdul Rashid Moten

ISLAM AND REVOLUTION: Contribution of Syed Maududi

FRONTIERS AND MECHANICS OF ISLAMIC ECONOMICS
(*co-editor with R. I. Molia, S. Gusau and A. A. Gwandu*)

NATURE AND METHODOLOGY OF ISLAMIC ECONOMICS
(*co-editor with M. O. K. Bajulaiye-Shasi*)

ISLAM IN AFRICA: Proceedings of the Islam in Africa Conference
(*co-editor with Nura Alkali, Adamu Adamu, Awwal Yaduda and Haruna Salihi*)

Political Science: An Islamic Perspective

Abdul Rashid Moten
Associate Professor and Head of Political Science
International Islamic University, Malaysia

First published in Great Britain 1996 by
MACMILLAN PRESS LTD
Houndmills, Basingstoke, Hampshire RG21 6XS
and London
Companies and representatives
throughout the world

A catalogue record for this book is available
from the British Library.

ISBN 0–333–64311–9

First published in the United States of America 1996 by
ST. MARTIN'S PRESS, INC.,
Scholarly and Reference Division,
175 Fifth Avenue,
New York, N.Y. 10010

ISBN 0–312–12711–1

Library of Congress Cataloging-in-Publication Data
Moten, A. Rashid.
Political science : an Islamic perspective / Abdul Rashid Moten.
p. cm.
Includes bibliographical references and index.
ISBN 0–312–12711–1
1. Islam and state/ I. Title.
JC49.M67 1995
320'.072017671—dc20 95–7827
CIP

10 9 8 7 6 5 4 3 2 1
05 04 03 02 01 00 99 98 97 96

Printed and bound in Great Britain by
Antony Rowe Ltd, Chippenham, Wiltshire

Contents

Preface xi

Acknowledgements xvi

1 Prologue: Islam, Secularism and the Muslim World **1**
Western secularism 1
Marxist secularism 3
Third World secularism 5
Islam and secularism 6
The shaping of secularism 8
Colonialism and elite formation 10
Nationalism 12
Secular political institutions 12
The economic system 14
Conclusion 15

2 Politics in Islam **17**
Politics defined 17
Politics in Islam 19
Islam and politics: the historical perspective 21
Encounter with the West and Muslim politics 25
Current trends 26
Conclusion 29

3 Islamic Methodology in Political Science **32**
Major traits of empirical social science 32
Reason and revelation 33
Social sciences versus natural sciences 35
The instrumentalist conception of politics 36
The Islamic framework for analysis 37
Facts and values 39
The structure of Islamic values 40
Madinah as the norm 42
Conclusion 44

4 Shari'ah: The Islamic Legal Order **46**
Sharī'ah and the law 46
Sharī'ah and *fiqh* 48
Sharī'ah defined 49

Sources of the Sharī'ah 51
The primary sources 51
The secondary sources 53
Rise and decline of Ijtihād 55
Essential features of the Sharī'ah 56
Sharī'ah in the Muslim world 59
Conclusion 61

5 Ummah: The Islamic Social Order 63
Terminological confusion 63
Ummah in the Qur'ān and the Sunnah 64
Essential features of the Ummah 66
Functions of the Ummah 68
Muslim Ummah: A historical perspective 71
The Periods of the Prophet (ṢAAS) and the *Khulafā al-Rāshidūn* 71
Ummah during the post-*rashidūn* period 75
The Contemporary Ummah 77
Nationalism and Islam 77
Arab nationalism versus the Ummah 79
Conclusion 81

6 *Khilāfah*: The Islamic Political Order 82
The state 82
Karl Marx on the state 83
Max Weber on the state 84
The notion of state compared with the Islamic system 85
The concept of 'state' in Islam 86
Essential principles of an Islamic political order 87
Islamic polity under the Prophet (ṢAAS) 90
The *khulafā al-Rāshidūn* 91
Polity under the Umayyad and Abbasid rule 93
Early Muslim jurists and thinkers 95
Contemporary Muslim thought and the structures of government 98
Organisation of the Islamic political system 99
Constitutional government 99
The executive 100
The legislature 101
The judiciary 102
Form of government 103
Conclusion 104

7 ***Muḥāsabah*: Accountability in Islam** **107**
The legislature: the representative body 107
Obedience to authority: the Qur'ān and the Sunnah 108
The *Khulafā' al-Rāshidūn* 110
Muslim jurists and thinkers 111
Grounds for impeachment 113
Legality 113
Legitimacy 115
Institutional apparatus for impeachment 116
The judiciary 117
The leadership council 118
The consultative assembly 120
Conclusion 123

8 ***Nahḍah*: The Islamic Movement** **126**
Fundamentalism versus *Nahḍah* 126
The *Nahḍah* and the Islamic world view 128
The Salafiyah movement 130
The Sokoto *Jihād* 130
The Mahdiyah movement 131
Various Manifestations of the Muslim *Nahḍah* 132
The Tablīghī Jamā'at 133
The Jamā'at-e-Islāmī 135
The revolution in Iran 136
A comparative perspective 138
Conclusion 138

Glossary 141

Appendix A: Framework of an Islamic State 155

Appendix B: Model of an Islamic Constitution 169

Appendix C: Profile of the Muslim World 186

Notes 191

Select Bibliography 211

Index 218

List of Tables

1.1	Islam vs secularism	7
5.1	The Pair of Brotherhood instituted by the Prophet (ṢAAS)	73
5.2	Nationalism and Ummah compared	79
6.1	Essential principles of the Islamic political system	87
c.1	Gazetteer of States in the Muslim World	186

List of Figures

Preface

When Europe was in the Dark Ages, Islamic civilisation was at its peak. A role reversal took place with the colonisation, during the eighteenth and nineteenth centuries, by European powers, of virtually the entire Muslim land from East Asia to West Africa. It destroyed the mosaic of Muslim culture and fragmented the Muslim Ummah by creating highly centralised, independent nation-states, governed by post-colonial, secular military-bureaucratic elites.

Muslims, for long, have been searching for ways to break out of this situation, to gain control of their collective lives and to link their past to the future. Some suggest a Western-style secular state; others advocate a Sharī'ah-governed society; yet others seek a synthesis of Islam, nationalism, democracy and modern technical capabilities. Each of these concepts has been the subject of several scholarly and popular publications. Some of these writings reflect biased scholarship as is generally the case with 'Orientalism'; others, the work of Muslim apologists, explain the errors, deny the allegations and challenge the malevolent representations of Muslim ideals and aspirations; still others, the work of theologians, are characterised by obduracy and closed to new methods of critical inquiry. In other words, there is a paucity of serious analytical works, especially by the students of political science.

The on-going world-wide Islamic reawakening, which has caused a bewildering array of mistatements and misrepresentations, provides an unparalleled opportunity to explain the teachings of Islam *vis-à-vis* politics to a much larger audience than was previously possible. Given the possibility of greater comprehension as well as the alarming rate of deliberate distortions, it is important to turn once again to the Islamic reality in the context of the Islamic world and the external ideas, concepts and forces which have continuously been playing a role in that world and to which that reality has continuously been responding. This task has to be accomplished with the knowledge and empathy of an 'insider' with a determination to highlight and uphold the priorities which the Islamic culture itself has selected. *Political Science: An Islamic Perspective*, is an attempt in that direction. Rather than concentrating on individual thinkers, it adopts an issue-oriented approach without ignoring the historical development of ideas. Using *ijtihād*, it shows through textual, intellectual and historical evidences, the linkage between

Islam and politics, the essentials of Islamic research methodology, the nature of the Islamic Law, the Islamic social order, the Islamic political order, and the strategies and tactics of various Islamic movements.

The approach adopted in this study is dictated by the nature of the subject itself. For each of the issues covered, first an attempt is made to analyse and understand the concepts by referring directly to the two fundamental sources of Islam: the Qur'ān, the revealed Book of Islam which is the literal word of Allah (SWT), and the Sunnah, the exemplary life of the Prophet (ṢAAS) embracing his sayings, acts and deeds as well as the acts and deeds of the companions that the Prophet (ṢAAS) approved explicitly or through silence.

Second, an analysis is made of the historical process in order to examine the extent to which the ideals, as deduced from the Qur'ān and the Sunnah, were applied, modified or neglected. Such an analysis also reveals the values and attitudes which characterised the Muslim community in history. Since the Muslims look upon the first four temporal successors of the Prophet (ṢAAS) as the rightly-guided leaders of the Muslim community and the ideal reference for both spiritual and temporal affairs, special attention is devoted to the period of the *Khulafā' al-Rashidūn*.

Third, the Muslim political and juristic writings revolving around the issues that developed since the Abbasid period have been discussed in the light of historical development and subsequent interpretations. Given the rich amount of literature, the range of inquiry had to be restricted to representative exponents of *Sunni* political thought of the classical and contemporary periods. The selection of thinkers was based partly on personal preference, and partly on the availability of others' scholarship.

Finally, in dealing with these issues, an attempt has been made to identify equivalent Western concepts, compare them with as much precision as possible and lastly to explain the meaning imparted by Islam.

Chapter 1 initiates the discussion by briefly sketching the social, economic and political problems of the Muslim world. It is concerned with different variants of 'secularism' and its impact upon Muslim society. Throughout, the West remains an important variable, and its corrosive effect on Muslim society, culture and political development is appropriately assessed. It is placed in the context of the overall struggle of Muslims for progressive transformation of their society. It shows quite clearly the kind of coalition building that took place during the colonial period and points out why it has been possible for secularism to achieve its hegemony and the tragic consequences of that hegemony for the Muslims.

Chapter 2 emphasises that any attempt to understand the true nature of political thought in the Muslim world must take into account the inherent link between Islam as a comprehensive scheme for ordering human life, on the one hand, and politics as an indispensable instrument to secure universal compliance with the scheme, on the other. Sufficient evidence of inseparability of religious faith and politics in Islam is shown by the very socio-political implications of rituals like *ṣawm* (fasting), *ṣalāt* (prayer), *ḥajj* (pilgrimage), *zakāh* (purification tax), *jihād* (holy war), and so on. It then examines this linkage as viewed by Muslim scholars and as it existed during the time of the Prophet (SAAS) and the *Khulafā' al-Rashidūn*. Most Muslim scholars would agree with Ibn Khaldun that a radical change took place with the emergence of the Umayyad caliphate which caused a deviation from the orthodox Islamic tenets about a just government. It shows that despite the relative weakening of the linkage, successive rulers refrained from publicly proclaiming the separation of religion and politics in Islam. The few who did so, did it at their own peril.

Chapter 3 attempts to draw a contrast between the Western and Islamic modes of political inquiry. It shows that the methodology and epistemology of Western political science is built around the seemingly limitless power of natural sciences. It exposes the subjective and ideological nature of political science in its own epistemic landscape. By identifying reason and revelation as the twin sources of knowledge, Islamic political science methodology is shown to have been associated with such Qur'ānic concepts as *tawḥīd* (the unity and sovereignty of Allah), *risālah* (messengerhood of the Prophet Muhammad), *khilāfah* (vicegerency), *'ibādah* (worship), *'adl* (justice) and the like. It concludes that Islam accords full freedom to experience and experiment and to rational and intellectual inquiry within the confines of the revealed knowledge. The universality of Islamic values grants a universal status to the discipline of political science which is subservient to the Islamic intellectual framework.

Chapter 4 deals with the 'sharī'ah: the Islamic Legal Order', the Islamic alternative to secularism. It differentiates the sharī'ah from Western law as well as the science of Islamic jurisprudence (*fiqh*) and explains the reasons for conceiving the Sharī'ah as the law. It defines Sharī'ah from various related perspectives, traces its development and assesses its impact upon the society. It argues that the law ceased to mould the society as a result of the classical legal theory which thwarted the exercise of independent reasoning. *Ijtihād* must be accorded its rightful place if an ethical restructuring of the society is to be accomplished.

Chapter 5, entitled 'Ummah: The Islamic Social Order', is a sequel to Chapter 4. It is possible to conceive of law without sanction but not without a social order. How has the society been conceived in the West and how does it tally with its Islamic meaning? How has it been defined in the Qur'ān, by Muslim jurists and thinkers and how did it evolve during the days of the Prophet (ṢAAS)? It discusses the role of the Ummah in the world at large and throws light on its internal constitution or structure. Finally, it compares the Ummah with the concept of nationalism and shows the differences between the two.

Chapter 6 is on '*Khilāfah*: The Islamic Political Order'. It begins by defining the state from a Western perspective and examines its validity for the Muslim world. It analyses various implications of the idea of an Islamic polity. It raises questions such as the unity and multiplicity of such polities, the nature of legislation and sources of power. Can an Islamic political order be democratic, if so, of which variety? Is the Western conception of democracy compatible with an Islamic polity? It discusses the basis of an Islamic political system; identifies it in terms of such fundamental principles as divine unity, justice, equality, freedom and consultation, and outlines its various structures and their relationships.

Chapter 7 follows naturally from the consideration of an Islamic polity and considers the problem of accountability in Islam. It examines the method for protecting the rights of the individual and for limiting the powers of public officials. It argues for the obligatory nature of installing a government, of subordinating the ruler to law, and the obligation of the ruled to disobey an unjust command. To this extent, it reproduces what has been written by others. It goes further, however, in considering the principle of determining the lawfulness of the command, the integrity of the ruler and the need for a procedure which could be followed to deal with a ruler who is found guilty of gross negligence and misconduct.

Chapter 8 looks at the Islamic movements which represent an important phase in the Ummah's reawakening and self-expression. Is this Islamic movement a single phenomenon or does it really comprise different responses to a variety of political situations? It argues that there are certain distinct features which are common everywhere but they never exhaust the richness of the movement. The Jamā'at-e-Islāmī of Pakistan, the Tablīghī Jamā'at which originated in India and the revolution in Iran are cases exemplifying variations in strategy and tactics. They represent unity within diversity and variation that leads to unity.

This work is not a comprehensive textbook. It includes substantive areas and themes of interest to students, academics and experienced professionals concerned with Islamic political studies. These themes have been placed in a historical and contemporary perspective. It should help us all understand the problematic relationship between Islamic and Western political thought, make us comprehend the contemporary Muslim world, and provide some clues for analysing a continuous chain of Islamic movements agitating the entire world.

International Islamic University, Malaysia

ABDUL RASHID MOTEN

Acknowledgements

In the preparation of this work I have benefited immensely from my students in the classroom through discussions, from scholars and activists through their writings, and from friends and colleagues through conversations and exchange of ideas. To acknowledge their contributions is not a matter of ritual, but a necessary recognition of the social nature of intellectual production. My debt to the authors of many works should be apparent from numerous quotations and footnote references. Special mention must, however, be made of Professor Sajjad ur Rahman, a kind and sincere friend, who offered invaluable advice and assistance both at personal and professional levels. I am also thankful to Professor Khaliq A. Kazi for his scholarly comments on various parts of the manuscript. Dr Shabbir Akhtar read the entire draft and made useful observations. I have sincerely heeded most of their comments. Dr Abdullah al-Ahsan and Br. Muhammad Yusuf were readily available to share their knowledge. Professor Mumtaz A. Anwar and his team of librarians at the International Islamic University Malaysia, assisted greatly by locating and quickly procuring requested materials. I am thankful to the Research Centre, International Islamic University Malaysia, for providing funds for typing the manuscript. Sr. Halimahtun bt. Ahmad diligently word-processed many drafts and redrafts of each chapter. Her patience and good humour deserve special commendation. I also want to thank most heartily my editor at Macmillan, Grāinne Twomey as well as production supervisor Keith Povey, for their dedication and hard work throughout the revision process. My thanks to all those people does not implicate them in any infelicities, errors and omissions, which remain my fault.

I wish to dedicate this book to my son, Ahmed Zaki. *Inshā'Allah*, he will find inspiration in his faith and culture and will inspire others to live by Islam in an age which is increasingly secular and materialistic. My wife Ramizah Wan Muhammad, has been very kind and gave me support to persevere under difficult circumstances. She lived, through patience and forbearance, the days when the pressures of publisher's deadlines made me even less sociable than usual.

May Allah, *subḥānahū wa ta'ālā*, reward them all, accept this work as a humble contribution, and forgive me for all errors and shortcomings.

1 Prologue: Islam, Secularism and the Muslim World

Secularism has made deep inroads into the Muslim world; it has become the standard mode of governing Muslim society. To be sure, Islam is the arch-enemy of the secularist's claim to universal acceptance and, therefore, the main target of secularism has been the Islamic faith and culture. It is precisely in these areas that the greatest erosion was caused by the triumphant march of secularism. Despite aping Western manners, and alien institutions, the Muslim world is nowhere closer to the millennium of self-sustained growth. On the contrary, they have become strangers to their own tradition and have become alienated from their own culture, values and belief system. This chapter discusses the nature of secularism, contrasts it with Islam, analyses the forces that shaped the secular idea and assesses the manner and extent of damage caused by secular domination of Muslim thought and life. Determined in the crucible of specific socio-political environment, secularism evinces many forms and shapes varying in contents, intents and origins. It is instructive, therefore, to discuss secularism by focusing upon its Western, Marxist and Third World varieties.

WESTERN SECULARISM

The word secularism has been used in a variety of ways and within a number of different perspectives. In all major Protestant countries, it is used to refer to the policy of separating church from state. In Catholic countries, the preferred term is 'laicism', which emphasises the distinction of the laity from the clergy.[1] Both terms, however, refer to two aspects of the same thing and hence are used in connection with the problems of duality, opposition or separation of church and state.

As a formal philosophical system, secularism was first proposed by Jacob Holyoake about 1846 in England.[2] Its most commonly regarded postulates are three: this-worldly orientation, Western science and liberalism. The first postulate sanctified humanity as the ultimate reality and argues that the significance and ultimate aim of human beings should be sought with reference to the present life and social well-being without reference to religion or to the life in the hereafter. Western science espouses a belief in natural causation and consequent emphasis on the generalisability and applicability of the methodological pattern of Newton's physics for the discovery of truth. The emphasis is upon reason, observation and experiment to the neglect of revelation, tradition or authority.[3] Liberalism, the third constituent, is founded upon humanism, a belief in the integrity and sanctity of the free individual and upon inherent human rights to life, liberty and pursuit of happiness.

The ultimate claim of the liberal was religious and hence, the ultimate freedom emphasised was the freedom of the individual to profess the faith as the conscience called. As John Stuart Mill remarked:

> The great writers to whom the world owes what liberty it possesses, have mostly asserted freedom of conscience as an indefeasible right, and denied that a human being is accountable to others for his religious belief.[4]

By emphasising the freedom of faith, the liberal creed has intended, in the words of Jefferson, 'to erect a wall of separation between church and state'. From this standpoint, a secular state came to mean:

> a state in which government exerts no pressure in favour of one religion rather than another religion: a state in which no social or educational pressure is exerted in favour of one religion rather than another religion or no religion; a state wholly detached from religious (or irreligious) teaching or practice.[5]

The model of the secular state was operationalised politically in terms of the system of elections, the press, and the executive, legislative and judicial arms of government.[6] The system of election was to ensure the liberty of the individual to choose people for various public offices. The press was to be the keeper of the conscience of the people while the three organs of government were to ensure that all active and legitimate groups in the population might make themselves heard in the process of decision-making. Economically, such a society is to be based on a self-regulating system of markets and harmony of interests. Its orientation is toward maximum efficiency, its essential characteristic is a capacity for self-sustaining growth, and it is to operate without much concern for religion, ethics or aesthetics.[7]

The institutions outlined above are evolved under a democratic system which, though stated in secular terms, is profoundly influenced by Christian ethics and morality. As W.C. Smith points out:

> Democracy comes from two main sources: the Greek tradition, and the Judaeo-Christian. It would be irrelevant for us here to pursue this beyond remarking that Western democracy is in an extremely meaningful sense Christian.[8]

Given the above, the wall of separation in the secular society could not and does not involve any hostility on the part of the state towards Christianity. The relationships between the two was, as Holyoake thought, that of mutual exclusiveness. Many liberals, unable to emancipate themselves from the preconception of Christian thought 'demolished the Heavenly City of St. Augustine only to rebuild it with more up-to-date materials'.[9] This eighteenth-century legacy continues to the present day.

Western secularism was well received in the Muslim world. Some Muslim rulers applied this secularist model, following either the authoritarian or liberal path to modernity. Mustafa Kemal Atatürk's scorched earth Westernisation of Turkey in the 1920s exemplifies the authoritarian approach. Turkey was proclaimed a secular republic; European clothes and alphabet were made compulsory, and shrines and religious brotherhoods were closed. Resistance to these policies was met with repression, even death. Habib Bourguiba of Tunisia followed a gentler programme. He maintained Islam as the state religion but prohibited women from wearing the *ḥijāb* (veil) and, in 1961, called upon the Tunisians not to fast in the month of Ramaḍān, in order to fight underdevelopment. In both cases, however, the seeds of secularism fell on barren ground as evidenced, in retrospect, by the active and organised Islamic movements of the last twenty years.

MARXIST SECULARISM

The progress made in the West in scientific, technological and material terms was considered as the outcome of secular moral values. None saw the consequences of the achievement of the West better than Karl Marx. Bourgeois civilisation, Marx wrote, left

> no other bond between man and man but naked self-interest and callous 'cash payment'. It has drowned the sacred awe of pious ecstasy,

> of chivalrous enthusiasm, of philistine sentimentalism in the icy water of egotistical calculation. It has dissolved personal integrity into exchange value . . . torn off the veil of feeling and affection from family relationships and reduced them to purely financial connections.[10]

Repelled by the rottenness of Western civilisation, Karl Marx propounded a political and economic theory of the inevitable course of social development leading to the establishment of a classless society. He clothed his ideas with the force of religious conviction and the certainty of apparently scientific proof. The end product is known as Marxism, which 'was the most powerful philosophy of secularisation in the nineteenth century'.[11]

It should be stressed at the outset that Marxist secularism is essentially the product of Western history, social organisation and the Western cultural outlook. Not merely did its founders and leading figures come from the West, but its entire philosophy rests upon the infrastructure of the Western bourgeois mode of production. Marxism, in essence, is a Westerner's reaction against the West. Consequently, essential principles of Marxist secularism are the same: this-worldly materialism, rationalism, scientism and humanism. The distinction is one of emphasis and on the operational procedure prescribed to redeem mankind from the worst vices of bourgeois civilisation. The humanism of Karl Marx emerges boldly in his condemnation of bourgeois culture, organisation and mode of production, which 'degrades the higher values of humanity' and in his attack on Christianity, which preaches 'cowardice, self-contempt, abasement, submission, dejection, in a word, all qualities of the canaille'.[12]

The claims of Marxism, like those of Western liberalism, are religious in their intensity. Whereas the West had thus far confronted religion only indirectly, Marxism is the first creed to assume a militantly hostile attitude. The preface to Marx's doctoral thesis contains: 'In a word, I hate all the gods'. Religion, to Marx, is unreal; it is the product of man's ignorance of the scientific laws of causality and of his psychological weakness. It sets the stage for man's bondage and alienation and dehumanises him by thwarting his captive impulses. It is both unreal and undesirable. Therefore,

> To abolish religion as the illusory happiness of the people is to demand the real happiness. The demand to give up on illusions about the existing state of affairs is the demand to give up on a state of affairs which needs illusions.[13]

Marx's atheism is, perhaps, the product of the deeply felt social deprivations of his Jewish infancy, a conscious reaction against priests frustrating his love affairs, and against the Lutheran religion which his father had been forced to adopt.[14]

Marxism was put into practice in the then Soviet Union, and in a modified form, in China. In these countries systematic official attempts have been made to suppress religion as anti-social. In almost all left-wing societies, the tendency has been towards ideological monopoly.[15] It means that these regimes carry out protracted and relentless campaigns to stamp out all religious faith in order to establish the Marxist dogma. Even many in the Muslim world considered the words of the Hebrew prophet, Marx, as the sacred text, accepted his ideas as revelation and looked upon him as the god who loathed all other gods.

THIRD WORLD SECULARISM

Secularism in the Third World, like other socio-political structures, was imported from the West and imposed from above. The leaders of the newly independent countries realised not merely that Marxist secularism is out of the question, but also that strict adherence to the Western model of secularism through the erection of an 'impassable wall' between religion and politics would result in their total rejection by the deeply religious populace of their respective countries. Secularism, therefore, had to lose its Western character and flavour. They began to argue about what they called the positive character of secularism. This is better explained in the Indian context by Gajendragadkar's argument that:

> Indeed, Indian secularism recognises both the relevance and validity of religion in human life. . . . In the context of the constitution, secularism means that all religions practised in India are entitled to *equal freedom and protection* (emphasis mine).[16]

Thus understood, secularism *does not mean* the absence of religion in the public arena. It simply means religious neutrality of the state, which is interpreted, in turn, to mean equal opportunity for all religions for state patronage and for participation in public affairs. Sadly, neither India nor any other country espousing this brand of secularism adheres to it in practice.

Although this positive brand of secularism was conceived and announced by Indian leaders, it received constitutional sanction in the predominantly Muslim country of Bangladesh. Sheikh Mujibur Rahman, the founding father of Bangladesh, not merely endorsed the idea but inserted 'secularism' as one of the fundamental principles of state policy in the very preamble of the Bangladesh Constitution which was promulgated in 1972. To cap it all, he even ordered readings from the holy books of Islam, Hinduism, Buddhism and Christianity at the opening of broadcasts by the state-owned Radio and Television networks. Given the inherent Islamic character of Bangladesh, Sheikh Mujib's call for secularism created a backlash among the Muslims, and when General Ziaur Rahman took over the state machinery in 1975, he scrapped secularism and gave the constitution an Islamic colouring.

Other Muslim countries which proclaim secularism include, among others, Gambia, Guinea, Niger, Nigeria, Senegal and Turkey. Though most of these states refrained from entering the word 'secular' into their constitutions, their secular character is, however, evident. Thus section 10 of the 1979 Constitution of Nigeria states that 'The State shall not adopt any religion as the state religion'. Though the wording is vague, the way religious affairs are handled in the country leaves no doubt that the proponents, and particularly those implementing this constitution, subscribed to the Indian version of secularism.

ISLAM AND SECULARISM

Secularism may, therefore, be considered as everything whose origin is merely human, that is, non-divine. Its metaphysical basis lies in the ontological barrier separating Man and God. In contrast, Islam is all divine. Its basis is the Qur'ān, the consummate and ultimate expression of divine will, and the Sunnah of the Prophet (ṢAAS). Its perspective is unitary: all aspects of life, as well as all degrees of cosmic manifestation, are governed by a single principle, *tawḥīd*, the unity and sovereignty of Allah (SWT). There is no being or reality other than the Absolute Being or the Absolute Reality and there is nothing outside the power of Allah (SWT).

Scholars have been at pains to show similarities between Islam and secularism. It is argued that secularism aims at enthusing mankind to strive by the most enlightened methods at its disposal to establish a humane order characterised by social justice and welfare for all.[17] Since Islam admits of such a striving, it could be described as secularistic. To be sure, Islam emphasises reason and critical inquiry in arriving at the truth; it grants qualified individuals the right to *ijtihād*; obligates

Table 1.1 Islam vs secularism

Secularism	*Islam*
Man–made in origin.	Divine in origin.
This-worldly orientation.	Emphasizes this world and the hereafter.
Emphasizes reason, observation experiment.	Emphasizes revelation, reason, observation and experience.
Believes in humanism.	Believes in humanism but within the framework of Sharī'ah.
Separates religion and politics.	Integrates religion and politics.
Relegates religion to personal sphere.	Islam governs all aspects of a believer's life.

acquisition of knowledge; enjoins the believers to do good and shun evil; and, declaring the believers to be the best of the Ummah, made it obligatory for them to organise a humane world order through wisdom and sound exhortations. In these integral features, Islam exhibits an anti-theocratic but not secularistic strain.

Secularism, as stated, is unconcerned with the life in the hereafter. It ignores and, in the case of the Marxist variety, denies the spiritual sphere. Though it rules out all idealism and Utopianism, there developed also a tendency to carry over into the secular realm a number of older idealistic elements which had been identified with religion.[18]

This does not create any common ground between Islam and secularism (see Table 1.1). Islam does not compartmentalise the human life into temporal and spiritual domains. Islam governs all aspects of the believer's life and it also constitutes the essential basis and focus of identity of the follower and his loyalty to the community. The emphasis in Islam is on unity, *tawḥīd*, which explicitly refers to the oneness of the Creator and His Lordship but implicitly provides for the totality and universality of the Islamic belief system. In Islam, as Iqbal points out,

> The ultimate Reality is spiritual, and its life consists in its temporal activity. The spirit finds its opportunities in the natural, the material, the secular. [Consequently] All that is secular is therefore sacred in the roots of its being.[19]

Finally, as Waterhouse points out, in secularism 'error lay in knowledge rather than intention'.[20] In Islam,

> an act, however secular in its import, is determined by the attitude of mind with which the agent does it. . . . An act is temporal or profane if it is done in a spirit of detachment from the infinite complexity of life behind it; it is spiritual if it is inspired by that complexity.[21]

Unlike Christianity, the church and the state are not two facets of the same reality; but 'one or the other as your point of view varies', since

> matter is spirit in space-time reference. The unity called man is a body when you look at it as acting in regard to what we call the external world; it is mind, or soul when you look at it as acting in regard to the ultimate aim and ideal of such acting.[22]

THE SHAPING OF SECULARISM

The shaping of secularist thought is generally explained in terms of a series of intellectual and social transformations on the European continent. The Renaissance, Reformation, Enlightenment and the French and Industrial Revolutions all acted in a cumulative way to create the secularist code.[23] The contribution of Christianity to these transformations, however, was not marginal. The seeds of secularism are found in the doctrine of 'dual swords' which urges 'rendering unto Caesar the things that are Caesar's and to God the things that are God's'. This is interpreted to mean that human society is divinely ordained to be governed by two authorities, the spiritual and the temporal, and that none under Christian dispensation can possess both *sacerdotium* and *imperium*. This, coupled with the Christian view of human history as sacred and divine, and belief in a Golden Age on earth in the future, gave stimulus to secularist concern with the things and happenings in this world. The church–state controversy, which initially caused great havoc throughout Europe, was resolved through reconciliation and rational reinterpretation of the Christian faith. As the writings of Immanuel Kant, Saint-Simon, Auguste Comte and others bear out, the secularists made Christianity or some version of Christianity the cornerstone of faith in progress. In this sense, Christianity is a factor in the formation of the modern European mentality.

Stressing the contribution of Christianity and internal European dynamics is only a partial answer to the emergence of the secular creed. A major part of the explanation is to be found in the attitude of Christianity towards Islam. Christianity, like its predecessor Judaism, was founded in an atmosphere of hatred, fear and a false complex of superiority towards other religions. Its hatred of Islam, however, was total. Islam not merely challenged its right to universality, but attacked the authenticity of its doctrine summed up in the oft-recited four-versed chapter (*Sūrah*) 112 of the Qur'ān. This was followed by a historically unprecedented rapid territorial expansion and conversion of Christians to Islam which caused 'the dissolution of the cultural unity of the Mediterranean basin' and heralded the beginning of the Middle Ages in Western history.[24] Consequently, Christians poured out their genius in vituperating and vilifying Islam, its Prophet (ṢAAS) and its revealed scripture, the Qur'ān.[25]

Armed with science, technology and manoeuvrability, European armies and enterprises overran the Muslim world and reduced all Muslim territories to a colonial or semi-colonial status. The history of Christianity and the history of modern, Western civilisation, thus forms one continuum with no visible interruption. The civilisational mission to 'win the world for Christ' came to be waged by the secular adherents of modernisation.

The task of the colonialists, as suggested in 1901 by Baron Carra de Vaux of the Catholic Institute, was

> to split the Muslim world, to break its moral unity, using to this effect the ethnic and political divisions. . . . Let us therefore accentuate these differences, in order to increase on the one hand national sentiment (*sentiment de nationalise*) and to decrease on the other that of religious community (*communauté religieuse*) among the various Muslim races. Let us take advantage of political conditions. Egypt, for example, governed today by British power must form a moral entity clearly distinct from French Sudan or from Arabia which remains free. Let us make of Egypt a barrier between African Islam and Asian Islam. In one word, let us segment Islam, and make use, moreover, of Muslim heresies and the Sufi orders.[26]

Eugene de Roberty, the Russian free thinker and sociologist, suggested that Europe should 'work on the Muslim elite . . . build railways in the world of Islam and to proceed with a secular colonisation of land and industry . . . [and] to segment the principal Muslim power, the Ottoman Empire'.[27]

COLONIALISM AND ELITE FORMATION

The major victim of the colonial domination was the Muslim's self-image and cultural identity. This was due to the colonial policy of 'progress' and 'enlightenment' which was interpreted to mean education and Christianity. Lord Macaulay's insistence that 'a single shelf of a good European library was worth the whole native literature of India and Arabia' marked the onset of an educational policy which replaced the Oriental with English learning.[28] In the African and particularly the Nigerian context, Lord Lugard held a similar opinion and pursued a similar policy. The educational policy was geared at transmitting the European cultural values to the natives and to make available to the British raj a class of clerks, collaborators and cronies to continue the cultural onslaught of the West. Lord Macaulay summed up the goal as that of forming 'a class who may be interpreters between us and the millions whom we govern; a class of persons Indian in blood and colour but English in taste, in opinions, in morals and intellect'.[29]

The policy was pursued with the full force of colonial might and economic pressure without 'any regard to religious institutions or local habits, or to the influence of other laws handed down from the remotest antiquity'.[30] It received strong support from the evangelical, liberal and utilitarian schools. The principal evangelical figure in the Indian context was Charles Grant; in Nigeria it was the Rev. Walter Miller who, along with Lord Lugard, came up with a unique secular school project called the 'Zaria Experiment' for 'educating the mallams and the Chief's sons in Zaria', Northern Nigeria.[31] With the resources of Western imperialism at the disposal of English language educational institutions, attempts were made to suppress Islamic education and to phase the Shari'ah out of existence. If Islamic education was permitted, it was made a private affair devoid of public funds. If public funds were made available, a secular curriculum was imposed in the name of progress and enlightenment.

The success of the three civilising agents, i.e., 'Christianity, Commerce and Colonialism',[32] can be seen in the inferiority complex it produced among Muslims. Feeling a sense of shame about their cultural heritage, the Muslims, and the colonised in general, embraced the values of an alien Western culture and began to ape the colonisers, emulating specific aspects of their life-style and attempting to shape the society on the model of the Western intruders. This is better expressed by the Indian Prime Minister, Jawaharlal Nehru:

> The height of our ambition was to become respectable and to be promoted individually to the upper regions. Greater than any victory of arms or diplomacy was this psychological triumph of the British in India.[33]

This is true for Africa and the Muslim world as a whole. The Muslims became a queer mixture of the East and the West, out of place everywhere, at home nowhere.

> To the extent that he Westernised himself, the Muslim has in fact barbarised himself. His life has become a conglomeration of styles, discontinuous with his past. He has made of himself neither Islamic nor Western, a cultural monstrosity of modern times.[34]

To be sure, the Western encroachment was felt and received by a small but influential number of Muslims; the great base of the social pyramid composed of the age-old peasantry was far removed from these Westernised segments of the population. From the beginning, a number of people were selected for higher studies and were educated in the colonial legal system. They were then entrusted with the task of running the educational institutions set up in the colonies to develop a new class of Western-educated elite. The traditional leadership was systematically destroyed. The Ulama', who had a virtual monopoly of the legal profession, were routed out in favour of those who studied Western law and education. A foreign-oriented local leadership was thus imposed which eventually became the heir of the imperial powers. It is this class which became voluntary or involuntary instruments of intermediate domination for the Westernisation of the Muslim society. They imbibed and implemented liberal ideas and institutions and incorporated them into their respective constitutions. These included, among others:

(a) the principle of nationalism which claims total, unconditional identification of oneself to the community in which one lives, to the extent of being prepared to lay down one's life in its defence;
(b) the corollary principle of the nation-state and the operation of its structures and institutions; and
(c) the pursuit of a capitalist economic system which transformed the country as part and parcel of the Western financial system and eventually made it dependent on it.

Nationalism

Nationalism, thriving on such diverse factors as territory, language, culture and racial superiority, is an alien concept unheard of in the world of Islam. Nationalism destroys the deeper bonds between human beings. It divides human beings into racial groups, sets up barriers of languages within one single religious community and demarcates artificial territorial boundaries. Yet nationalism found a receptive audience in the Muslim world in the wake of colonialism. The recipients were the Westernised elites because it served as a vehicle for achieving certain goals. 'These goals are usually of special importance to a particular elite within a society'.[35] It was the tool used by colonialists to dismember the Muslim world and to shatter the religious unity of Islam into pieces. The Westernised local leadership adopted it to unite, for a time, the divergent elites and to mobilise much-needed mass support for independence from colonial rule. Nationalism eventually led to the structure of the modern nation-states, each replete with national frontiers, flags, anthems and its own interests in preference and at the cost of all others. These nation-states were carved out without any reference to geographical factors, the availability of economic activities or lines of communication. As a result, many Muslim communities were partitioned into two or more states. Thus, the Hausa/Fulani Muslims of Africa are partitioned into Niger, Nigeria and Chad; the Somalis between Kenya, Ethiopia and Somalia, and the like. Its results are the estrangement of man from his fellow man, frequent conflicts and wars between nations and the dismemberment of the political power of Islam. That these nation-states are unstable, weak and forever on the verge of collapse is a testimony to the fact that these states are artificial creations carved out for the 'natives' without any input from the latter. Yet the ruling elites never, not once, asked whether their national boundaries are rational and are conducive to their viability and potential for progress and development. Maintained by internal oppression and external imperial support, none of these states has solved any of its people's problems. Rather, in this age of a hegemonic world order of power states, Muslim powers have become third-ranking client states.

Secular political institutions

Within these nation-states, the prime concern of the ruling elites has been to perpetuate and exploit the inherited liberal democratic principles and institutions, i.e., the election system, the media and the three arms of government. It is generally agreed that these principal institutions of secular society were an import from Europe, but as implemented in the colonies, these institutions were a travesty of the Westminster model. The system of free and fair elections was not made available in the colonies. The franchise was restricted, controlled and at times coerced to obtain majority support for the government.

> The whole legislative arrangement was an elaborate hoax. . . . There was no freedom which was not suppressed by the judiciary so long as the law was not violated. . . . The executive objectivity which was a guarantee for the citizen at home became a justification for servility in the colonies. The press, an instrument of free expression of views at home, was used to control and influence the intelligentsia in the occupied territories.[36]

Trained in the art of manipulating the secular institutions, the ruling elites of the newly independent nation-states discovered that their holding on to the power position depended on the perpetuation of these institutions. Any attempt at radically altering these institutions, therefore, drew powerful protests since the socio-economic position of the elite is linked with the survival of the inherited system. These institutions, as such, continue and operate as an extension of colonial rule albeit in a more heightened form than before.

Elections in the Muslim world have been notorious for the way in which the dominant political forces have suppressed opposition parties, coerced the masses and workers into voting for the approved candidates, used goon squads to harass political rallies, and miscounted ballots or conveniently lost entire ballot boxes in hostile precincts. On numerous occasions, the army has stepped in to nullify elections after the vote showed an unacceptable party or candidate on the verge of winning. Algeria provides the latest example of such a manipulation. Given this attitude, the ruling elites cannot be expected to share the Westerner's aversion toward centralising power in the hands of a single institution or person. Consequently, one notices the lack of an independent legislature or parliament to act as a check on the power of the executive. In most cases, the legislative branch has been summarily dissolved or suspended indefinitely. In many others, the legislature consists solely or largely of persons appointed by the President or military ruler. In instances where the legislature is elected, it usually has such little real power that it is reduced to the task of ratifying the decisions made by the executive.

Civil liberties are non-existent and the governments are making an increasing use of press censorship to prevent criticisms of their policies and decisions. The 'free' press of these countries is under such an assault that it may not survive at all. As for the judiciary and the judges who insist on donning wigs and robes, they tend to perform an eminently legitimising function for the state and its ruling elite. Indeed, so supportive of the given political regime is the judiciary that any new government makes sure that it makes a clean sweep of the judges of the old regime if the new government is convinced that they will not be enthusiastic at legitimising the new power-holders.

The ruling elites are so obsessed with obtaining and retaining control of the government, and of mustering coercive force to suppress dissent, that there is little in the way of resources, energy or time left to devote to bettering the life of their citizens. The masses find themselves dominated by hierarchically organised corporate bodies accountable only to themselves yet capable of endless manipulation of the political environment for their own advantage. They have acquired an unchallengeable sense of self-importance and omnipotence. For the masses, politics has become a zero-sum game in which they lose all without making any gain whatsoever.

The economic system

In the economy too, the ruling elites adored Western civilisation as the ideal type. The model being followed is that of the West: industrialisation is its firmly entrenched goal, and a capacity for self-sustained growth its major characteristic. Their attempt at rational and scientific control of man's physical and social environment, however, has been unsatisfactory.

Available statistics on 52 Muslim majority areas present a horrifying picture of the contemporary Muslim world. They occupy about 26 million km of land distributed between larger Arab (14 mkm), Asian (6.8 mkm) and smaller African (5.8 mkm) countries. Their combined GNP and GDP figures are respectively US \$786m and US \$746m; and their average per capita income is about US \$1000 only, thus placing them in the category of underdeveloped countries. The labour force as at 1991 in terms of total population was about 17 per cent, 53 per cent and 33 per cent respectively for Arab, Asian and African countries. The larger proportion of it was in the agricultural sector. No Muslim country is truly industrial, as the average industrial labour force is about 20 per cent, with the African group contributing a meagre 10 per cent. Within the international system of economic stratification, the majority of the Muslim population is located in the low income and poorer countries. They are moderately urbanised, have a relatively high rate of inflation, low rate of economic growth, low life expectancy and a very high level of adult illiteracy (see Appendix C).

In general, Muslim countries have not improved their lot despite over three decades of formal independence. On the contrary, poverty has increased, the gap between the rich and poor has widened, agriculture is in ruins and more and more peasant farmers are put off the land. Cultural values have eroded. The sexual code has relaxed, letting young people enjoy increasing freedom to meet and to mate.

The development strategy aimed at economic growth and material prosperity has resulted in the rising incidence of urban crime, prostitution, corruption, misuse of power and other aspects of decadence in general. They are equally the product of technical and professional education which ignore moral and spiritual values. In short, not only are the Muslims poor, they are alienated from their traditions and cultural roots as well. The encouraging sign, however, with increasing militancy, is that they are becoming aware of this miserable plight and are now revolting against modernisation and all its works.

CONCLUSION

Secularism, once triumphant, is now under attack. Many Muslim countries have become progressively ambivalent toward the ideals and institutions of secular society, inappropriate transplants from an alien culture with a different sense of history and values. Secularism has failed to meet the political and social needs of Muslim societies. Problems of political legitimacy and authoritarianism continue to exist. Grievous socio-economic disparities, the breakdown of traditional life pattern and a spiritual malaise characterised by widespread corruption are attributable to the blind following of a valueless social change.

To be sure, attempts at emulating the Western model of modernisation were confined to small elites which, when in power, expanded the functions and powers of the inherited nation-state and its institutions at the expense of the religion and its institutions and invariably allied themselves with foreign powers to the detriment of their respective societies. True to their education and training, they made Islam the handmaiden of the parochial nation-state, manipulated the socio-political institutions to the detriment of their own people and served to undermine the values, beliefs and attitudes of Muslims.

The challenge before the Muslim world is to reassert its identity and reach for its destiny. This is possible only by adhering strictly to the ethics and values of Islam. This requires a firm faith that in the plight of the Muslim world today the values of Islam can help shape priorities of what can and must be done to make society better according to an Islamic scale of values. It warrants as well challenging the power of the nation-states and a turning round of the inherited colonial institutions so that they become servants of the popular will within the framework of Sharī'ah. Despite all these efforts, secularisation has yet to succeed to any significant degree in most of the Muslim world. The victory of the Muslim party in the 1994 municipal elections in Turkey and the triumph of the Islamic Salvation Front in Algeria's aborted parliamentary elections are two recent examples of the shattered secularist dream. Likewise, the rapid rise of Islam as a faith in central Asia indicates the failure of communism to impose secularism and to stamp out the 'opiate of the people'.

2 Politics in Islam

Muslim societies in all of their social, structural and cultural variety are, as Donald E. Smith points out, 'organic' societies characterised by organic religious systems. In these societies, religion tends to permeate all institutions rather than to be differentiated and/or autonomous.[1] The vast body of literature produced since the departure of the colonialists from the Muslim lands suggests, however, either the implicit existence of the dichotomy or at least the feasibility and advisability of radical separation between the spiritual and temporal realms. The seriousness of the issue, evidenced by an outpouring of studies, calls for an examination of the dynamics of the relationship between Islam and politics in order to determine what has changed and what has remained unchanged. This entails, first, an understanding of the meaning and nature of politics from the Western perspective to facilitate a comparison.

POLITICS DEFINED

The word 'politics', originating from the Greek word 'polis', meaning a city, and confined to the study of the state, has acquired a variety of meanings. This has led E.E. Schattschneider to call political science 'a mountain of data surrounding a vacuum'.[2] There are many who question the wisdom of defining politics, arguing that its definition is contextually determined. They adhere to the view that politics is what the political scientists say it is, a position well summarised in Bernard Crick's trite comment that 'politics is politics'.[3] Despite this tradition of disinterest, many definitions have been offered which throw some light on the core meaning of the political scientist's subject matter.

Plato and Aristotle viewed politics primarily in terms of the moral purposes that the decision-makers ought to pursue. The polis, for both, existed to seek its common good, civic virtue and moral perfection. Aristotle saw 'the highest good' as 'the end sought by political science'.[4] Although focusing on the moral purposes that the leaders ought to pursue, Aristotle did not ignore the importance of political structures. He paid particular attention to the ways in which officials were selected for governing the state, the manner in which their authority was determined and the nature of ends or interests they pursued.[5] Many political scientists, in recent times, hold the same position and identify political activity with moral beliefs. They consider the conflict about the nature of the good life as constituting the 'core of politics'.[6] Though their conceptualisation of the good life varies from the realisation of freedom to a combination of freedom with goodness,[7] they subscribe to politics as the art of living and working together.

Robert A. Dahl considers Aristotle's definition of politics as too restrictive since it ties it to state-organisations. He, therefore, reformulates it to read 'any persistent pattern of human relationships that involves, to a significant extent, power, rule or authority'.[8] Dahl criticises the idealised Aristotelian notion of the self-sufficiency of the state for pursuing the good life. His definition broadens the political relationships to include patterns of behaviour that are not co-extensive with national societies. He does follow Aristotle, however, in defining and observing 'offices' or 'roles' in complex political systems.

What Dahl implies is made explicit by David Easton. His identification of 'political acts' as those that 'authoritatively allocate values in a society' has provided many political scientists with what he calls a 'conventional guide' for political analysis.[9] Like Dahl, he sees politics as a set of human interactions, but limits it by emphasising 'authoritative allocations' for an entire society. Furthermore, Easton focuses attention, not only on the goals of policy-makers trying to alter the distribution of scarce resources or values in a society, but also on the authority or power relationships involved in it. As pointed out by Alan C. Isaak, this is 'a compromise position which is neither too restrictive nor overly broad'.[10]

The stress on the value allocation process and policy outcomes reappears in the writings of Harold Lasswell, who defines politics as being concerned with 'who gets what, when and how'.[11] Lasswell's definition is wide in scope, enabling the enquirer to look for politics in many social settings, including that of state organisations. It contains both authoritative relationships and the implication of power and conflict in the distribution process. The difference between Easton's and Lasswell's conception is largely in emphasis: the former focuses attention on the entire political system while the latter concentrates on individuals with power. It is hardly surprising, therefore, to find Lasswell describing politics generally as the 'shaping and sharing of power'.

Clearly, the subject matter has undergone a transformation from an emphasis on state structures to a set of human interactions concerned with the allocation of scarce resources which are considered desirable. Additionally, the nineteenth-century positivist and empiricist tradition has replaced the classical or medieval preoccupation with the search for a good society with a search for the laws of behaviour. Even the notion of power and/or conflict which binds the classical and modern definitions of politics has changed its meaning. The ethical, normative content of power which characterised classical political philosophy has been made irrelevant and redundant by the triumphant march of materialism and behaviouralism. Defined as 'the ability of its holder to exact compliance or obedience of other individuals to his will on '*whatsoever basis*' (emphasis mine),[12] power has been made absolute and omnipotent. Such power could hardly co-exist with the possibilities of human freedom and dignity. Consequently, state power has grown on an unprecedented scale, leading, in most cases, to the subjugation of peoples, the manipulation of their thought and culture, and the erection of fascist, totalitarian states.[13] Politics, therefore, came to be seen, in the words of Isaac D'Israeli, as 'the art of governing mankind by deceiving them'.[14]

POLITICS IN ISLAM

The pejorative image of politics resulting from Western conceptualisation has no relevance to politics as conceptualised in Islam. However, if the essence of politics is the striving for the 'good life', a life lived in worship and in seeking the pleasure of the One and only Allah (SWT) then politics is central to Islam. Four of the five fundamental pillars of Islam, i.e., prayer, fasting, alms-giving and pilgrimage are, 'perfectly suited to promoting *esprit de corps* and group solidarity among its followers'.[15] These pillars of Islam are not meant for pure spiritual upliftment, but have socio-economic and political significance as well. They are closely related to human behaviour and activity. Thus, in the prayers, which are incumbent upon the faithful to be conducted at appointed hours (Al-Qur'ān, 4:103), preferably in congregation, a believer executes a variety of actions which combine rational reflection, emotional stimulation and physical movements. The believers stand shoulder to shoulder with each other, elect one of them (the *imām*) to lead the prayer and obey him for its proper performance, draw his attention to any impairment, and having first glorified the Lord, ask Him, individually and collectively, to 'Guide us to the straight path'. Inherent in the prayer, therefore, are the principles of the good life: of social solidarity and equality; of leadership and obedience; responsibility and responsiveness; and of universal brotherhood. The same goes for the other pillars of Islam and they are in the nature of a course of training in societal living. 'The more assiduously we follow the training', wrote Sayyid Mawdudi, 'the better equipped we are to harmonise ideals and practices'.[16]

Politics is also central to Islam if it is defined in its narrow sense to mean the art of government. Qur'ānic exhortations of 'enjoining the good and forbidding the evil', of upholding justice and other Divine values and criteria, require the participation of all members of society in the affairs of government to ends laid down by Allah (SWT). The Qur'ān condemns anarchy and disorder (2:205), and the Prophet (ṢAAS) stressed the need for organisation and authority in society. Similarly, 'Umar, the second caliph, considered an organised society impossible without an *imām* (the leader), and added that there could be no *imām* without obedience.[17] The *Khulafā al-Rāshidūn* and their companions recognised that the divinely mandated vocation to realise the will of Allah (SWT) in history was communal as well as individual. They held an organic, holistic approach to life in which religion was intimately intertwined with politics, law and society. This is well expressed by Ka'b, as quoted by Ibn Qutaybah, saying,

> Islam, the government and the people are like the tent, the pole, the ropes and the pegs. The tent is Islam; the pole is the government; the ropes and pegs are the people. None will do without the others.[18]

Politics is even more central to Islam when it is defined in the realist perspective as a struggle for power. To profess faith in Allah (SWT) and to proclaim *tawḥīd* is to call unequivocally for the repudiation of *ṭaghūt*, i.e., those who claim absolute right and power which is due only to Allah (SWT) and, therefore, to banish *ẓulm* (oppression and injustice) from the face of the earth. The *tawḥīdī* society Islam desires can brook neither a rival nor a compromise. The Qur'an enjoins the believers to shatter the absolutism of demi-gods and false deities; to divest them of any leadership roles; to wrest power for the righteous; and to reinstate good in place of evil. It was on the urging of the Qur'ān that the Prophet Muhammad (ṢAAS) came out of his seclusion and fought all those who rebelled against the prophetic guidance. One of the major objectives of his *hijrah* (migration to Madinah) was to establish political authority in accordance with the Divine will. Similarly, all the earlier prophets were engaged in conveying the Divine guidance, and reminding the faithful to eschew *ṭāghūt* (Al-Qur'ān 16:36). Islam is thus actively concerned with power, a power through which the world can be transformed to be in accord with Islamic tenets and principles to benefit humanity as a whole. *Jihād fī sabīl Allāh* (utmost exertion in the way of Allah, SWT) is but another name for the attempt to establish the Divine Order. The importance of securing power for the righteous is so fundamental that the Qur'ān declares *jihād* to be a touchstone of belief.

Power is sought in Islam, then, not for its own sake nor for personal or collective aggrandisement. Islam puts power in an active moral framework. It is not an end but a means to serve Allah (SWT); to earn a blissful eternal life and thus a source of mercy and justice for humanity. Such a conceptualisation totally transforms the nature, scope and purpose of power as conceived in Western theory and practice.

The foregoing points to the fact that the fusion of religion and politics is the dictate of Islam and cannot be disregarded. The choice between the Creator and Caesar *simply* does not arise. For Islam, there is no Caesar, there is only Allah (SWT) and His Messenger. The Shari'ah (the Islamic Law) incorporates the temporal with the spiritual. In Islam, ethics sets the tone for politics and the rules of political behaviour are derived from the ethical norms of Islam. Thus the major concerns of politics, i.e., striving to control the state structure, to wrest power for the righteous, to root out evil and bring about the good life are all relevant to and encouraged by Islam. Islam accords centrality to these activities, with the difference that the political life has to be situated within the larger frame of the religious and spiritual life. Religion and politics, as such, are not 'two sides of a single coin in Islam'.[19] Neither can they be rank-ordered, making one the independent and the other the dependent variable in the relationship. The truth, as Muhammad Iqbal puts it, is that 'Islam is a single, unanalysable reality which is one or the other, as your point of view varies'.[20]

ISLAM AND POLITICS: THE HISTORICAL PERSPECTIVE

The intertwining of religion and politics in its perfect form is exemplified by the last Prophet of Islam, whom the Qur'ān describes as the noble paradigm (*uswah ḥasanah* 33:21). One of the momentous events of his life is the migration to Madinah (*ḥijrah*) undertaken, *inter alia*, to restructure power relationships and make them subservient to the Divine will. Here was established the first Islamic polity of which Prophet Muhammad (ṢAAS) was the spiritual and temporal head. He led public prayers, commanded the army, acted as a judge and formulated public policies. The rightly guided caliphs, *al-Khulafā' al-Rāshidūn* (1–40 AH/622–659 CE), who headed the four successive polities, emulated him in every detail. They, as leaders of the community, executed the Shari'ah, defended the religious doctrine and maintained its purity. By the time of the third caliph, 'Uṭhman, Islamic civilisation had extended from the 'Trans-Oxus' to the 'shores of the Atlantic' in the West.[21]

There is unanimity among scholars that the political system established in Madinah is a model (defining the principles to actuate an Islamic polity) for all Muslim societies to adopt and follow. With the emergence of the Umayyads, however, there ensued a new variant in Muslim history – dynastic rule which sometimes degenerated into unbridled monarchy.[22] Their authority, for all practical purposes, was arbitrary. Yet, they were considered to be the defenders of the faith, protectors of the honour of Islam, and warriors against forces hostile to the Islamic way of life. They were bound not to flout the Shari'ah with impunity.

The movement which transferred the caliphate from the Umayyads to the Abbasids rested mostly on the close kinship ties which the latter had with the family of the Prophet (ṢAAS). On assuming power, they wore the cloak that was thought to have been once worn by the Prophet (ṢAAS) and kept his cloak and sacred relics whose possession was considered a powerful element of their legitimacy. For a variety of reasons, they inflated the religious aspect of the caliphate and in public statements expressed their wholehearted adherence to the Shari'ah.

To prove their regard for religion, most of the ruling heads of state suffixed the words of Allah and *dīn* (religion, way of life) to their names and titles such as al-Muntasir bi-Allah, al-Qahir bi-Allah, Ṣalāḥ al-Dīn, Muḥyi al-Dīn, and so on. Thus, although the later caliphs ruled without reference to Shari'ah and practised separation of Islam from their politics, they were never allowed to rule unreined, and, publicly at least, confirmed the close connection between faith and power. In any case, the *de facto* separation practised by Muslim rulers cannot form the basis for arguing that Islam permits the separation. The Islamic stand should be understood and evaluated by its principles rather than by deviations perpetrated by its practitioners.

Barring a few exceptions like the Umayyad caliph 'Umar ibn 'Abd al-'Azīz, who subjected his rule to the Sharī'ah and lived frugally and simply like a saint, power during most of Muslim history has not always been subject to the divine will and has been exercised for ends other than establishing justice among the people. This situation gave rise to three major trends in Muslim intellectual history. Some, like certain

Ṣufīs (mystics) and others, disengaged themselves from public affairs and withdrew into quieter shells. Thus Abu Layth al-Samarqandī, a Hanafi theologian, quotes Anas saying that 'ulama (the religious scholars) 'are the depositories of the prophets; yet when they draw near to the rulers and take part in the dealings of the world, they betray the prophets'.[23] Withdrawal, in effect, meant spiritual renovation carried out by a host of *Ṣūfī* orders which emerged around the sixth and seventh century of the *Hijrah*, and which exist right up to the present day. Their beliefs, moral attitudes and rituals of different types conformed to Islam but there also crept in non-Islamic practices which eventually subverted everything from top to bottom. Yet, it must be admitted, they helped preserve many precious values and saved the faith from caving in under the impact of alien world-views.

The second trend is represented by those thinkers and jurists who extended a type of *de facto* recognition to the prevailing order, on the plea of preserving the unity and stability of the Ummah, the community of believers. Paradoxically, most of these jurists distanced themselves from the seats of powers, refused to accept public offices, disqualified oaths under compulsion and supported the rebels who defied public authority in the name of Islamic ideals. The founders of the four schools of jurisprudence (*madhāhib*) kept contact with the authorities, but their relations were much less than cordial. They followed, to borrow Manfred Halpern's terminology, a policy of 'antagonistic collaboration'[24] for which they suffered persecution, harassment and, one of them, Imam al-Shāfi'ī, narrowly escaped execution. Muslim thinkers did justify the status quo, not because these regimes reflected the ideals of Islam, but because the alternative was chaos and civil disorder. Hence, they advised obedience to a ruler as long as their orders did not lead to sin. Such an attitude was tantamount to accepting secularism in practice and did cause confusion among the believers, but it also shows their abhorrence of secularism in theory, their sense of realism and their concern for minimising suffering and the disruption of the community's peaceful existence.

The third trend is represented by the 'Ulama' who shouldered the burden of 'carrying Islam in the absence of state support and through the vicissitudes of social upheaval'.[25] They were content with reforming individuals, hoping that this would lead eventually to the transformation of society along Islamic lines. Most of their efforts were concentrated on rituals and on the original purity of the faith by reference to the Qur'ān and the Sunnah. They propagated spiritual values, like sincerity, truthfulness, love and brotherhood, respect for parents, and indeed patience.

Admittedly, the role of Islam in politics has become increasingly complex, reflecting the growing complexity of the Muslim society subsequent to the period of *Khulafā' al-Rashidūn*. It also reflects the rapidly changing world in which the jurists, the *Ṣūfīs* and the 'Ulamā' have had to operate. The seeming separation of the realms, spiritual and temporal, never meant a divorce in the sense that each went its separate way. Although some *Ṣūfī* teachers disengaged themselves from politics, the great ones have always combined contemplation and action. They practised asceticism, but they were also actively engaged in politics, often came into conflict with the rulers, and eventually generated powerful socio-political movements. The intellectual disciple of al-Ghazālī in the sixth century, AH, Muhammad ibn Tūmart, is a case in point.[26] The doctrine he preached formed the basis of the Muwahhid empire (524–667 AH/1130–1269 CE) which embraced the whole of the Maghreb and enjoyed 'for two generations a peace and well-being it had not known since Roman times'.[27] Their predecessors, al-Murabiṭūn, the inmates of the *ribāṭ* (a place where warriors of faith live and worship), waged a successful *jihād* and founded the al-Murabit empire (448–541 AH/1056–1147 CE) which extended from Senegambia to Algeria.[28] Examples could also be cited of Naqshbandis in Turkestan, the Mahdiyyah in the Sudan, and many more, in the recent past.

Similarly, the 'Ulamā' who accepted the status quo never did so as *de jure*, as the true fulfilment of Islam. Their generally held concept of temporal and spiritual unity was eloquently expressed in al-Ghazāli's saying that 'religion and temporal power are twins'. To him, politics aims at 'man's welfare in this world and bliss in the next'.[29] The ideal state, whether of the jurists (like al-Māwardī and al-Ghazālī), of the philosophers (e.g., Nasr al-Dīn al-Fārābī and Fakhr al-Dīn al-Rāzī) or of the writers of mirrors for princes (such as Niẓām al-Mulk and Husayn Wa'iẓ Kashfī),[30] remained one that provided opportunities to all its citizens to 'live the good life' – a life 'as would fit them for participation in the future life, by due performance of their religious and ethical duties, by mutual cooperation in their respective functions according to the ordinances of the Sharī'ah, and by the development of their moral personalities on the lines ordained by God'.[31] Even Ibn Khaldūn, who has been extolled by the orientalists mainly for the secular aspects in his writings, attached great significance to the intertwining of religious and political aspects of the ideal Islamic polity. Like al-Māwardī, he defined *khilāfah* as 'a substitute for Muhammad' for the protection of religion and administration of the world.[32]

Thus there has, in principle, never been any disjunction in thought between faith and political action. Islam being an all-inclusive system of temporal and spiritual percepts cannot and does not leave societal and political life outside its jurisdiction. Yet, the various trends discussed above gave rise to paradoxical notions about power and socio-political goals which were aggravated by the Western domination of Muslim lands.

ENCOUNTER WITH THE WEST AND MUSLIM POLITICS

Islam's encounter with the West in the nineteenth and twentieth centuries shook the confidence of Muslims in their own civilisation. Their analyses of historical reverses and their prescription for remedial action produced three different perspectives referred to by Khurshid Ahmad as modernists, traditionalists and *tajdīd*.[33] Yvonne Haddad prefers to call them acculturationists, normativists and neo-normativists.[34]

The modernists, according to Cantwell Smith, are either Westernised Muslim thinkers groping for a veneer of Islam to legitimise their alien views or Muslims tied to their traditions yet desirous of importing certain Western ideas which they justify by constant reference to Islam.[35] Its able representatives include Sir Sayyid Ahmad Khan (1232–1316 AH/1817–1898 CE), Jamal al-Din Asadabadi alias al-Afghānī (1254–1315 AH/1839–1897 CE), his intellectual disciple, Sheikh Muḥammad 'Abduh (1260–1323 AH/1845–1905 CE), and others. They denounced *taqlīd* (blindly following tradition), advocated adoption of Western scientific knowledge and technical know-how, and placed reason at the crux of Islamic thought. Their notion of reason was highly secular, positivist, and divorced from the intellect as traditionally understood in Islam.[36] Modernism eventually became the fountain-head of secularism among certain Muslim intellectuals.

The most vocal representative of secularism among Muslims was Sheikh 'Alī 'Abd al-Raziq (1304–1384 AH/1888–1966 CE), a graduate of al-Azhar University, who, for some time, had also studied law and economy at Oxford. His *al-Islām wa-usūl al-hukm* (*Islam and the Principles of Government*) is extolled by E.I.J. Rosenthal as providing 'the theoretical basis for the radical separation of Islam as religion . . . from the affairs of state which are the exclusive concern of man'.[37] 'Abd al-Rāziq conceived of Islam purely as a religion to the exclusion of all political affiliations and pretensions. The Prophet (ṢAAS), he argued, was a *rasūl* (messenger) with a purely religious message untarnished by any inclination to rule or by any summons to organise a state.[38] Islam is the perfect universal religion for people as a whole and

Muhammad (ṢAAS) is the undisputed religious or spiritual leader whose political activity, 'for the sake of state (*mulk*), and towards consolidating the Islamic polity', was merely incidental and not related directly to his prophetic mission.[39] The Qur'ān repeatedly warns the Prophet (ṢAAS) not to act as the agent (*wakīl*), guardian (*ḥāfiẓ*) or holder of absolute authority (*musayṭir*) over the Muslims, for he was assigned to admonish and to communicate the divine message through wisdom, beautiful sermons and logical argumentation.[40] In short, Islam and politics are worlds apart and must, therefore, be kept apart.

The corollary of the above contention was to nullify the theory of the caliphate as having any religious sanction either in the Qur'ān, the Sunnah or the *ijmā'*, (consensus of the community). The caliphate was founded on 'brute force' and maintained by oppression. The caliphs denied Muslims the freedom, 'in the name of religion', to do research 'in the science of politics . . . for fear it might assail the very foundation of [their] rule'.[41] 'Abd al-Rāziq acknowledged the necessity of government for implementing Islamic ideals and for promoting people's welfare, but he argued that religion does not prescribe any particular form; it could take 'whatever form' be it 'despotic, democratic, socialist, or bolshevist'.[42] 'All political functions are left to us, our reason, its judgements and political principles'.[43] Muslims must participate in politics and organise their state on the basis of most modern achievements in statecraft.

The fierce opposition which *al-Islām wa uṣūl al-ḥukm* provoked resulted in its condemnation by the Grand Council of al-Azhar. The Council stripped its author of his al-Azhar diploma and unceremoniously terminated the judicial appointment he held. One may question the severity of the punishment meted out to 'Ali 'Abd al-Rāziq. There is no mistaking, however, that he misconceived, under the impact of secularism, the prophetic mission which included not merely the creation of a just society but also the founding of a state. Rationalism, behaviouralism and scientism which formed the foundation of modernist and secularist thought were direct challenges to the whole notion of faith and the inviolability of the tenets of religion which have constituted the very definition of belief in Islam.

CURRENT TRENDS

Modernism rejected the absolute authority of religious doctrine while its off-shoot, secularism, sought to ostracise the power of religion in the politics and life of the society. Based upon Western norms and values, the entire acculturationistic package was foreign to Islam and the cultural system associated with it. To justify this innovation (*bid'ah*) through a reinterpretation (*ta'wīl*) of the doctrine was, in the eyes of the 'Ulamā,' nothing short of heresy. Given such denunciation, and devoid of the popular support which lay behind the 'Ulamā,' acculturationists could not become a salient intellectual force in Muslim societies.

Hamid Enayat, referring to 'Abd al-Rāziq's emphasis on the exclusively religious character of Islam, lamented that the issue was not allowed 'to develop in a free and honest debate' and thus missed an opportunity for 'an overdue analysis of . . . the question of self-subsistence of moral values'.[44] He blamed the modernists for their 'over-confident, intemperate mood' which

> lent plausibility to the traditionalists' charge that what the modernists sought was not a simple modification of religious attitudes, but the very eradication of Islam as an all-inclusive system of moral, social and political guidelines.[45]

The 'Ulamā', i.e., the normativists, did not merely find acculturationists hostile to their institutions and ideas, but worse still, they found them too primitive to be worthy of a serious intellectual dialogue. Compared to great Muslim orientalist scholarship, the works of Sheikh Muḥammad 'Abduh and others suffered from a poverty of thought. Indeed, they seem to display a superficial knowledge of the heritage of Islamic social, philosophical and political thought. Rosenthal, who otherwise applauds 'Abd al-Rāziq's treatise, notes its inconsistencies and incoherences and finds its author to be 'obviously unaware of the political treatises of al-Farābī, Ibn Sīnā and Ibn Rushd in particular, and of others among the *falāsifah*, the Muslim philosophers'.[46]

Malcolm Kerr's verdict about the acculturationists' knowledge is unequivocal: 'they had no sufficient ideological basis on which to build new doctrines, other than a dimly understood Western one'.[47] They could not formulate an Islamic response to the challenges of the West, nor could they conceptualise complex contemporary problems within the framework of their own culture.

The richness of thought necessary for providing such responses is present in Islam and this hinders the acceptance of Westernisation and its value system *in toto*. The need was to accept the challenge which was shouldered by the neo-normativists who

> responded with new zeal, interpreting Islam for modern man. The literature they have produced evidences assimilation and integration of some new tools of hermeneutics and explication, but the content of what is affirmed is the eternal message of Islam, the same message given to man at creation, valid for today and forever. What is being advocated is a new articulation of the faith relevant for modern challenges, but not a new Islam.[48]

They are referred to by Fazlur Rahman as neo-fundamentalists. He criticises them for their failure to engage in the systematic interpretation of the scripture and the Sharīa'h needed to relate Islam to the modern world. He, however, was not oblivious to the intensity of neo-fundamentalism: 'It is vibrant, it pulsates with anger and enthusiasm, and it is exuberant and full of righteous hatred. Its ethical dynamism is genuine, its integrity remarkable'.[49] They are the ones in the forefront of the on-going Islamic movement in the Muslim world. Sayyid Abul A'lā Mawdūdī (1322–1399 AH/1903–1979 CE), Sayyid Qutb (1324–1386 AH/1906–1966 CE) and a host of other contemporary scholars have advocated the universality of Islam. To Mawdūdī, secularism, by relegating religion to the personal realm, encourages men to give way to their bestial impulses and perpetrate evil upon one another. To Sayyid Qutb, secularism is the hall-mark of the ignorant (*jāhilī*) culture which must be replaced by a dynamic and integrated Islamic system. Their point of departure is *tawḥīd*, the unity and sovereignty of Allah (SWT), *risālah*, the messengership of the Prophet (ṢAAS), and *khilāfah*, the vicegerency of man. In their approach to social, economic and political problems, they begin from the fundamental premise of spiritual and temporal unity. 'The religious ideal of Islam', Iqbāl points out, 'is organically related to the social order which it has created. The rejection of one will eventually involve the rejection of the other'.[50] Basing his ideas upon a *ḥadīth*, 'The whole of this earth is a mosque', Iqbāl asserts that in Islam: 'All that is secular is therefore sacred in the roots of its being' for 'All this immensity of matter constitutes a scope for the self-realisation of spirit'.[51]

The Western theoretical distinction between God's domain and that of Caesar does not exist in Islam. In Islam, there is no Caesar, there is only Allah (SWT) who is the Creator, the Cherisher, the Sustainer and the Lord of the entire universe. The emphasis in Islam is on unity: the unity of Allah (SWT), the unity of the community of the faithful, the Ummah, the unity of life as a totality, and the unity of the temporal and the spiritual. Contemporary trends in Islamic political thought, as in the past, gravitate around this idea of unity. This is the predominant trend. This is the *ijmā'*, the consensus of the Muslim Ummah.

CONCLUSION

Islam is not a religion in the sense commonly understood as no more than the sum of several beliefs, rituals and sentiments – but rather a system of life that deals with all aspects of human existence and performance. It is a well-ordered system, a consistent whole, comprising a set of universal principles and pan-cultural values for the socio-economic, political and moral guidance of humanity. The Qur'ān teaches, as Sayyid Mawdūdī points out, not simply 'to preach' Islam but 'to act upon it, promote it, and actually enforce it'. Politics, no matter how it is defined, forms a part and parcel of Islam; the two form one indivisible realm. This is precisely the reason that

> Traditionally, Muslims rarely studied politics in isolation from related disciplines. Problems such as the nature of the state, the varieties of government, the qualifications of rulers, the limitation on their power and the rights of the ruled were discussed as part of the comprehensive treatises on jurisprudence and ideology – all securely within the unassailable walls of the Shari'āh.[52]

This interlocking of the spiritual and the temporal was exemplified in the roles donned by the Prophet (ṢAAS) and by his successors – the *rashidūn* caliphs.

The Madinah model exemplifies the principles of an Islamic polity in its pure and perfect form. Since then, as Ibn Khaldūn argues on the basis of historical evidence, a radical change took place which caused a deviation from the true Islamic governance decreed by the Qur'ān and the Prophet (ṢAAS). Starting with the Umayyads, the governments throughout Muslim history embodied only some aspects of Islamic doctrines. Yet, the dynastic rulers publicly recognised the supremacy of the Sharī'ah and sought the legitimacy of their political rule in the doctrines of Islam. During those turbulent years, the Muslim thinkers grappled with the onerous task of fostering in the believers an authentic religious spirit and in conjunction with this an insistence on the implementation of all the injunctions of the Sharī'ah. Their lives exude a mutually enriching togetherness of spiritual striving and effective socio-political reform activity.

During the nineteenth century, Islam experienced a particularly grave crisis. The Muslim world succumbed militarily, economically and politically to Western Christendom, which challenged the very meaning of Muslim history. As a way out, one group, the normativists, advocated holding fast to Islamic tradition and its legacy and a total withdrawal from the processes of Westernisation. The Westernising Muslim modernists, even if they meant well in their desire to defend Islam, in fact presented a truncated and deformed Islam. The interaction between the two has spawned a vibrant and modern interpretation of Islam by the neo-normativists, who emphasise the totality of Islam as the divinely mandated alternative to the materialism and secularism of the West.

The call for a return to the original message of Islam, to discover its relevance to the existing milieu and to strive to change the status quo to conform to the tenets and principles of Islam, is not something new but a perennial phenomenon in Islamic history. What distinguishes the twentieth-century Islamic movements is the geographical spread and consistent and vigorous championing of Islam in the politics of the Muslim world. There is an almost continuous chain of Islamic movements operating in all parts of the Muslim world. Their call, which is integral to the Jamā'at-e-Islāmī of Pakistan, the Muslim Brotherhood of Egypt and other Islamic movements, is for a comprehensive reform along Islamic lines in all aspects of life including politics. Religion, which under the impact of secularism lay dormant for a while, has re-emerged in Muslim politics and society. This has been so vigorous that even those Muslim leaders who long championed the cause of secularism and modernisation, like Zulfikar Ali Bhutto of Pakistan, have had to retreat and are forced to pay lip service to the popular aspiration for an Islamic socio-political order.

Such was the strength of this aspiration that it destabilised the governments of Muhammad Riẕa Pahlavī, Shah of Iran, and Z. A Bhutto of Pakistan. Subsequently, it is Islam which gave legitimacy to their successors, the Ayatollah Khomeini and General Ziaul Haq. Under Zia, Pakistan came to be regarded by the Muslim world as the most Islamic-oriented polity after Iran. Brunei, attaining independence in 1984, proclaimed itself as the Sultanate of Brunei Darussalam, declaring thereby its identity as part of the Muslim Ummah in its official designation. Even in Turkey, which drastically broke its spiritual bond with the Islamic world in 1924, there is evidence of a modest reawakening of Muslim identity.

There are, nevertheless, varying degrees of constitutional espousal of Islamicity as well as differences in the degree to which the Muslim societies have adopted the values enshrined in the Qur'ān and the Sunnah. The basing of legislation on the Sharī'ah will, however, have no magical effect unless a total transformation of society takes place. This requires bringing politics within the fold of Islam, such that people's political life is always situated within the larger frames of their religious and spiritual life. In this sense alone, politics, could be made to promote, in the words of al-Ghazālī: 'Man's welfare in this world and bliss in the next'.[53] This, in turn, necessitates knowing about everything that the word politics connotes. Political science provides that knowledge. It is the disciplined, systematic study of ideas, behaviour, institutions, policies as well as the formal and informal processes involved in politics at all levels and contexts. Creating a humane world order, an Islamic order, necessitates studying politics seriously within the framework of the Sharī'ah with the ultimate goal of seeking the pleasure of Allah (SWT).

3 Islamic Methodology in Political Science

Islamic science once imparted life and motion to Islamic civilisation and society. It is now confined within the walls of old schools and classical tomes. Having embraced the new sciences and accepted Western behaviourial modes of thinking, some 'Muslim' intellectuals have made Islam into an abstract theory fossilised inside traditional forms of mere customs, rites, and rituals. This situation alone provides enough justification to reconstruct the methodology of Islamic sciences; the continuing Islamisation movement makes the attempt even more pertinent.

This chapter attempts to explain Islamic methodology in political science. This is accomplished by identifying, through a contrast with Islamic principles, the weaknesses of key concepts moulded in the crucible of Western culture and civilisation. This is needed because Islamisation warrants liberating Muslims from the theological worldview of the West so that they may strive toward that state of perfection reached in Madinah under divine guidance during the time of the Last Prophet (ṢAAS).

MAJOR TRAITS OF EMPIRICAL SOCIAL SCIENCE

Western empirical social science is based upon the assumption that human behaviour is patterned and that these regularities can be scientifically investigated and expressed as generalisations that approximate to the universality of scientific law or theory in the physical sciences.[1] Confining the long tradition of social and political theory to 'the dog house'[2] for living 'parasitically on ideas a century old',[3] the new science believes in the applicability of empirical and scientific methods to every field of inquiry. It marks the rejection of every form of knowledge that has its basis in the supposition that there is no reality beyond inner-worldly existence. The new science became synonymous with the movements of logical positivism and linguistic philosophy, which subsequently set the pace for the powerful growth of an intellectual movement which believes in a complete separation of 'facts' and 'values'.

> By the beginning of the twentieth century, particularly under the impact of Weber's ideas, the social scientist had accepted as axiomatic and unquestionable what he had learnt as a callow student; namely, that political values must be vigorously excluded from empirical research.[4]

Such empirical science has been characterised by its attempt to free nature from religious overtone, to abolish sacral legitimation of political power and authority, and to base its instruments of knowledge exclusively upon human reason, which enables man to discover laws of development inherent in a 'rationally ordered' world. It has eschewed moral or ethical questions and has aspired to make science objective and value-neutral, 'stating all phenomena . . . in terms of the observed and observable behaviour of men'.[5] Consequently, it has been concerned with methodology and observation, classification, and measurement. Research techniques have been borrowed from biology, mathematics, physics and other similar natural sciences.

The growth of positivism in the social sciences generated fresh confidence among its proponents, but that proved false and short-lived. Faced with mounting structural deformities in relations between the north and the south, increasing incidence of authoritarian rule and frequent perpetration of inhuman atrocities in Lebanon, Kashmir, the Gaza Strip and the Gulf, society is in a state of decay and dissolution.[6]

The need is to replace this paradigm with one which studies individual behaviour within the context of an entire social system. Islam, as a total civilisation, looks upon human life as an organic whole and approaches its problems in the light of moral values and social ideals enshrined in the Qur'ān and the Sunnah of Prophet Muhammad (ṢAAS). Based upon Islam, the methodology of Islamic social sciences cannot but be theocentric, which stands totally opposed to the Western conception of man and nature in all its details and ramifications and needs to be clearly spelled out.

REASON AND REVELATION

As pointed out by S.H. Naṣr, Western social science is anthropomorphic in nature in that it accepts individual human existence as the criterion of reality, to the total neglect of any higher principle. For the same reason, Western social science is reductionist, for it not only separates reason from revelation but rejects the latter as a means of knowledge.[7]

Based upon Graeco-Roman cultural tradition and rational philosophy, it accepts nothing which cannot fit the scale of reason and human intellect and, abiding by the same standard, it considers nothing as moral if it fails to yield maximum returns in material terms.[8]

In contrast, the civilisation of Islam is rooted in divine revelation. As revelation is a distinguishing feature of the methodology of Islam, Muslim scholars took a keen interest in disentangling the various issues connected with it. However, the truth of revelation was always appreciated in the light of reason. From the very beginning, revelation's relation to reason continued to be of central importance in all philosophical and theological debates. Even al-Ash'arī (270–330 AH/873–941 CE), before whom the system of rationalist *Kalām* crumbled, strongly defended the use of reason, or *Kalām*, in explaining standard formulations of doctrine. It is also well known that Imām Abū Hanīfah and his celebrated followers al-Ṭahāwī, al-Māturīdi and, indeed, al-Ghazāli adopted the principles and methods of reasoning as an avenue to knowledge.[9]

This is in accordance with the Qur'ān's repeated exhortations to reason out and weigh rationally all matters to enable one to follow the right way (see Al-Qur'ān, 59:2, 7:86, etc.) Rather than posing a problem 'in the form of contrast between Divine Law and human reason,' as argued by Rosenthal, revelation and reason are complementary to each other.[10] For, without reason, the truth of revelation cannot be appreciated. Nor would its divineness be recognised and acknowledged as such. Unlike some religious texts that present doctrine in mysterious language beyond rational comprehension, the Qur'ān, in no less than 750 verses, exhorts the believers to observe, think, and ponder, to reason, comprehend, and understand nature, history, and human societies. However, as al-Māturīdī has pointed out, reason and sense organs have their limits and at times 'human intellect is obscured and influenced by internal and external factors' and thus 'fails to give us true knowledge of things that are within its own sphere'.[11] Revelation enlightens man, provides direction and purpose, and widens the scope of knowledge to include not merely the proximal world but the unseen everlasting abode as well. Divine revelation provides the landmarks and guideposts and thereby saves mankind the tragic cost of falling victim to inadequate knowledge, ignorance, and stagnant traditions. As the epistemologies of al-Ghazālī and Ibn Khaldun show, Muslims, for centuries, pursued knowledge through blending reason with revelation and heralded the Golden Age of Science in Islam during the twelfth century. 'What we call science arose as a result of new methods of experiment, observation, and measurement which were introduced into Europe by the Arabs. . . . (Modern) science is the most momentous contribution of the Islamic civilisation'.[12]

SOCIAL SCIENCES VERSUS NATURAL SCIENCES

The world has suffered from the folly of the social sciences following indiscriminately the model of the natural sciences, with the result that technocratic solutions are being imposed even on problems with purely moral and ideological overtones. Imitation of the natural science model was based on the desire for increased social prestige, the achievement of scientific respectability, and the quest for social status on a par with that of natural scientists.[13] In so doing, behaviourial political scientists have assumed not only the stance of the physical model but also its epistemology and its assumptions about the nature of knowledge and the means of knowledge as well. They considered human behaviour in an artificial manner, stripped the variables of their meaning in order to operationalise them, and have tended to bend, reshape, and distort the political map to fit the model they use to investigate it. As Deutscher puts it:

> We concentrate on consistency without much concern with what it is we are being consistent about or whether we are consistently right or wrong. As a consequence, we may have been learning a great deal about how to pursue an incorrect course with a maximum of precision.[14]

The conclusion to be arrived at from the above analysis is that political science must abandon claims to approximating natural science without ceasing to aspire to comprehensive knowledge.

To be sure, the place of the two sciences in the scheme of human knowledge is one and the same, i.e., to unfold and comprehend the Divine pattern. In the Qur'ānic scheme, this knowledge (*'ilm*) is to be obtained through revelation or divinely ordained absolute knowledge (*ḥaqq al-yaqīn*), rationalism or inference based upon judgement and appraisal of evidence (*'ilm al-yaqīn*), historical reports, description of life-experiences and the like (*'ayn al-yaqīn*).[15] Thus, the Islamic way of knowing accords full freedom to experience and experiment and to rational and intellectual inquiry within the circumference of revealed knowledge. It is indeed advisable to benefit from the best offered by one field for the better understanding of the other, but one must recognise the distinction between the two fields, which is in terms of research strategy and techniques.

THE INSTRUMENTALIST CONCEPTION OF POLITICS

By virtue of their orientation to the model of the natural sciences, the empirical political scientists have limited the scope of their inquiries to observable behaviour. Politics came to be defined either as the 'study of who gets what, when, and how' (Lasswell) or 'the authoritative allocation of values' (Easton). Similarly, political association or state is conceived as an instrumental apparatus for the pursuit of contingently determined ends that can be calculated according to a strategic-instrumentalist conception of rationality, i.e., expediency, gross national product, and utilitarian considerations.

It hardly needs mentioning that the instrumental conception of political association is not universal but culturally specific. Originating in the West, it reflects and at best fits only that particular society. Given such a conception, it is but natural for the Western commentators to regard the Iranian revolution, the Muslim resistance in Afghanistan, the freedom struggle in Kashmir, and the like as irrational and myopic simply because these are not averse to subordinating GNP to other considerations. Devoid of moral contents, politics in the West have become a 'dirty game' in which self-centred, power-seeking individuals vie with each other to acquire or augment power and privilege through alliance formation, manipulation, intimidation or elimination of rivals.[16] When power becomes the goal of politics devoid of other purposes, it becomes cynical, brutal and dehumanising.

The instrumentalist conception of political association is at variance with the Islamic way of life, which is purposive and goal-oriented. Islam, therefore, stresses the need for organisation and authority for the realisation of its goals. The Qur'ān condemns disorder and anarchy (2:205) and the Prophet (ṢAAS) stressed the need for organisation and authority in Muslim society. This emphasis has also been vividly expressed by scholars through the ages. 'Umar, the second caliph, believed that there could be no organised society without an imām to be obeyed. Imām Ibn Hanbal concurred and held the opinion that in the absences of an imām, anarchy and disorder would certainly ensue.[17] The towering Muslim political thinker al-Māwardī went further in stating that the existence of an imām, was as necessary as the striving for truth and the acquisition of knowledge.[18]

The reason for such a heavy emphasis on organised authority, as explained by Fakhr al-Dīn al-Rāzī (543–606 AH/1149–1209 CE), is that 'without political social organisation man cannot reach his destiny.'[19] To Ibn Taymīyah (661/728 AH/1262–1328 CE), moreover, 'religion cannot exist without it.'[20] Sayyid Abul Al'ā Mawdūdī maintained that the ultimate goal of an Islamic polity is neither to maintain peace and raise the standard of living of its inhabitants nor to defend its frontiers. Its ultimate purpose is 'to enforce and implement with all resources of its organised power that reformatory program which Islam has given for the betterment of mankind'.[21] The Islamic polity is ideological, its approach is universal and all-embracing, and its mission is to establish virtue and justice in accordance with revealed guidance. In short, the polity in Islam 'is only an effort to realise the spiritual in human organisation.'[22]

Thus, in Islam, the polity is conceived not as a means to ends that are separable from the state but as itself the locus of religious-cultural purposes. Such a conception leaves no room for separating religion from politics. Rather, it blends the two, conducts politics in accordance with revealed guidance, and uses the political science as a servant of the Creator 'inviting all to the good, enjoining virtue and forbidding vice' for the purpose of achieving piety (Al-Qur'ān, 3:104;5:3). It is this ideal which inspired and sustains the struggle for the liberation of Palestine and Afghanistan. For the Kashmīrī Mujahīdīn as well as for the Palestinians, from the Islamic point of view, the polity is not an instrumentality for the pursuit of other extrinsic ends. Rather, it is itself the focus of profound religious-cultural purposes which would allow them to fashion their life according to the revealed principles of individual and social behaviour and would impart a sense of their own dignity. The West needs to be exposed to this Islamic conception of the polity for a more informed and more articulate response to Muslim aspirations.

THE ISLAMIC FRAMEWORK FOR ANALYSIS

The foregoing conception of the polity is based upon the fact that Islam is a comprehensive system of life. Islam does not divide the world artificially and arbitrarily into social and profane or into religious and secular. In Islam religion and polity are one organic unity that coheres into an undifferentiated social and political unity. As al Faruqi points out:

> The Ummah is like an organic body whose parts are mutually and severally interdependent with one another, and with the whole. For the part to work for itself is for itself to work for each of the other parts as well as for the whole, and for the whole to work for itself, is for itself to work for each of the parts.[23]

The Prophet (ṢAAS) has described the Ummah as 'the well-settled and consolidated building, each part of which buttresses the other' and he compared it to 'a body which reacts *in toto* with discomfort and fever whenever a part of it is hurt'.[24]

Given the organic nature of the Ummah, the appropriate framework for analysing the political phenomenon is to try to place the parts within a wider context. The individual, for instance, cannot be understood on its own terms, inasmuch as individual purpose and identity are constituted by participation in family relations; the family in turn must be placed in the wider context of social and political relationships and so on. Individuals can have a sense of themselves as individuals to the extent that they can relate their own purposes to wider social groups such as family, community, and the polity, and they can sustain a sense of individual identity so long as these wider groups maintain themselves as coherent wholes. It is for this reason that the Qur'ān devotes much attention to the issues relating to family – the essential social unit, flanked by the individual on the one side and the universal Ummah on the other. Indeed, many Muslim thinkers consider family and society as synonymous since in an Islamic setting one is not feasible without the other.

To understand contemporary politics, it may be necessary to begin by observing that the traditional social symbols, which have informed every dimension of community life for centuries, have been assaulted by technological civilisation to the extent that individuals, being less and less sure of family roles, are subjecting the axioms and assumptions of parenthood and parental responsibilities to constant redefinition. The crisis of authority at the family level is accompanied by the relative absence of compelling and widely shared overall social purpose, with the result that individuals lack a clear sense of their duties and obligations as members of the Ummah. Consequently, political relationships are characterised by cynicism, mistrust, and frustration, and the polity experiences an increasing legitimacy crisis, which eventually renders any given government poorly equipped politically to cope with socio-economic and political crises. An analysis of the political phenomena in an Islamic framework then proceeds by constructing an organic model of the Ummah with each separate part – politics, economics, social framework, etc. – in a defined organic relation to all the component parts.

The proposed organic model broadens the scope (i.e., a conception of the nature of its subject matter) of the discipline of political science, for justifiable reasons. First, the 'parts' in a functional sense are equivalent to the whole in that they maintain order: integrate, define, and try to attain goals. Second, the smaller units are easily accessible for investigation and often accommodate advanced methods of study. Third, placing parts within wholes widens the horizon of knowledge. It permits learning a great deal about macrocosms. Finally, since Islam obligates every conceivable part of the society to seek actualisation of the Divine Will, it is not appropriate for the investigator to restrict his or her study to any one or two aspects of the social order to the detriment of the other parts and of the whole.

Facts and values

One of the implications of the Islamic methodology outlined above is that political science cannot be based upon facts alone, for facts of human behaviour are not dead, but alive. Facts take on meaning or significance only to the extent that they can be situated within a significant whole which provides a theoretically informed context for their interpretation. The simple recording of the fact, by itself, contributes very little to the understanding of political life unless it is related to other facts in an overall explanatory or descriptive account, that is, when it is placed within an ordered theoretical whole. The fact that a peace treaty was signed between Israeli Prime Minister Begin and Egyptian President Anwar Sadat or between Israeli Prime Minister Rabin and Palestinian Chief Yasser Arafat could mean either a great deal or little depending upon its place within a much wider interpretive matrix. All facts relating to man are relative, as human behaviour depends on human volition, which is shaped by beliefs and ethical ends. A fact does not describe itself; it does not perform according to mathematical formulae and equations. It is the analysts who give meaning to the fact by determining how it should be fitted into existing concepts and beliefs, and how far the exiting concepts and beliefs should be modified and extended to accommodate it.

To emphasise the need for an interpretive matrix is to stress, in essence, the importance of values. The myth of value-free political science was exploded with finality by scholars like Thomas Kuhn, Seyyed

H. Nasr, Naqib al-'Attās, and by one of the past presidents of the American Political Science Association.[25] To make such a pretence reflects either hypocrisy or self-delusion. Value-free political science is a myth because values provide a matrix which shapes the selection of subjects for investigation, formulation of concepts, and selection of data for analysis and interpretation. If the knowledge is to be given and used for the right purposes, values must be restored to their central position.

To be sure, Western political science is not value-free. Maintaining a demeanour of rigorous value-neutrality, most Western political scientists affirm the sanctity of Western liberal democracy, with its sole concern for profits and profit maximisation. To put it mildly, 'they confuse a vaguely stated conventional democratism with scientific objectivity'.[26] The knowledge thus produced is not neutral but 'subtly fused together' with the character and personality of Western civilisation, 'so that others take it unawares, *in toto*, to be real knowledge *per se*'.[27]

It is clear that all political actions are guided by some values or normative considerations and that all practitioners of political science have a set value system or some conception of the proper human ends. Understanding of the ordinary terms of political discourse presupposes acquaintance with the kinds of ends implied in common political experience. As such, values or normative considerations cannot be excluded from analysis.

The structure of Islamic values

While Western political science confuses or conceals normative considerations, Islam states its values explicitly. The Stockholm Seminar of 1981 on 'knowledge and values' identified ten concepts which generate the basic values of an Islamic culture: *tawḥīd*, *khilāfah*, *'ibādah*, *'ilm*, *ḥalāl* and *ḥarām*, *'adl*, *ẓulm*, *istiṣlāḥ*, and *ḍayā'*.

The essential comprehensive characteristic of Islam and its primary basis is *tawḥīd*, the unity of Allah (SWT), which affirms the radical monotheism of Islam. Allah (SWT) is One, He has no partner, and there is none worthy of worship except Him. *Tawḥīd* extends to all of creation and thus signifies the unity of Allah (SWT), the unity of the community of the faithful, the unity of life as a totality, and the unity of the temporal and the spiritual. *Tawḥīd* provides one, single direction and guarantees a unified spirit for its adherents. It perfects the ethical consciousness of mankind and endows humanity with the hidden power of 'wisdom' which nurtures and perfects it.

A corollary of *tawḥīd* is *khilāfah*, mankind's vicegerency of Allah (SWT). As a vicegerent, mankind is free but also responsible and accountable to Allah (SWT). One's vocation and destiny, therefore, is the service of Allah (SWT), or the fulfilment of Divine Will. Allah (SWT) has 'not created mankind and jinn but to serve Him' (Al-Qur'ān, 51:56). The *khilāfah* consists of the fulfilment of the responsibility of sustaining the self and other creatures in accordance with the will of Allah (SWT). The faithful execution of this sublime responsibility is, in fact, the true nature of *'ibādah* (worship or service to Allah SWT).

The concept of worship, *'ibādah*, is very wide in Islam. It does not mean merely ritual or any specific form of prayer, but a life of continuous prayer and unremitting obedience to Allah (SWT). *'Ibādah* encompasses all activities of life – spiritual, social, economic, and political – provided they are in accordance with the rules as laid down and if their ultimate objective is to seek the pleasure of Allah (SWT).[29] As a *khalīfah*, man's activities may be grouped under two headings: *ḥaqq Allāh*, i.e., duties and obligations due directly to Allah (SWT), and *ḥaqq al-'ibād*, duties to oneself, to fellow beings, and to other creatures for the pleasure of Allah (SWT).

Among the many manifestations of *'ibādah* and a prerequisite to its effective performance is *'ilm*, knowledge. In its totality, the concept of *'ilm* in Islam is very vast. It ranges in its meaning from the *Ṣufi* understanding of the term *marifah* (gnosis) to the interpretation of knowledge as it concerns everyday activities of the individual.[30] *'Ilm*, in general, is divided into two categories: revealed knowledge, which basically includes the Qur'ān and the Sunnah, and science-derived knowledge, which is acquired through experience, observation, and research. The former category is further sub-divided into *farḍ al-'ayn*, which is binding on every individual Muslim, and *farḍ al-kifāyah*, which is binding on the community as a whole but which can be discharged on its behalf by some members of the community.[31]

'Ilm is mentioned in the Qur'ān with unusual frequency and has been paired, in verse 30:56 with *īmān*, faith, which according to verse 3:71, follows upon knowledge. The pursuit of *'ilm*, according to a *ḥadīth*, is incumbent upon every Muslim even if it entails travelling to China. However, *'ilm* becomes a value only if it is pursued within the value-framework of Islam. Unlike the Western hackneyed phrase of 'knowledge for knowledge's sake', or that entire convoluted argument that 'all knowledge is good', Islam considers *'ilm* as a value and an act of *'ibādah* only when it is pursued for the benefit of the individual or the community and ultimately for gaining the pleasure of Allah (SWT).

'Ilm has to be value-based and must have a function and a purpose. In other words, knowledge is not for its own sake but serves as a way to salvation, and not all kinds of knowledge would serve the purpose. Consequently, Muslim scholars throughout history have occupied themselves in sifting out the kinds of *'ilm* which are sanctioned in Islam. This led to the categorisation of knowledge into *ḥalāl* and *ḥarām*, permitted and prohibited, or the praiseworthy and the blameworthy. *Ḥalāl* includes all knowledge and activity that is beneficial for an individual, society and the environment. *Ilm* which is *ḥalāl* seeks to promote *'adl*, social justice, and *istiṣlāḥ*, public interest. *'Adl*, in all its multidisciplinary facets, and *istiṣlāḥ*, with its wider dimensions, ensure that knowledge is pursued to promote universal equity, individual freedom, social dignity, and values that enhance the well-being of Muslim society and culture.

Ḥarām or blameworthy research includes all that is destructive for man and his environment in its physical, intellectual, and spiritual sense. Research promoting alienation, dehumanisation, environmental destruction, and others which are *per se* evil are, therefore, rejected. These activities are tyrannical, or *ẓulm*, and are categorised as *ḍayā'*, wastage. Even astrology, which is part of knowledge, falls under this category. Its practice was declared unlawful by the Prophet (ṢAAS), since the evil in it was greater than the good it contained. Mankind as the best of Allah's creation is endowed with conscience, wisdom and discretion and is 'inspired to strive together toward all that is good, to eradicate *ẓulm*, and to establish justice and faith in Allah' (Al-Qur'ān 2;148, 193).

It should be evident that the matrices of values outlined above are organically related to each other, and impart a unique character to the epistemology of Islam. The discipline of political science that emerges following such a strategy is able to rank a variety of human ends by reference to an overall sense of what is important and what is good in general. It introduces a principle of coherence into otherwise disparate human sciences; it reflects upon what is important and meaningful in human life. It thus offers a basis for discriminating between what is relevant and irrelevant, significant and insignificant, virtuous and vicious, which a political science conceived merely as a partial catalogue of facts cannot answer.

Madinah as the norm

As a system of values, Islamic methodology does not rest solely on facts, nor does it exclude normative considerations from analysis. The concept of what something 'is' cannot be separated from a conception of what 'ought to be'. Thus the concept of 'political order' is analogical to the concept of an 'ideal order' in that the former cannot be judged and evaluated without understanding the latter. Pre-behaviourial Western social science did realise the need for such a model and hence attempted a kind of utopianism found in the writings of Saint-Simon, Robert Owen, Charles Fourier, and, of course, the 'classless society' of Karl Marx and Frederick Engels.

For the Muslims, however, there is no need to resort to utopian idealism. There is unanimity among the Muslims that the political system founded by the Prophet Muhammad (ṢAAS) in Madinah and later governed by the *Khulafā' al-Rashidūn* was the best ideal polity ever found on earth and hence provided a normative standard. As well-defined by Sayyid Quṭb:

> That was a remarkable period, a sublime summit, an exceptional generation of people, a bright beacon. It was, as we have stated, decreed and willed by Allah SWT, so that this unique image might be materialised in the situations of real life and recourse might later be had to it, in order to repeat it within the limitations of human capacity.[32]

This standard is independent from changing conditions and specific contexts and it is available as a criterion to be used for judging the value of existing conditions and institutions. Islamic political science is but a perpetual struggle toward the ideal of the Prophet (ṢAAS) as the Perfect Man and his Madinah as the Perfect Polity. It is the mysterious touch of the ideal that animates and sustains the real.

It is well known that Muslim scholars of note worked within the parameters of Islamically defined knowledge giving equal status to all forms of scholarship. The *fuqahā'*, jurists, of the classical period, wrote al-Fārūqī, were real encyclopedists, masters of practically all the disciplines from literature and law to astronomy and medicine. They were themselves professional people who knew Islam not only as law, but as ideal and theory, as system of thought and life lived by millions of humans in actual practice.[33]

The political theorising that emerged from these early scholars' pens is value-laden. Almost all of them invariably began their treatises with an inquiry into the purposes of political life and sought a theoretically grounded rational foundation for understanding political relationships. Their reflections are based upon deduced logic from Islamic ideals and principles. Sharī'ah was never lost as the ideal. Thus they placed normative considerations at the centre of their descriptive and explanatory analysis.

The achievement of early Muslim scholars is in part a result of their starting out by asking some of the right questions: What is politics and political association and what is it for? Their limitations were largely methodological – a void which was filled, for the time being, by the sociological analysis of Ibn Khaldūn (732–808 AH/1332–1406 CE), with his emphasis on observation, comparison, meticulous use of reason and a multidisciplinary approach to untangle the complexities of social and political life.[34] In so doing, Ibn Khaldūn never wavered in finding out the correlation between the kinds of political association and the nature of human ends and purposes realised by these associations. In other words, Ibn Khaldūn was engaged in moral reflection, which is in conformity with the Islamic insistence that *politics must be a quest for ethics* and that the two are inseparably linked with each other. This is one of the most valuable contributions of Islam to human society. The quest for ethics in politics is the first step toward the creation of an equitable, humane universal order.

CONCLUSION

The contrast attempted here between the Western mode of political inquiry and the Islamic alternative helps illuminate not merely the deficiencies inherent in the former, but, more importantly, highlights the characteristic set of features inherent in the latter. The picture that emerges is that Western political science, its methodology and epistemology as the final product, is built around the seemingly limitless power of natural science. The subjective and ideological nature of political science has been effectively exposed from its own epistemic landscape and real life situation. There is no such thing as knowledge for the sake of knowledge. The image of a dispassionate, objective, and value-free political science is no longer in vogue. The instrumentalist conception of political community, theoretical formulation, empirical verification, and final packaging of knowledge are all coloured with the social, cultural, and historical experiences of Western Christianity which is also, paradoxically, materialistic and secular to the core. Such a science has not fulfilled and cannot fulfil the needs and requirements of Muslims and as such it cannot take social and cultural root in the Muslim society.

The Islamic alternative considers the pursuit of knowledge within the value framework of Islam. It abandons all claims to approximating natural science and its consideration of the nature of political association is guided not by the instrumentalist conception of the community but by the question of ends for which it exists. The decisive basis of political science is the distinction between part and whole and that of fact and value. The part takes on significance by being situated within an encompassing whole with its matrix of eternal values enshrined in the Qur'ān and the Sunnah of the beloved Prophet Muhammad (ṢAAS). Finally, Islamic political science aims at approximating the values and spirit of the Madinah model, an association which embodied understanding of human ends. Where human ends are at issue, there is moral reflection. As such, political science in Islam is not a value-free enterprise. Islam insists that politics must be a quest for ethics and that political association, as well as individuals, have an obligation to act morally. Ethics and politics are inseparably linked – a lesson mankind must learn anew if it wants to restore sanity to the world gone awry.

'Ilm, or knowledge, in Islam is an obligation enjoined upon mankind by the Creator. This knowledge can be acquired through revelation as well as reason, from observation as well as intuition, through tradition as well as theoretical reflection. These diverse ways of studying political phenomena must, however, be subservient to the eternal values of divine revelation. This entails associating the pursuit of knowledge with such Qur'ānic concepts as *tawḥīd*, *khilāfah*, *'ibādah*, *'ilm*, *'adl*, *istiṣlāh*, and the like. Only the knowledge pursued within the matrix of eternal values of Islam, as *khalīfah* and ultimately for the pleasure of Allah (SWT), attains the status of *'ibādah*. This means, *inter alia*, avoiding all *ḥarām* activities promoting *ẓulm* and *dayā'*.

The values enshrined in the Qur'ān impart a universal character to Islam. This universality of Islamic values grants a universal status to a discipline subservient to the Islamic framework. In any case, the Muslim community which is under obligation to enjoin good and forbid evil has no viable future without recasting its discipline into an Islamic framework.

4 Sharīʻah: The Islamic Legal Order

The Sharīʻah is the core of Islam, the divinely ordained way of life for man. It is the instrument for building the Islamic socio-political order. Being divine in origin, it is the ultimate source of authority providing the sanctions as well the moral basis for the Islamic body-politic. It epitomises 'the goal towards which Muslims are restlessly trying to advance in quest of their destiny'.[1]

The concept of the Sharīʻah is, however, widely misinterpreted, ill conceived and misunderstood, giving rise to intense feelings of fear, hostility and ridicule, not only among the opponents of Islam, but among the Westernised Muslim intellectuals as well. For them, the Sharīʻah is time-bound and obsolete, reflects the ideas and the socio-political and moral attitudes of bygone ages and is out of tune with contemporary reality. Consequently, it must be modified and repealed, formulating new laws instead to cater for the new needs. Part of the antagonism towards the Sharīʻah is attributable to the prejudice commonly found in Western thought which is based upon the traumatic experience of the 'Crusades' upon the western mind. Part of the blame must also rest with the situation presented by the forces of bigotry and conservatism among the Muslims, on the one hand, and the abuse of the Sharīʻah by Muslim despots and leaders who find it expedient to espouse the cause of the Sharīʻah. Hence the need for and the desirability of, elucidating and deepening the understanding of this pivotal concept of Islam; its conceptual basis, sources, primary objectives and essential features. First, it is essential to clarify the difference in meaning among the terms Law, Sharīʻah, *fiqh* and Islamic Law which are erroneously considered as synonymous and interchangeable.

SHARĪʻAH AND THE LAW

The Sharīʻah has often been described by Muslims and non-Muslims alike as the 'Islamic Law' which is eternal and sacred. Such a conception of the Sharīʻah should not be confused with the term 'law' as is found in modern, Western usage. Among the numerous theories, the positive theory of law, which owes its origin to Thomas Hobbes, re-emphasised by John Austin and later by Kelsen, is widely prevalent in the West. They conceive of law as the command of the sovereign in the form of edicts or fiats. The sociological school, under the guidance of Ehrlich, expanded the idea to include not only what the state enacts but also the customs and mores of the community enforced by the state. Despite variations, law in the Western sense may be referred to as a 'rule of conduct' prescribed through legislation, judicial decisions and the like for enforcement by constituted authority within a recognised territory. Law has nothing to do with morality, it is conceived as it 'is' and not as it 'ought' to be. Such a definition of law is inapplicable in the case of the Sharī'ah for the bulk of its content is ethical and moral rather than legal.

Law in the Islamic sense is the entire scheme of moral and social guidance directed toward the divine purposes of the Creator. It covers every aspect of human behaviour and deals extensively with the intention as it does with rituals and civil and criminal matters. It is primarily normative and is designed for moral education as well as legal enforcement. The Muslim scholars and jurists call it 'the law' because they conceive of the divine revelation as the command from the Creator to which a Muslim, as a *khalīfah* of Allah (SWT), must willingly submit. As a *khalīfah* man is given the ability to manage and control his world as a trust (*amānah*) through which he achieves what is his worth and thus decides his eternal destiny in the hereafter. In other words, man's conduct, as a trustee, is subject to arbitration by Divine Judgement and reward and punishment will be meted out for the entire course of human life. Seen from this perspective, every human act is charged with 'legal' consequences and responsibilities which provides ample justification for the 'legalism' of the Sharī'ah.

From the foregoing, the distinction between the Western and Islamic notion of law should be clear. First, Sharī'ah as the law is the expression of the Divine will, while the Western law is the creation of the human mind. Second, the Western system of law grew out of social circumstances and changes in society. Islamic law, being prior to the society and the polity, moulds and fashions society itself. Third, the Western law is generally confined to the regulation of man's relationship with his fellow beings and with the state, the Islamic law includes as well his relationship with his Creator and his own conscience. Finally, the ability of Western law to regulate social behaviour is limited by, and contingent upon, the performance of other institutions like the state, religion, morality, education and the like. The law, as such,

> is not an effective instrument for the formation of human character or the development of human potentialities. It has a very limited power to make men into acceptable social members or to help them become accomplished individuals.[2]

In contrast, the Islamic law has a pervasive and far-reaching impact on society because it is an all-inclusive system combining both the legal and moral realms. 'The Sharī'ah is operative by internal manifestation and works on human conscience'.[3] Some of its provisions may require the sanction of a political authority for enforcement; the bulk of it, however, depends upon human conscience. The believer remains under the obligation of the Sharī'ah even in the absence of any authority to enforce it.

SHARĪ'AH AND *FIQH*

The Sharī'ah has also often been equated with the term *fiqh*. Though related and hence used synonymously, the two concepts are analytically different.[4] Unlike the *sharī'ah* (note the italics and the small letter s) which is divine in origin, *fiqh* is a human product, a body of rules and injunctions based upon the Qur'īn and the Sunnah but arrived at through jurisprudential interpretations, deductions and other principles and methods of classical jurisprudence (*uṣūl*) to regulate social and individual behaviour. *Fiqh* is better designated as applied *sharī'ah* since it is meant to represent the intention of the revealed Will of Allah (SWT) in a detailed and applied way. It has been often presented as an application of general rule indicated in the Qur'ān and the Sunnah or as an analogue to a particular rule in the Divine sources. As such, the *sharī'ah* and *fiqh* appeared as equal parts of the Sharī'ah and were incorporated together in the major encyclopedic works of the jurists. What needs stressing is that though the Sharī'ah does not exclude *fiqh*, they are not identical. The *sharī'ah*, the corpus of law and precepts embodied in the two revealed sources, is sacred, eternal and immutable. The *fiqh*, evolved by Muslim jurists and scholars, on the basis of their understanding, is time-bound and therefore cannot have eternal or universal validity. It nevertheless represents a brilliant jurisprudential accomplishment which can be always inspiring and enlightening Conceived as such, Islamic law contains two basic elements:

the divine, which is unequivocally commanded by Allah or His Messsenger (i.e., the Qur'ān and the Sunnah) and is designated as the *sharī'ah* in the strict sense of the word; and the human which is based upon and aimed at the interpretation or application of the *sharī'ah* and is designated as *fiqh* or applied *sharī'ah*.[5]

Thus, the *sharī'ah* is divine, *fiqh* is human; the former is eternal while the latter is temporal. The divine *sharī'ah* is immutable, the human *fiqh* is subject to change and adaptation, it represents the dynamic aspect of the Sharī'ah.

SHARĪ'AH DEFINED

The Sharī'ah is an Arabic word which literally means a path or a way leading to a watering place. As applied to a divine legal system, this could be taken to mean a 'way to the very source of life'. Indeed, in Islam, it signifies the way to Allah (SWT) as ordained by Allah (SWT). The root word is *shara'a* which literally means 'to pave the way' but conceptually it denotes enacting laws or devising a system. Consequently, its various derivatives like *al-shāri'a*, *tashrī'* and *shari'* are used in the sense respectively of the law, the legislation and the legislator or the law-giver.[6]

Sharī'ah has usually been defined by Muslim scholars in two different but related senses. In its broader sense, Sharī'ah refers to all those institutions and injunctions which Allah (SWT) has ordained to guide the individual in his relationship to Allah (SWT), the Creator; to his own self; to his fellow beings and to everything around him including resources and bounties which the Creator has bestowed at his service.[7] It is a jural order regulating the life and thought of a believer, according to the Divine Will as revealed to the Prophet (ṢAAS). It is 'a complete scheme of life and an all-embracing social order where nothing is superfluous and nothing is lacking'.[8] It is 'the way' which encompasses the totality of man's life. It is in this sense that the Qur'īn (45:18) reminds the Prophet (SAAS):

> Then We set you (O Muhammad) on the Way (Sharī'ah) pertaining to the affairs (of your Dīn); therefore, follow it, and follow not the likes and dislikes of those who do not know.

As pointed out by al-Qurṭubī, the word Sharī'ah is used in the above verse to indicate the total system of life comprising the *tawḥīd*, *'ibādāt*, *mu'āmalāt* and other noble deeds.[9]

The Sharīʻah, therefore, is the entire corpus of divinely revealed law ordering the Muslim believers' entire life from cradle to the grave and ensurings his worldly prosperity as well as happiness in the hereafter. It prescribes the modes of worship for the individual and gives guidance for personal morality and action. It also prescribes directives for their collective life which touches upon such varied subjects as family relationships, socio-economic affairs, duties of citizens, decision-making structures, laws of war and peace and international relations.[10] It is a well-ordered system, a consistent whole, embracing all the various departments of life.

Thus understood, the Sharīʻah is virtually synonymous with the word *dīn* and Islam. *Dīn* denotes submission and obedience to Allah (SWT); to accept with the heart as well as the tongue and to comply with the commands of Allah (SWT).[11] Literally, it means 'the way of life' in which a believer, recognizing Allah (SWT) alone as the possessor of all power and majesty, submits himself to His authority and holds himself accountable only to Him for all his actions.[12] Islam is the name of this *Dīn* while the Sharīʻah is the divinely ordained way of life to serve Him alone. Fazlur Rahman has translated Sharīʻah as 'the ordaining of the way', indicating the law's divine source and purposeful direction. True enough, in the Qur'ān there are far more frequent references to *dīn* and *Islam* than to the Sharīʻah and that its extensive use came into vogue much later.[13] This is natural, since in the early days the terms Islam and *dīn* were employed to convey the same meaning as the Sharīʻah.

As stated, the Sharīʻah has also been defined in a more restricted sense to mean all those commandments and injunctions set down for creed and rituals, social and family affairs, crime and punishment and inheritance and business transactions. To al-Ṭabarī, Sharīʻah is comprised of the laws of inheritance, the *ḥadd* punishments, and commandments and prohibitions.[14] The Qur'ānic verses dealing with these rules and regulations are known as *āyāt al-aḥkām*. Couched in modern terminology, these portions of the Sharīʻah include penal and civil laws, constitutional and administrative laws, international laws and the like. These require the backing of a political authority for their enforcement. Such *āyāt al-aḥkām* in the Qur'ān are very few, exceeding no more than 500 verses. According to ʻAbd al-Wahhāb Khallāf, 70 verses of the Qur'ān deal with family laws; 70 with civil matters; 30 for penal law; and 10 on economic and financial matters.[15] Such an enumeration has to be approximate since legal bearings of some injunctions are debatable, while there are injunctions which apply simultaneously to several spheres of law.[16]

It must, however, be noted that the Muslim jurists, while emphasising these *aḥkām*, always kept the organic nature of the Sharī'ah in view. In other words, these *aḥkām* have no independent existence and can neither be enforced nor understood apart from the total system of life to which they belong. This explains why canonical punishments like amputation of hands for theft and stoning to death for an adulterer are hedged around with conditions. These 'conditions' are not advanced as an apologia, as argued by G.H. Jansen,[17] but to emphasise the organic nature of the Sharī'ah, to uphold the highest standard of justice which is the prime objective of the Sharī'ah and to deter the people from bringing false or unsubstantiated accusations.

In sum, no matter how it is defined, the word Sharī'ah covers every conceivable act of human behaviour and thinking. It deals with rites and rituals, civil and criminal matters, as well as with the intentions behind every action. As the Qur'ānic verse 16:89 maintains:

> We revealed the Book to you as an exposition of all things, and a guidance and mercy and glad tidings for those who have surrendered to Allah.

SOURCES OF THE SHARĪ'AH

The distinction made between the terms *sharī'ah* and *fiqh* suggests that the sources of Islamic law can be discussed under two categories: the primary and the secondary.

The primary sources

The primary sources of the Sharī'ah include the Qur'ān and the Sunnah. These two constitute the foundation as well as the essence of Sharī'ah. 'I leave two things for you', said the Prophet (ṢAAS) in his farewell address, 'you will never go astray while holding them firmly: the Book of Allah and the Sunnah of His Prophet.'[18]

The Qur'ān is the principal source of the Sharī'ah. It is literally the word of Allah (SWT), purely divine, incomparable and inimitable. It was revealed in a piecemeal fashion to facilitate the understanding of the text, appreciate its relevance, implant gradually but firmly its norms and to smooth the path of its implementation.[19] The revealed book was preserved, word for word, in its complete and original form to serve as a source of guidance for all times. It provides a general theoretical framework for Islam, containing universal and particular rules (*aḥkām kullīyah wa far'iyah*), principles, exhortations and commandments which are manifest (*mubīn*), sublime (*'ālī*) and blessed. Being divine, it is sacred, eternal, unconditionally binding, and irrevocable for the faithful.

> He who follows my guidance shall not go astray, nor shall he be unprosperous. But whosoever turns away from My remembrance, his shall be a life of narrow scope, and on the Resurrection Day, We shall raise him blind. (Al-Qur'ān, 20:123–4)

The Qur'ān contains three types of instruction: the articles of faith, the ethical and legal instructions, and the regulations concerning state and society. As previously stated, the bulk of its content is ethical and moral. The legal prescriptions comprise only about 10 per cent of the entire Qur'ān, and this gives mankind a wider scope to determine their socio-political affairs through the use of *ijtihād*, *shūrā* and *ijmā'*.[20]

The Sunnah consists of all the authentic reports of the acts, utterances and silent approval of the Prophet (ṢAAS). Initially, there existed a distinction between the term Sunnah, referring to the practices of the Prophet (ṢAAS), and the *ḥadīth* denoting his utterances as narrated by his companions. Gradually, however, the entire Sunnah was reflected in the *ḥadīth* to such an extent that, by the fifth century AH, the two terms became completely synonymous.[21] Mostly recorded in the six *ṣiḥāḥ* (authentic collections), the Sunnah forms the second fundamental source of the Sharī'ah.

As explained by Ibn Qayyim al-Jawzīyah, the Sunnah is secondary with respect to the Qur'ān because:

> The Qur'ān is definitive as well as final and authoritative as a whole and in its detail, the Sunnah is neither definitive nor final or authoritative in its detail, but must be taken as a whole. There are three possible relations of the Sunnah to the Qur'ān. The first is where the Sunnah agrees with the Qur'ān in all respects, and in this case, the two corroborate and reinforce the given point. The second is where the Sunnah explains and illustrates the Qur'ān and the third is where the Sunnah legislates on a matter on which the Qur'ān is silent. No other possibilities exist for the Sunnah can never run counter to the Qur'ān.[22]

The Sunnah derives its authority from the Qur'ān which calls Prophet Muhammad (ṢAAS) the inspired Prophet (63:3–4). He was entrusted with the Holy Scripture (the Qur'ān) and the message (Islam). The Qur'ān calls him the interpreter and preceptor of the Qur'ān (16:44), the teacher and the guide (3:48), the ruler, the legislator and the judge (44:59) and the 'ideal role model' to be emulated by the believers. The Sunnah, is the practical manifestation of *tawḥīd* and is fully grounded in the eternal virtues of the Qur'ān. Therefore, the Qur'ān declares: 'whosoever obeys the Messenger, he has indeed obeyed Allah' (4:80) and the Prophet (ṢAAS) confirmed by saying: 'whoever followed me followed Allah, and whoever disobeyed me disobeyed Allah'.[23]

Clearly, Allah's commandments and directives have been bequeathed to mankind in two forms: the Qur'ān, and the Sunnah, the ideal conduct of the Prophet (ṢAAS). The Sunnah is better seen not as 'another' source but as an explanation and detailed elaboration, through words and deeds, of the general principles enshrined in the Qur'ān. The Qur'ān is the soul, the Sunnah the body; the former provides the norms, the latter explains and practicalises these norms. The two taken together constitute the supreme law of the real sovereign known in Islamic terminology as the Sharī'ah.

The secondary sources

The secondary sources of the Sharī'ah include all those methods and procedures employed by Muslim jurists and scholars to comprehend and operationalise the Divine Will as contained in the Qur'ān and the Sunnah. Contemporary scholars consider these as part of the all-encompassing concept of *ijtihād*.

Ijtihād, literally means 'effort, exertion or endeavour' but technically it signifies exerting the utmost effort to ascertain the injunctions of Islam and its intent through the efficient use of jurisprudential evidences (*adillah*) and principles (*qawā'id*). Mohammad Iqbal defined it as exerting one's self 'with a view to form an independent judgement on a legal question'.[24] The decisions arrived at through *ijtihād* should neither contravene the Sharī'ah nor 'distort its brilliant clarity' and it should be resorted to only in the absence of an applicable text of the Qur'ān or the Sunnah. Epistemologically, *ijtihād* involves both induction and deduction to the extent that it uses the existing body of knowledge (i.e, the Qur'ān and the Sunnah) and pure logical reasoning. It presupposes an ultimate agreement between reason and revelation with the provision that the former is subservient to the latter.

Ijtihād, if exercised loosely, may result in a wide variety of opinions. The jurists, therefore, developed another method as a restrictive tool on the exercise of *ijtihād*. This is known as *qiyās* (analogical reasoning), i.e., the method of extending the legal injunction found in the divine sources regarding one case to the parallel cases.

An *ijtihād* of an individual or a group may gain the consensus of the learned scholars ('Ulamā') or of the Muslim Ummah and thus attain the status of an *ijmā'*. *Ijmā'* is essentially a consensus of the Ummah in understanding, interpreting and applying the teachings of the Sharī'ah. It is a process that links reliable knowledge to universal agreement. *Ijmā'* carries the double significance of acting as a practical check upon the free flight of the individual as well as according a recognition to the creative breakthrough achieved by the individual.

Khurram Murad maintains that any 'consensus which has a historical continuity from the days of the four caliphs and the companions of the Prophet (ṢAAS) is accepted to be binding'.[25] Given their admitted piety, knowledge of the Sharī'ah, closeness to the Prophet (ṢAAS) and the strong *muttaqī* (pious) leadership of the first four caliphs and their strict adherence to the letter and spirit of the Sharī'ah, their consensus is considered as authoritative. The disintegration of the central institution of *shūrā* (consultative assembly) for the achievement of consensus after the period of *al-Khulafā' al-Rāshidūn* made it difficult to ascertain the claim of the *ijmā'* on any point. All such claims may serve as strong precedent but may be subjected to re-examination relative to changes in human and social conditions. It is worth noting that though there exists some consensus on matters dealing with rites and rituals, there has been no absolute consensus on major issues confronting the contemporary Muslim Ummah. Even on issues with consensus, 'there is continued controversy in the different schools of jurisprudence'.[26] The jurists of different schools have developed various other principles for establishing a new law when the text is silent on a particular matter. These include

(a) *Istiḥsān* (juristic preference): the legist's adoption of a course which he considers better than the one suggested by the analogy (*qiyās*) of the fixed, legal provisions.
(b) *Istiṣlāḥ* (public good) or adoption of a course which is considered to be in the best interest of the community.
(c) *Istisḥāb* (continuance or performance) or considering the continuation of a given judicial situation previously existent unless it can be proved that it no longer exists or has been modified.
(d) *'Urf* (customs or usages) of a particular society which conform to the Sharī'ah.

From the above analysis, one may conclude that the primary sources of the Sharī'ah are the Qur'an and the Sunnah. As for the secondary sources, traditionally only *qiyās* and *ijmā'* were included in this category. Contemporary scholarship consider the above two and the rest under the category of *ijtihād*. The laws derived through the secondary sources are regarded as legal because all these laws, in the final analyses, are rooted in the primary sources, i.e., the Qur'ān and the Sunnah.

RISE AND DECLINE OF IJTIHĀD

Ijtihād, according to Iqbal, 'is the principle of movement in the structure of Islam'.[27] It enables the system to adjust to change and provides continuous development and progress within the framework of Sharī'ah. In fact, it is a key element in ensuring the dynamism of the Sharī'ah.

The principle of *ijtihād* has its origin in the well-known verse of the Qur'ān: 'and to those who exert, We show our path' (19:61). There is also the well-known *ḥadīth*, the tradition of Mu'ādh ibn Jabal, wherein the Prophet (ṢAAS) clearly approved of Mu'ādh's resolve to the exercise of *ijtihād* in cases where the Qur'ān and Sunnah were silent. With the expansion of the frontiers of Islam, the companions of the Prophet (ṢAAS) and scholars trained by them made extensive use of *ijtihād* to confront the new situations and to meet the socio-political exigencies of the time. Realising that the principle of *ijtihād* as constant and progressive was imperative, they strove hard to discover the law to apply it to the actual situation in life. This position is even stressed in a *ḥadīth* which asserts that Allah (SWT) is pleased with one's striving despite its ineptness and that He is doubly delighted when the 'effort' results in a true understanding of His law.

The giant intellectual upsurge generated through the use of this principle, by great jurists like Abu Ḥanīfah (80–150AH/699–767CE) Malik ibn Anas (97–179AH/716–801CE), Muhammad ibn Idrīs al-Shafi'ī (150–204AH/767–820CE), Ahmad ibn Hanbal (164–241AH/780–855CE) and others have few parallels in history. Examining the problems of the Ummah in the light of available knowledge and prevailing circumstances, they gave their judgements to uphold the truth. They repeatedly emphasized, however, that their rulings were their best judgements and 'never claimed to possess a binding authority over Muslims'.[28] With the passage of time, these judgements were elevated to the status of eternal law leading eventually to the establishment of various schools of jurisprudence. Subsequent inter-school debates and arguments led to a hardening of positions. The fall of Baghdad in the middle of the seventh century AH, and the eventual subjugation of Muslim lands by European powers added fuel to the fire. The instinct of self-preservation led to, what Iqbal calls, the 'over-organization' of legal thought characterised by 'jealous exclusion of all innovation in the law of Sharī'ah as expounded by the early doctors of Islam'.[29] Consequently, most of the people consciously or unconsciously became captives of blind imitation (*taqlīd al-a'immah*), which limited everything to the literal observance of the Islamic precepts and to blind obedience to past decisions.[30] Such an excessive preoccupation with 'memory and imitation' had generally weakened the impulse of creativity and change. Transformed into an ossified body of laws and confined to procedural and technical matters to the neglect of substantive questions, Sharī'ah ceased to produce the living, dynamic civilisation it once created in the golden days of Islam. The decline of Islam has been due to the decline and suspension of *ijtihād*, and preoccupation, not with the essentials, but with the externalities and minutiae of religion. The implication of the above observation is that *ijtihād* must be accorded its rightful place if an ethical restructuring of the society is to be accomplished.

To be sure, *ijtihād* can be practised only by those virtuous people who combine the knowledge and insight in the teachings of the Qur'ān and the Sunnah with a thorough understanding of the contribution of early jurists and awareness of contemporary reality.[31] Since these conditions are 'well-nigh impossible of realisation in a single individual", Iqbal suggests as an alternative, the institutionalisation of *ijtihād*.[32] The institution may be constitutionally empowered to make laws through *ijtihād*. This must be elected on the basis of ability such that its members together would fulfil the requirements laid down for a *mujtahid* (one who exercises *ijtihād*). 'In this way alone,' maintained Iqbal, 'we can stir into activity the dormant spirit of life in our legal system and give it an evolutionary outlook.'[33]

ESSENTIAL FEATURES OF THE SHARĪ'AH

The foregoing discussion on the nature and sources of Sharī'ah makes it possible to delineate some of its essential features. The example of divergent thinking given above justifies the need for such an elucidation to help clearly understand and appreciate the significance of Sharī'ah.

To begin with, first, the Sharī'ah is divine. It is the Divine will of Allah (SWT) revealed to the last Prophet of Islam (ṢAAS). Basically, it rests on the authority of divine sources, i.e., the Qur'ān and the Sunnah. Stated differently, the source of the Sharī'ah is Allah (SWT) 'Who has created the heaven and the earth . . . . Verily, to Him belong the creation and the sovereignty' (Al-Qur'ān, 7:54). To Him alone, therefore, as his only Lord and Master, man must submit his entire being. Since Allah (SWT), in addition to being Omnipotent, is Omniscient, human actions are judged according to intentions or *nīyah*. This being the important feature of the Sharī'ah, the believer in Islam is required to observe it with sincerity and good faith. Therefore, the Law, as Ibraheem Sulaiman puts it, 'is a "Believer's Law" in the sense that it is binding primarily on those who believe in it'.[34] It rests, therefore, on faith or conviction. Being divine, the Sharī'ah is eternal and just, designed for all times and all climes.

Second, the Sharī'ah is primarily normative rather than prescriptive. It is a set of value-oriented guidelines expressing the divine purposes of Allah (SWT). It offers a set of values and standards of behaviour with the object of creating that standard of character which takes pleasure in rendering service to humanity. The basic motives of civilised society such as the creation of a moral frame of mind capable of discerning virtue and vice; compassion for the weak, the deprived and the helpless; fairness in commercial transactions; protection of women against all types of exploitation; incorruptibility in the administration of justice; governing through mutual consultation and the holy texts, etc., are enjoined upon man.[35] Intoxicants, *ribā* (usury or interest), gambling and similar acts are forbidden. The objective of the Sharī'ah is to relieve people of hardships by providing necessities of life (*ḍarurīyāt*), conveniences (*ḥājiyāt*) and luxuries or refinements (*taḥsīnīyāt*). It aims at ordering the individual and collective life on the basis of virtues or *ma'rūfāt* and to purge humanity of vices or *munkirāt* (Al-Qur'ān, 3:104).[36] Consequently, all acts are categorised into two: *ḥalāl* and *ḥarām*, each having several gradations. In fact, the Sharī'ah divides the code of behaviour and conduct, its moral quotient, into five categories: the mandatory (*farḍ* and *wājib*), the recommendatory but not enjoined (*mandūb*), indifferent hence permissible (*mubāḥ*), the reprehensible but not prohibited (*makrūh*), and the prohibited (*ḥarām*).[37] Reflecting the varying levels of moral demand placed on human acts, these norms and rules help shape the society in a way conducive to the unfettered growth of righteousness and truth in every sphere of human activity. Since the Sharī'ah deals with value-judgements and principles, its commands can be applied to innumerable human and social conditions with precision and flexibility.

Third, the Sharī'ah is comprehensive. At the individual level, it covers the spiritual, moral, intellectual, aesthetic and physical dimensions of the human personality. At the level of collectivity, the Sharī'ah guidance covers the social, economic, political and other relevant aspects of societal behaviour. It regulates all aspects of human experience for prosperity here and salvation in the hereafter. As S. Parvez Manzoor puts it:

> All contradictions of *internalized* ethics and *externalized* law, of concealed intentions and revealed actions, indeed of faith and deeds, are thus resolved in the all-embracing *actionalism* of the Sharī'ah. . . . It is both a *doctrine* and a path. It is simultaneously a manifestation of divine will and that of human resolve to be an agent of that will. . . . It is an all-embracing system of religion, morality, law, sociology and even politics that is the most formidable achievement of the religious genius of Islam (all emphasis original).[38]

The Sharī'ah injunctions are not confined to external behaviour. It extends its application to overt and covert behaviour of man, to his manifest acts as well as to his innermost feelings and intentions. Some injunctions are of personal nature, some are societal, others purely political, yet others moral. The combination of the general and particular, of moral and political, is what distinguishes the Sharī'ah from other legal systems.

Fourth, and most importantly, the Sharī'ah is an organic and integral whole whose many aspects and provisions all flow logically and ineluctably from the same basic principles of *tawḥīd* and *risālah*. The religious, the political, the economic, and the social are not separate systems but form part of the same system co-ordinated with and gaining strength from each other. It is like the body-politic of the Muslim Ummah in which, as described by the Prophet (ṢAAS),

> The believers are to one another like a solid edifice (reinforcing one another) each in the likeness of a (live) body where each and every member in it is alerted to a state of feverish solitude the moment one of its members is afflicted.[39]

The Sharī'ah recognizes no division between religion and other aspects of life including politics. There is no area of man's activity which the Sharī'ah does not address with specific guidance. This guidance may be clear or unclear, hard as in its *farā'iḍ* and *muḥarramāt* or soft as in its categorisation of *mandūb*, *makrūh* and *mubīḥ*. But nothing escapes its guidance. From the perspective of the Shārī'ah, life is a seamless whole that must be lived in its entirety. The different parts of the Sharī'ah cannot be viewed in isolation from one another. It can function smoothly and efficiently if the entire scheme of life is practised *in toto*. Thus, as pointed out by Mawdūdī, the penalty of amputating the hand for the commitment of theft is meant to be promulgated in a full-fledged Islamic polity where virtues thrive and vices are proscribed, where each and every citizen is provided with equal privileges and opportunities to seek economic livelihood. It is not meant for a society characterised by gross injustices, class distinctions and distressing economic disparities. Similarly, punishment for adultery and fornication are not meant for 'that filthy society wherein sexual excitement is rampant, wherein nude pictures, obscene books and vulgar songs have become common recreations'.[40]

Finally, Sharī'ah strikes a balance and harmony between the elements of permanence (stability) and change (flexibility). This is suggested in the Qur'ānic verse 5:48 which reads: 'To every people have we ordained a Divine Law and an open road'. Thus, the Lawgiver has ordained not merely a law but has permitted within the area of Sharī'ah an 'open road' for temporal legislation to meet the various exigencies of time and place. Things that fall in the categories of *wājibāt* and *ḥarām* are strictly demanded of the believers. These obligatory and prohibitory commands are few and a major part of man's day-to-day life falls in the *mubāḥ* category which accords a vast expanse and degree of latitude to individual choice, freedom and initiative under varying socio-economic and political circumstances. It is this part of the Sharī'ah which is flexible and which endows it with wide possibilities of growth and advancement and makes it progressive. The jurists have laid down rules and procedures on the basis of which changed human conditions can be catered for. Most of these procedures can be subsumed under the concept of *ijtihād* which has to be exercised within the framework of the Qur'ān and the Sunnah.

THE SHARĪ'AH IN THE MUSLIM WORLD

Sharī'ah is the core of Islam. It is the chief arbitrator of all norms, actions and policies and the defining element of an Islamic political order. Yet, the Sharī'ah has been forgotten or neglected by Muslims for most of their history since the days of the rashidūn caliphs. During the period of *al-khulafā' al-Rāshidūn*, Sharī'ah enjoyed the position as the pivot of Muslim civilisation. The caliphs saw to it that Islamic law was faithfully administered and obeyed. The reality of government over the many centuries thereafter bore little relation to these ideal models. The Umayyad and the Abbasid caliphs sought to compensate for this gap by associating themselves with symbols of Islamic legitimacy and to bolster their prestige by patronage of Islamic institutions and services to the Islamic cause. The *post facto* acceptance by many Muslim jurists of the dynastic rule and its later rationalisation under the doctrine of necessity meant that political authority slowly slipped out of the purview of the Sharī'ah. It was a logical culmination of this bifurcation that the colonial powers found it easy to relegate Sharī'ah to a very limited sphere and supplant it with the law of their own making.

> Under the policies of Austin's imperative theory, European codes of Civil Law were introduced into legal, procedural and judicial affairs. In French possessions, the *Code Napoléon* and in those of the English the *Common Law* were introduced and codified and made law for the Muslims. A new national legal system was developed in each Muslim area; lest the religious susceptibilities of the people may be offended, the law relating to family affairs was left largely intact.[41]

The emergence of Muslim nation-states after the Second World War did not improve the matter. The established trend has been the Westernisation of the legal system and confinement of the Sharī'ah to matters of personal status, and that, too, with drastic modifications or reforms. Turkey has for long replaced the Sharī'ah with a non-Islamic legal system *in toto*. Others have relegated the realm of the Sharī'ah to distorted versions of personal law maintaining in force the criminal and general civil laws based upon European models. Countries like Saudi Arabia and the peninsular Emirates, though they concede the Sharī'ah to be the law of the land, permit practices contrary to the spirit of Islam. In the dominant judgement of the Islamically committed scholars, emirates and monarchies do not represent the style of government demanded by the Sharī'ah. Iran, under the late Ayatollah Khomeini, tried to overhaul the common laws to conform to the comprehensive version of the Sharī'ah. The hostile external forces and the critical shortage of manpower militated against her attempts at operationalising the Sharī'ah.

Thus, there exists not a single Islamic republic which may be acknowledged as representing a model of Islamic governance in the sense of a government constituted according to Islamic requirements. The only visible gain made by the on-going global demand for the implementation of Sharī'ah is the insertion of Islam as a 'state religion' clause in some of the constitutions of the Muslim world and constitutional provisions indicating that the Sharī'ah is either 'a source' or 'the source' of all legislation in about 26 Muslim countries. It may be noted that the Sharī'ah does not have any provision requiring that Islam be designated as the state religion or that Sharī'ah be the source of legislation. An Islamic constitution *ipso facto* implies the supremacy of Islam and the Sharī'ah and hence any such designation is not merely tautological but actually uncalled for. The idea of a 'state religion' is a European formulation and has been imported into the Muslim land to provide an Islamic cover to the existing secular constitutions. The fact that Islam is or is not formally made the 'state religion' does not by itself have any influence in determining the role Islam actually plays in a given country. These designations have more symbolic than practical significance and have been designed as a gesture to placate the Islamically committed critics of the established secular order led by the Westernised, educated elite.

Implementation of Sharī'ah is not a matter of getting away with cosmetic change and minor adjustments in the existing secular structures. It entails a total readjustment of social and political machineries as well as of directions in legislative thinking and procedures to conform to Islamic way of life. It calls for the mobilisation of the entire community to dethrone the alien mode of thinking and living, to put an end to political and cultural imperialism and to inculcate Islamic values in order to usher in an Islamic socio-political order.

CONCLUSION

Sharī'ah is often misunderstood and has wrongly been equated with the law as understood by many in the West. It has been equated with *fiqh* or jurisprudence. The two terms, though related, are not identical: *sharī'ah* is divine in its origin, while *fiqh* is a human product, outcome of attempts to understand, interpret and apply the will of Allah (SWT). The Qur'ān and the Sunnah define the Divine Will, the *fiqh* spells out that Will and establishes the methods to derive and apply its rules to regulate individual and collective behaviour. In common usage, however, the two appear as equal parts of the Sharī'ah.

Sharī'ah is an entire scheme of life ordained by the Lord, the Creator, and sustainer of the Universe. Divine in its origin, the Sharī'ah is largely prescriptive, comprehensive, and organically balanced in nature. It sets forth and regulates man's relation with and obligations to Allah (SWT), to himself, to his fellow beings and to other creatures. It may narrowly be defined to imply do's and don'ts. These commandments have always been viewed within the perspective of an entire scheme of life covering all spheres of human activity. What is presently known as Islamic law or introduced under the Islamisation programme is only part of the larger whole which has no independent existence and cannot be enforced apart from the total system to which it belongs.

Sharī'ah is based on the principles of: (1) the centrality of Allah (SWT) in everything (*tawḥīd*); (2) the prophethood of Muḥammad (ṢAAS) (*risālah*); (3) the vicegerency of man on earth (*khilāfah*); and (4) the doctrine of enjoining virtue and forbidding vice (*amr bi al-ma'arūf wa al-nahy'an al-munkar*). *Tawḥīd* implies the unity and sovereignty of Allah (SWT) Who alone has the right to regulate man's behaviour. Hence the revelation of the Qur'ān. The appointment of the inspired prophet is a *sine qua non* to interpret the Qur'ān and to guide the believers through his personal examples, sayings and approvals referred to as *Sunnah*. To derive positive rules from the Qur'ān and the Sunnah and to expand their application to new situation there emerged the all-embracing concept of *ijtihād* which subsumes various categories of endeavour such as *ijmā'*, *istiṣlāḥ*, *istiḥsān*, *istisḥāb*, and *'urf*.

Sharī'ah, the dominant moral and legal code of Muslim societies, facilitated the social growth and development of the Muslims to such an extent that it culminated in the establishment of the geographically vast civilisation of Islam. This dynamism of the Sharī'ah is largely due to the role played by *ijtihād*. It is well known that the companions of the Prophet (ṢAAS) and the majority of scholars during the formative period of Islam, including the founders of the schools of jurisprudence (*madhāhib*), did exercise and called for the extension of *ijtihād* to all qualified Muslim scholars. Soon, however, *ijtihād* ceased to play its role as the guiding force that inspired Muslim creativity and ingenuity and that nurtured the growing spirit of the Muslim community. *Taqlīd* came to be the generally accepted mode of analysis. The contemporary realisation that *taqlīd* resulted in intellectual decline, social decadence and eventual acquiescence to the Western mode of civilisation had led to a renewed call to reopen the gate of *ijtihād* to proceed to the work of reconstructing a dynamic, thriving civilisation of Islam.

5 Ummah: The Islamic Social Order

The Islamic social order, the Ummah, as a bearer of 'witnesses (to the Truth) before all mankind' (Al-Qur'ān, 2:143) is the dynamic vehicle for the realisation of the Divine Will in space-time, in history. Recognising this necessity, the Shari'ah has apportioned the larger portion of its expansive corpus to the treatment of the social order, leaving only a tiny fraction concerned with rituals and personal ethics. The Islamic tradition, likewise, has placed much emphasis on the idea of the Ummah. Being part of the Ummah is a central part of being a Muslim. The Islamic era begins not with the birth or death of the last Prophet of Islam (ṢAAS) nor with the first revelation of the Qur'ān, but with the *Hijrah* of the Prophet (ṢAAS) and his companions to Madinah. This was the point when the Muslims of Makkah opted to place their loyalty to Allah (SWT) before the ties of kinship. Muslim lives become significant only through belonging to this 'justly balanced' Ummah which is indispensable for their salvation, in the hereafter. This explains why the concept of Ummah occupies the most pivotal position in the lexicon of Islamic political theory. What then is the Ummah? How has it been conceived in the Qur'ān and the Sunnah? How did it emerge in history? What are its essential features? Finally, how does it compare with the concept of nationalism?

TERMINOLOGICAL CONFUSION

Ummah is a unique concept having no equivalent term in the Western languages. The earlier attempts at equating Ummah with nation or nation-states has been abandoned in favour of 'community' which has recently gained currency among the Western political science circles. The term nation or nation-state is of relatively recent origin, borrowed from the West, and pressed into use by native intellectuals whose Western education has led them to admire and emulate their foreign mentors. It is equally wrong to use community as a synonym for Ummah.[1] The similarities between the two terms are superficial.

The term community has been defined rather widely to 'mean any circle of common life' and would, as such, range from a small 'locality group' to 'any area of social life' such as a village, a town or a country.[2] It is a 'complex social system with both a physical locus and a socio-psychological consensus.'[3] Stated simply, a community is a group of people who have common attachments to a given area and who possess strong ties of identity. This sense of communal identity may arise out of blood, kinship-ties, common culture, common territory or, most commonly, out of some combination of these.

As defined, the term community has nothing in common with Ummah. The deciding basis for Ummah is neither race, language, history or any combination of them, nor is it determined by geographical considerations. Ummah transcends race, language and geography. It is a universal order enclosing the entire collectivity of Muslims inhabiting the globe, united by the bond of one strong and comprehensive ideology of Islam. It is indispensable for the actualisation of the Divine Will in space-time and for the achievement of happiness in this world and salvation in the hereafter.

UMMAH IN THE QUR'ĀN AND THE SUNNAH

As used in the Qur'ān, Ummah is a comprehensive concept and carries many senses.[4] In some verses, it refers to a 'people' or 'nation' thus making it an approximate synonym of *qawm* or *sha'b* held together solely by ties of kinship (40:5; 49:13). It is also used to refer to a group of people within a larger community (7:159) as well as to a group of 'men who were watering" (28:23). In verse 10:19, the whole of mankind has been referred to as a single community, *ummah wāḥidah*. This community got divided as its members held 'divergent views' on Divine Guidance. In the strict legalistic sense, however, the term Ummah denotes a group of people united in religious belief and practice (Al-Qur'ān,7:159), a group of people who having listened to a prophet, believe in him (Al-Qur'ān, 10:47) and make a covenant with Allah (SWT) to serve Him alone. It is especially in this sense that the Qur'ān speaks of the followers of the Prophet Muḥammad (ṢAAS) and addresses them as 'you are the best of Ummah evolved for mankind; enjoin the right, forbid the wrong and believe in Allah (3:110). Thus understood, Ummah refers exclusively to the believers (*mu'minūn*) and are contrasted with the unbelievers (*kuffār*), the Jews and the polytheists (*mushrikūn*). Thus: 'We have divided them into *umam* (plural of Ummah) on earth. Some of them are righteous and others are the opposite'

(7:168). The *shahādah* in Islam is not merely a testimonial of faith in the unity of Allah (SWT) and the prophethood of Muhammad (ṢAAS) but an oath of allegiance to the *ummah Muslimah* as well. This Ummah extends to the whole of mankind as the message of the last prophet of Islam is addressed to mankind as a whole. 'Say O men, I am sent to you all as the messenger of Allah to whom belongs the dominion of the heavens and the earth; there is none worthy of worship save He . . .' (7:158).

The term Ummah occurs most frequently in various traditions of the Prophet (ṢAAS). He is reported to have referred to his followers as Ummah and stressed greatly preserving the organic unity and psychological cohesion of the nascent social order. The conceptualisation of the Ummah was, however, sharpened by the Prophet (ṢAAS) in what Hamidullah calls the first written constitution in the world, the constitution of Madinah.[5] This is a document regarding which 'even the most critical minds do not cast doubt about its authenticity'.[6] This is the fundamental document establishing the Muslim Ummah and is the first treaty between them and the scripturaries, *ahl al-kitāb*, here, of course, the Jews of Madinah.

Beginning with the invocatory formula 'In the name of Allah the Merciful, the Mercy-Giving', the document clearly spells out that the believers and Muslims of Quraysh and Yathrib and those who follow them and join them and strive with them are a single Ummah to the exclusion of the rest of mankind.[7] They are *mawālī* (patrons, clients, friends) of one another;[8] act as a corporate body and are contrasted with the unbelievers (*kuffār*), the Jews and, in one place, with the polytheists (*mushrikūn*).[9] Alongside the believers there stood another community, the Jews, whose members' lives were to be ordered in accordance with the precepts of Judaism.

Despite such clear statements, attempts have been made to prove that 'the Ummah as described in the Constitution of Madinah in fact has a territorial basis'.[10] Rosenthal joins Montgomery Watt and believes that the Constitution uses the term Ummah in a 'religious, social and political sense, granting certain privileges to and imposing certain duties on all its members, Muslims, Jews and pagans'.[11] The basis of such misgivings is the statement in the Constitution: *Inna Yahūd Bani 'Awf Ummatun ma'a al-mu'minīn'* which is translated as 'the Jews of Bani Awf are an Ummah along with the believers', meaning that the Jews and Muslims together form one Ummah in Madinah. Such an interpretation is unacceptable for several reasons. First, it violates the concept of the Ummah in the Qur'ān. Second, it contradicts the first article of the Constitution which singles out the believers, the Muslims, and those who follow them and strive with them as forming a single Ummah and contrasts them with both Jews and pagans. Finally, throughout the document, the Jews are ranged alongside the believers, never among them. Where the need was felt to discuss the two groups collectively, the Constitution coined and used the phrase *ahl hadhihī al-ṣaḥīfah* (the people of this document). Thus the Jews of Bani Awf are to be considered an Ummah by the side of the believers. The Muslim Ummah, as defined by al-Fārūqī, is therefore,

> a corporate organic, civic body, which is not limited to land, people, race, culture; universalist, totalist, and responsible in its corporate life as well as in that of every one of its members; and indispensable for every man's achievement of happiness in this world and the next, for every actualization of the divine-will in space-time.[12]

ESSENTIAL FEATURES OF THE UMMAH

Ummah, as defined, denotes a group of people having certain features in common and agreeing to certain conditions. First, the Ummah Muslimah defines its membership and distinguishes itself from the rest in terms of its belief and attitudes *vis-à-vis* the Lord, the Creator, Cherisher and Sustainer of the Universe. The entity of believers should, in principle, constitute a solid unity among themselves and against those who reject the faith. They profess their faith in the unity of Allah (SWT) and in the finality of the prophethood of Muḥammad (ṢAAS). They acknowledge one book, perform the prescribed rituals and follow the Shari'ah. In short, Islam is the essence of the Ummah which binds all its elements into one integrated whole and separates them from the rest of mankind. The Jews of Madinah were declared a separate Ummah in the constitution of Madinah precisely because they professed a different faith and adhered to a different ideology.

Second, Islam which gives identity to the Ummah, obligates it as well to be universal rather than particularistic. The Qur'ān loudly proclaims that all men descended from one and the same pair, asserting simultaneously that they were constituted into tribes and nations that they may fraternise and mutually enrich one another (49:13). From the very beginning, the audience of the Qur'ān and of the Prophet (ṢAAS) was the whole of mankind. Being squarely based upon the universal creed of Islam, the Muslim Ummah cannot but be universal. It can never restrict itself to any caste, class or colour. On the contrary, it must ceaselessly strive to embrace the entire Muslims. 'This Ummah of yours,' declares the Qur'ān, 'is one Ummah' (21:92; 23:53), and it must, therefore, actualise the will of Allah (SWT). To emphasise universalism is not to proscribe the natural groupings of humans into tribes and communities nor to rule out the desirability of territorial demarcation into units or states for administrative convenience and efficiency. It demands, however, that such groupings and administrative divisions do not become the ultimate measure of everything; that in it the Sharī'ah must reign supreme and that they must move continuously toward making Allah's way supreme on earth. The Muslim Ummah is not a matter of biology, geography and linguistic affinity. Islam recognises these groupings as divinely ordained. Beneath the seeming social, cultural and ethnic diversity lies the fundamental homogeneity of Islamic civilisation enclosing the entire collectivity of Muslims. Muslims may belong to numerous territories and to various communities, their acceptance of the *shahādah* and of the Shari'ah smooths these differences and makes them *ipso facto* the members of the Ummah.

Third, the Muslim Ummah, in addition to being universal, is organic in nature. It is like a well-ordered system characterised by cohesion among its component parts; the parts fit and stick together, and form a recognisable whole. The believers, men and women, are *awliyā'* of one another (Al-Qur'ān, 9:71). They are *anṣār* (assistants) and *a'wān* (helpers) to each other;[13] 'their hearts are united in friendly relations and in loving one another'.[14] This *wala* relationship is concretised further by the concept of *ukhūwah* (brotherhood). 'The believers are but brothers' whose hearts have been wound up around Him in mutual love of one another (Al-Qur'ān, 49:10; 48:29). This brotherhood is not one of lineage but of religion (*dīn*) and sanctity (*ḥurmah*) and is characterised by love and co-operation among its members.[15] This bond of brotherhood is expressed in their performance of prayers in congregation, acceptance of invitations from brother Muslims and in joining to carry the bier of a deceased fellow believer. In other words, the members of the Ummah are mutually and severally interdependent with one another and with the whole. This organic solidarity is the element capable of making the Ummah Allah's witnesses on earth. This is the meaning of the Prophet's (ṢAAS) analogy of the believers as a 'body' wherein each member cares for the other. It is the same idea inherent in analogy of a 'solid edifice' wherein the elements reinforce one another,[16] and all adhere together by the Prophet (ṢAAS), as the fingers are connected to and through the hand. Again and again, the Prophet (ṢAAS) has emphasised the seriousness of this point: 'You shall not enter paradise until you have faith and you cannot attain faith until you love one another,'[17] and he said, 'Every Muslim is brother to a Muslim, neither wronging him nor allowing him to be wronged.'[18]

Fourth, in emphasising the organic nature of the Ummah, Islam did not espouse the evils of regimentation or collectivism, nor does it give free rein to individual idiosyncrasies. Instead, Islam strikes a delicate balance between individualism and collectivism and declares its purpose to be the attainment of perfection for the individual as well as for the Ummah. The Shari'ah through its concepts of *fard al-'ayn* and *fard al-kifāyah* arbitrates between the collective pursuit and the individual freedom.

The final feature of the Ummah is its political expression in the 'political system', not in the Western sense of a sovereign, nationalist, territorial entity but as the political dimension of the collective endeavour of Muslims to actualise the Divine will. The 'polity' in Islam is Allah's (SWT) 'polity' and the believers constitute the party of Allah (*ḥizballāh*) which is the synonym used in the Qur'ān for the Muslim Ummah (5:56). The ideological basis of this polity is *tawḥīd*; in it, the ultimate allegiance is owed to Allah (SWT) Who alone is the sovereign; it is subject to the rules and norms of the Shari'ah; and in it, common affairs are undertaken through mutual consultation and discussion (*shūrā*) among the members of the Ummah, and decisions ideally are arrived at through *ijmā*. 'An Islamic political order as such, is a participatory association whose various organs act as instruments of the Ummah to establish the Sharī'ah through *shūrā* and *ijmā'*. In this sense, the Ummah is equally the political order known historically as *khilāfah*, the caliphate.[19] It was this institution which upheld the Divine Order of justice and symbolised the unity of direction of the Ummah.

FUNCTIONS OF THE UMMAH

To emphasise the unity of Ummah, the Qur'ān provided them common direction, *qiblah* or *ka'bah*; its symbolic form in the institution of *ḥajj*, and the means for fulfilling its purpose through *jihād*. The three terms are mutually closely connected and are mentioned in the Qur'ān in the context of the Ummah (2:143, 145; 22:77–78). Having a direct bearing on the life and constitution of the Ummah, it is perfectly natural for the Qur'ān to simultaneously specify the task and functions of the Ummah.

The 'sole objective' for which the Ummah has been evolved, says Sayyid Mawdūdī, 'the *raison d'être* of its existence' is to bear witness, before mankind, to the Truth and guidance which Allah (SWT) has bestowed upon them.[20] The Qur'ān proclaims:

> And thus we have made you an Ummah of the middle position (*wasaṭ*) so that you may be witnesses (to the Truth) before all mankind, and the Messenger may be witness (to it) before you (2:143).

The truth to be witnessed is the *shahādah*, the profession of Islamic faith which asserts that there is none worthy of worship except Allah (SWT) and that Muhammad (ṢAAS) is His Messenger. The *shahādah* 'encompasses the whole truth' and is the proclamation of and commitment to the lordship of Allah (SWT) over everything including all human life. It means as explained by Sayyid Mawdūdī,

> to teach human beings the proper way of conducting their lives, the code of behaviour that they should adopt to win Allah's favour, the acts that they should perform, the acts that they should avoid, and the things for which they will be brought to account.[21]

This witnessing to the Truth should be by word as well as by actions. The former is to be carried out through speech and writing, rational discourse and convincing evidence, by using all possible methods of education, communication and propaganda. The witness by actions implies doing and living Islam in its integral and comprehensive manner. It means moulding the individual and collective lives so that they become a living embodiment of Islam and to be actively engaged in *jihād* to establish justice and to make the Divine way prevail over everything else.[22]

The term *wasaṭ* in *sūrah* (chapter) 2, *āyah* (verse) 143, according to the Qur'ānic commentators, has reference to the balance of the two sides of a scale for upholding justice. The idea, then, is that the Muslims, unlike the rigidity of Jewish particularism and the accommodating nature of Christianity, do not exaggerate in their religion. They, instead, follow the 'right path' (*al-ṣirāt al-mustaqīm*) as revealed to the last prophet of Islam (ṢAAS).[23] In functional terms, Muslims are to act as judges to determine the extremes and as modifiers to smooth out those extremes. The former is a diagnostic function, an intellectual enterprise, while that of the latter is an operational one, a practical activity.

Verse 41 of *sūrah* 22 in the Qur'ān reads: 'Those (are Muslims) who when we give them *power* on earth, establish prayers, pay *zakāh* and enjoin virtue and forbid vice – and to Allah belongs the end of the affairs'. The task of the Ummah, as per above verse, is to establish on earth a socio-political order for effectively prohibiting evil and commanding good on the basis of a unique and only Lord, Allah (SWT). The object of the polity is clearly spelled out in both the negative and positive sense. The polity would not only prevent people from exploiting and suppressing each other and protecting them from foreign aggression, it would simultaneously evolve and develop a well-balanced system of social justice as enshrined in the Qur'ān and the Sunnah.[24] *Āyah* 104 of *sūrah* 3 says to the same effect: 'Let there be of you an Ummah to call to the good, to enjoin virtue and forbid the vice, these are the ones to be felicitous.' As explained by Yusuf 'Alī, this is a call to submit to the will of Allah (SWT).

> This implies (1) faith, (2) doing right, being an example to others to do right, and having the *power* to see that the right prevails, (3) eschewing wrong, being an example to others to eschew wrong and having the *power* to see that wrong and injustice are defeated (emphasis mine).[25]

It should be evident from the wordings of the passages as well as the commentaries that the task of establishing a socio-political order and of witnessing unto mankind are fundamentally interdependent and neither is possible without the other.

The task of witnessing is assigned to the entire believers. However, the words 'let there be of you an Ummah' can be interpreted either to refer to 'the entire Ummah' or 'a group', implying the religious leadership, from among the Ummah charged with the duty and responsibility of inviting mankind to comply with the Sharī'ah and stand as a judge or arbiter to diagnose and smooth out the extremes. Al-Tabarī and al-Qurṭubī adopted the latter interpretation while Ibn Taymīyah, Ibn Khaldun, and contemporary commentators cast their vote for the former option. There are passages in the Qur'ān calling upon Muslims to produce a group from among themselves who would acquire a deep understanding of the faith and would then diffuse it through teaching and preaching as in *sūrah* 9, *āyah* 122. The specific function, of acquiring an understanding of the faith and preaching it, assigned to 'a group' cannot be generalised to include the comprehensive task designated by the term witness. On the contrary, the Qur'ān abhors the idea of elitism and hence states in unequivocal terms that all Muslims, men and women, are the bearers of this responsibility. Thus *āyah* 7 of *sūrah* 9 categorically asserts that

> Believing men and believing women are friends and supporters of each other; they enjoin virtue and forbid vice, establish prayers, pay *zakāh* and obey Allah and His Messenger – these are the ones upon whom Allah will have His mercy, for Allah is Mighty and Wise.

Given such a categorical statement, it was not difficult for Ibn Taymīyah to assert that the injunction of commanding the good and forbidding the evil is the very end of religion and of all governments and that this is enjoined upon every capable Muslim. It is a duty incumbent upon the collectivity and may be discharged by its entrusted agents or organs of the Ummah. Failing that the act of witnessing becomes a personal responsibility incumbent on every able Muslim man and woman.[26]

There are several implications of the responsibility of 'witness' to the Ummah as a whole. For one, it negates elitism, which in the eyes of the Qur'ān is so abhorrent that it explicitly and emphatically states that 'believing men and women' are bearers of this responsibility. Next, it is also in conformity with the conception of the Ummah as laid down in the Qur'ān, a *tawḥīdī* Ummah which is universal, organic and egalitarian based on goodwill, cooperation and brotherhood. Finally, the acceptance of this responsibility by the Ummah has served, throughout Muslim history, as a great impetus for revolution and change in the Muslim world.

MUSLIM UMMAH: A HISTORICAL PERSPECTIVE

The origin of Muslim Ummah is not buried in a legendary past nor does its reconstruction require a philosophical reasoning. It could be found emerging slowly from the life of the Prophet (ṢAAS), his ceaseless struggle to establish Islam and the biographies of his companions.

The Periods of the Prophet (ṢAAS) and the *khulafā' al-Rāshidun*

The small group of Muslims, cut off from tradition by their obedience to the prophetic call, were the foundation stone of the Ummah. The Prophet (ṢAAS)'s wife Khadījah, his cousin 'Ali ibn Abī Ṭālib, his friend

Abu Bakr and his freedman Zayd ibn Ḥārithah constituted the first nucleus whose centre was the person of the Prophet (ṢAAS). They were joined, during the years 610–622 CE by others. They professed *shahādah* and thus accepted the belief which was expressed in a new mode of living shaped within the 'limits set by Allah' (Al-Qur'ān: 2:187).

The Ummah at Makkah existed in a kind of negative relationship to the well-entrenched merchant 'republic' that stood for tradition-rooted pagan social values. The Quraysh, the leading tribe in Makkah, subjected the members of the new Ummah to extreme and ceaseless persecution, seducing some from their new faith, exiling others from their city and eventually chalking out a plan for the outright murder of the Apostle. Under the Divine command, the Prophet (ṢAAS) migrated, along with his companions, to Madinah, which ushered in the beginning of the civilisation of Islam.[27] With this act, the Muslims secured a territorial base, acquired political authority and control and supplanted the tribal complex of Arabia by the Islamic norm of loving one another in the spirit of Allah (SWT).[28] In short, with the *Hijrah*, there emerged a new way of life, a new people and a new political order – all fused together by the compelling idea of a universal, organic, *tawḥīdī* Ummah.

One of the first acts of the Prophet (ṢAAS) in Madinah, was to inaugurate a virtual brotherhood (*mu'ākhāt*) among the believers which became stronger than blood ties. The prophet (ṢAAS) set the example by taking 'Alī ibn Abi Ṭālib as his brother. Hamzah, the Prophet's uncle, became the brother of Zayd ibn Ḥārithah, the Prophet's freedman. Others followed suit (see Table 5.1).

This was followed by the promulgation of *ḥajj*, the famous change of *qiblah* from Jerusalem to Makkah (see Al-Qur'ān, 2:144), and most important of all, the promulgation of the document, the Constitution of Madinah. With this document, there emerged two distinct and opposite entities: *dār al-Islām* (abode of peace) and *dār al-ḥarb* (abode of war).[29] The salient principles of the Muslim Ummah are summed up eloquently in the Prophet (ṢAAS)'s sermon at the last pilgrimage which is well worth quoting in full.[30]

> O men, listen well to my words, for I do not know whether I shall meet you again on such an occasion in the future. O Men, your lives and your property shall be inviolate until you meet your Lord. The safety of your lives and of your property shall be as inviolate as this holy day and holy month. Remember that you will indeed meet your Lord, and that He will indeed reckon your deeds. Thus

Table 5.1 The pair of brotherhood instituted by the Prophet (SAAS)

Abu Bakr with Kharija ibn Zubayr
‘Umar with Itban bin Malik
‘Abu ‘Ubaydah, Amir ibn ‘Abdullāh with Sa‘d ibn Mu‘ādh ibn al-Nu‘man
Abdul Rahman ibn Auf with Sa‘d al-Rabi
Al-Zubayr ibn Awwam with Salama ibn Salāma ibn Waqsh
‘Uthman ibn Affan with Aus ibn Thābit ibn al-Mundhir
Ṭalha ibn Ubaydullah with Ka’b ibn Malik
Sa‘d ibn Zayd ibn ‘Amr ibn Nufyal with Ubayy ibn ka‘b
Masud ibn Umayr with Abu Ayub Khalid ibn Zayd
Abu Ḥudhyfa ibn ‘Utba with Abbad ibn Bishr ibn Waqsh
‘Ammar ibn Yasir ally of B. Makhzum with Hudhayfa ibn Yaman
Abu Dharr, Burayr ibn Junada al-Ghifārī with al-Mundhir ibn ‘Amr
Hatib ibn Abi Balta‘a, ally of B. Asad ibn Abdul Uzza with Uwaym ibn Sa‘diab brother of B. ‘Amr ibn ‘Auf
Salman the Persian with Abu Darda
Bilal freedman of Abū Bakr with Abū Ruwayah ‘Abdullāh ibn ‘Abdullāh Rahman al-Khathami

Source: Ibn Isḥāq, *The Life of Muhammad: A Translation of Ibn Ishāq's Sirat Rasūl Allāh* tr. Alfred Guillaume (London: Oxford University Press, 1967), pp. 234–5.

do I warn you. Whoever of you is keeping a trust of someone else shall return that trust to its rightful owner. All interest obligation shall henceforth be waived. Your capital, however, is yours to keep. You will neither inflict nor suffer inequity. God had judged that there shall be no interest and that all the interest due to ‘Abbas ibn ‘Abd al Muṭṭalib shall henceforth be waived. Every right arising out of homicide in pre-Islamic days is henceforth waived. And the first such right that I waive is that arising from the murder of Rābi‘ah ibn al Ḥārith ibn ‘Abd al Muṭṭalib. O men, the devil has lost all hope of ever being worshipped in this land of yours. Nevertheless, he still is anxious to determine the lesser of your deeds. Beware of him, therefore, for the safety of your religion. O men, intercalation or tampering with the calendar is evidence of great unbelief and confirms the unbelievers in their misguidance. They indulge in it one year and forbid it the next in order to make permissible that which God forbade, and to forbid that which God has made permissible. The pattern according to which the time is reckoned is always the same. With God, the months are twelve in number. Four of them are holy. Three of these are successive and one occurs singly between the months of Jumāda and Sha‘bān. O men, to you a right belongs with respect to your women and to your women a right with respect to you. It is our right that they not fraternise with any one of whom you do not approve, as well as never to commit adultery. But if they do, then God has permitted you to isolate them within their homes and to chastise them without cruelty. But if they abide by your right, then to them belongs the right to be fed and clothed in kindness. Do treat your women well and be kind to them, for they are your partners and committed helpers. Remember that you have taken them as your wives and enjoyed their flesh only under God's trust and with His permission. Reason well, therefore, O men, and ponder my words which I now convey to you. I am leaving you with the Book of God and the Sunnah of His Prophet. If you follow them, you will never go astray. O men, harken well to my words. Learn that every Muslim is a brother to every Muslim and that the Muslims constitute one brotherhood. Nothing shall be legitimate to a Muslim which belongs to a fellow Muslim unless it was given freely and willingly. Do not, therefore, do injustice to your own selves. O God, have I conveyed Your message?

The sermon contains principles of great significance:

1. It abolishes blood relationship as the principle of loyalty, identity and vengeance.
2. It prohibits usury and all interest-based transactions.
3. It proclaims family relationship to be based upon the principles of love, equality and justice.
4. It declares life, property and family to be trusts from Allah (SWT) which must not be betrayed.
5. It emphasises Muslim solidarity as constituting one brotherhood.
6. It reminds the Muslims of following the Sharī'ah for salvation. All these injunctions are sealed by invoking Allah (SWT) as a witness.

It is the consensus of the Muslim scholars that a part of the Prophet (ṢAAS)'s authority had passed to the caliphs who possessed neither the divine power of making laws nor the prophetic function of proclaiming them.[31] A temporal ruler and the defender of the faith, the caliph was charged with the responsibility of keeping intact the heritage of the Prophet (ṢAAS) – the religion, the political order and the Ummah within the framework of the Sharī'ah. It was in this restricted sense that he was the successor to the Prophet, and had a total control over the Ummah. The caliph was the centre and the symbol of the political unity, an expression of the unity of the whole Ummah.

Ummah during the post-*Rāshidūn* period

Politically, the Ummah muslimah was united under one suzerainty during the golden age of faith, truth and right – the periods of the Prophet (ṢAAS) and the *Rāshidūn* caliphs. With the passage of time, the simplicity of manners and fervid religiosity of the companions gave way to pomp and grandeur and laxity in the observance of Sharī'ah. The Islamic concept of universal brotherhood and human dignity of the individual receded to the background, making way for the assertion of tribal practices of lineage and identity. The Umayyads consequently incurred an opposition that ranged from khawarij and Shiites to the jurists and non-Arab Muslims. They contrasted an idealised Madinan Islamic community with the decadent socio-economic and political realities under the Umayyad rule which gave rise to numerous verbal and physical assaults. The Umayyads, during the last days of their rule, reverted back to the Islamic universalist view assimilating Arabs and non-Arabs. The move, however, came too late to assuage and check the grievances of the *mawālī*, the non-Arab Muslims. The latter joined forces with the Abbasids and terminated the Umayyad rule in 132 AH (750 CE).

The Abbasids, riding a wave of popular sympathy against the Umayyads, proclaimed piety as the basis of their rule and replaced race with religion as the foundation of the new polity. The principle of social equality, according to Syed Ameer 'Alī, 'helped the early sovereigns of the house of 'Abbās to build up a fabric which endured without rival for five centuries, and fell only before a barbarian attack from without'.[32] This is, however, deceptive. During the reigns of the first seven caliphs (132–218 AH/749–828 CE), the Abbasid caliphate had reached its height, symbolised by the reign of the famous Hārūn al-Rashīd (170–194 AH/786–809 CE). Then, the slow, fitful decline characterised by ethnic group rivalry, political intrigues, palace coups and the dwindling of caliphal authority began. Around the year 390 AH/1000 CE, the Abbasid areas were splintered into Fāṭimīd, Ḥamdānids, Buwayhid, Samānid, and Ghaznavid sultanates. There was no unity of purpose and action among the different rulers, no coherence in their approach and no adherence to any set of principles. In fact, from 132 AH/750 CE to the end of the Ottoman caliphate in 1343 AH/1924 CE, the course of Muslim history has been one of political fragmentation of *dār al-Islām* and eventually the abolition of the caliphate system.

The destruction of the universal caliphate did not lead to the disintegration of the Ummah. In fact, as argued by Ibn Taymīyah, there is no juridical authority obligating the establishment of a unitary, universal caliphate. The Muslims, he argued, should form their independent entities with Sharī'ah as the directive law. They may then confederate and achieve the political unity of the Ummah.[33] Most Muslim jurists have been censored by contemporary scholars for their deviations from the ideal theory of the caliphate. What needs to be emphasised is that for the jurists the most important guarantor of the well-being of the Ummah was the presence and the application of the Sharī'ah. Even if naked force was allowed to legitimise itself under the framework of the Sharī'ah, the unity of the Ummah could be preserved and its disintegration thwarted. Ibn Taymīyah, however, completely ignored the office of the caliph and concentrated on the Ummah and its proper maintenance in accordance with Sharī'ah. The shift has not been from the '*khilāfah* as the ideal Muslim polity to the Sharī'ah binding the Ummah' as Rosenthal believed.[34] Rather the shift has been from the *khilāfah* as an instrument of the Sharī'ah to the Sharī'ah binding the Ummah.

The monolithic unity of the Ummah was predicated upon the application of the same Islamic law than upon having a unitary caliphate. It is the Sharī'ah which provided the Muslims with the sense of continuity and tradition and has been a powerful force in maintaining integration and involvement for the Muslims. 'It may rightly be said', according to Ismā'īl al-Fārūqī, 'the Sharī'ah or Islamic Law, is both the spearhead and spine of Muslim unity across the world'.[35] This sense of unity is reinforced by the spread and perpetuation of the instruments of socialisation together with the pervasiveness of the ethical-social code. Everywhere Islam went, writes Marshall Hodgson,

> there has been a continuous pressure toward persuading all Muslims to adopt like standards, like ways of living based on the Islamic ideals prevailing at a given time . . . everywhere Muslims are noted for their keen consciousness of the world Muslim community . . . and maintain in the most diverse geography not only the essential distinctive Islamic rites . . . but also, to some degree, a sense of a common cultural heritage.[36]

The monolithic unity of faith, of both material and higher culture and a unified world-view appeared to prevail throughout the *dār al-Islām* until the onset of colonial incursions upon the Muslim world.

THE CONTEMPORARY UMMAH

During the humiliating phase of colonialism and total Western hegemony, the Ummah suffered not only the political misfortunes, but its ideology, the very basis of its identity, was undermined. The colonialists abolished the institution of *zakāh* and the economic system built around it. The only part of the Sharī'ah which they conceded willy-nilly was the so-called law of personal status; all others were systematically dismantled. Consequently, contrary to its aspirations, there is division, dissension and strife within the ranks of the Ummah.

Currently, there are some 52 countries which may be considered as falling within the fold of Muslim Ummah. Among these states, there are varying degrees of constitutional espousal of Islamicity as well as differences in the degree to which Islamic values and Sharī'ah have penetrated the interstices of the social fabric. The range varies from Sudan, with its proclaimed policy of implementing a comprehensive version of the Sharī'ah at one end, and, Turkey which drastically broke its ties with Islamic culture in the 1920s, at the other end of the spectrum. There are in addition one-third of the world's Muslim population living as minorities in non-Muslim states.

The political fragmentation of the Ummah, as discussed in Chapter 1, was achieved by the imposition of the nation-state system and its acceptance by the elite as a vehicle for upholding its freedom and independence and for achieving self-sustained growth and political development. It has triggered an ideological controversy among Muslim intellectuals and it has centred around the basic contradiction between nationalism based upon traits peculiar to a group and Ummah espousing the universal brotherhood of believers.[37]

Nationalism and Islam

Often vague and mysterious in character, the concept of nationalism admits of no single definition. To Carlton Hayes it is 'modern emotional fusion of two phenomena – patriotism and nationality', to Shafer 'it is a varying combination of beliefs and conditions partly founded on myth and partly on reality', and to Hans Kohn 'it is a state of mind, an act of consciousness, the individuals's identification of himself with the "we-group" in which the loyalty of the individual is felt to be due the nation-state'.[38] However, this national 'we' has to a considerable degree, been defined by contrast to an alien 'they'. It is 'essentially an anti-feeling . . . [which] feeds and fattens on hatred and anger' directed against a competitor group.[39] Nationalism is an ideology in the secular sense of the term and its indoctrination implies replacement of other ideologies, particularly those of a religious nature.[40]

Nationalism was used as a tool by colonialism 'to shatter the religious unity of Islam in pieces'.[41] It gained currency in the wake of colonialism and was propagated, after the gradual withering away of the colonial system, by a new class of Western-educated elite. It 'has rarely been the conscious credo of the Muslim masses'.[42] It is an instrument of continued Western control and domination over Muslim areas of the world.

Nationalism represents a parallel ideology to that of Islam. In their spirit and aims they are diametrically opposed to each other. It is incompatible with the concept of Ummah on several grounds. First, nationalism is a form of glorified tribalism which was rejected outright by the Prophet (ṢAAS) saying: 'He is not of us who claims and who dies in the cause of tribal partisanship'.[43] According to another *ḥadīth*,

> people are of two kinds: believers who are aware, or transgressors who do wrong. You are all children of Adam and Adam was from clay. People should give up pride in their nations because that is a coal from the coals of hellfire. If they do not give this up Allah will consider them lower than the lowly worm which pushes itself through filth head foremost.[44]

Second, nationalism is based on linguistic, geographical, cultural, racial and similar other factors which is contrary to the Qur'ānic conception of Ummah. *Ummah Muslimah* transcends geography, language, race or history and is based upon *tawḥīd*. The Qur'ān asserts categorically that 'this Ummah of yours is one, united Ummah and I am your Lord. Serve Me' (21:92). Third, nationalism, giving rise to the structure of the nation-state system, demands the promotion of its own interests to the exclusion of and, at times, at the cost of all others. The Qur'ān demands of the Ummah, instead, promotion of virtue and eschewing of vice, to cooperate 'for the good, to the purpose of achieving piety' . . . 'and to disagree with and oppose one another so as to prevent evil, to avoid crime and stop aggression' (5:3). Fourth, nationalism intensifies the cultural plurality and social antagonism between various units and sub-units of the Muslim world. It militates against the idea of Muslim unity which is the essential feature of the Ummah. The Ummah is a universal system 'with one strong and comprehensive ideology, a world-government and a world-army to enforce its decision'.[45]

Table 5.2 Nationalism and Ummah compared

Nationalism	*Ummah*
Promotes loyalty to the nation.	Promotes loyalty to the Ummah.
Considers the nation and its institutions as the source of sovereignty and legitimacy.	Considers Sharī'ah as the ultimate source of legitimacy.
Based upon ethnic, linguistic, racial or other considerations.	Based upon belief in *tawḥīd*, the unity and sovereignty of Allah (SWT).
Demarcates artificial territorial boundaries.	Destroys contrived divisions.
Destroys bonds between human beings.	Promotes universal brotherhood.
Dismembered the Ummah into nation-states.	Promotes the unity of the Muslim world into one Ummah.

The arguments advanced above and summarised in Table 5.2, formed the basis for Muslim scholars like Sayyid Mawdūdī, Ḥasan al-Bannā, (1324–1369 AH/1906–1949 CE) Sayyid Quṭb and others to take an unequivocal stand against nationalism of all kinds. To them, as expressed by Mawdūdī, nationalism is the 'root cause of all those calamities and troubles in which humanity is involved today'.[46] They even object to the use of nationalism as a vehicle for mobilising mass opinion to resist foreign domination.[47] Nationalism with its emphasis on popular sovereignty, secularism and narrow particularism was contrary to the Sharī'ah-based system and universalism of Islam. The views advocating nationalism seem to have receded since the beginning of the 1970s as the Tajdīd-Iṣlāh movement has intensified. This does not, however, mean that nationalism has disappeared or waned from the Muslim psyche.

Arab nationalism versus the Ummah

The argument against nationalism in general applies with equal force against the advocacy of, among others, Arab nationalism which, according to 'Abd al-Raḥmān al-Bazzāz, is based upon 'linguistic, historical, cultural and spiritual ties and fundamental interests in life' adding further that Islam was 'revealed primarily, and essentially for Arabs'.[48]

Similarly, Sāṭi'al-Ḥuṣrī, the spiritual father of Arab nationalism, advanced the doctrine of *al-din lillāh wa-waṭan lijamī'* meaning" religion is for Allah and the fatherland is the concern for all.[49] Implied in this nationalist message is for the Arabs to conceive of themselves as ethnically apart from other Muslim people. Admittedly, though Islamic universalism is irreconcilable with all forms of national and ethnic pluralism, it does have special affinities with the Arabic language and culture. As a moral doctrine, however, Islam explicitly proscribes and castigates all sentiments of ethnic pride associated with Arabism as *jahilīyah* – ignorant. It is true that the Qur'ān is an Arabic revelation; that certain elements of pre-Islamic Arabic culture did pass on to Islam; and that the Prophet of Islam (ṢAAS) was himself an Arab. What is equally true and which is not being emphasised by the advocates of Arab nationalism is that the Qur'ānic usage of Arabic language was for its effective potential to appeal to the emotions of the audience and to stir their intuitive faculties; that Arab acceptance of Islam resulted in the replacement of Arab tribal culture by the world brotherhood under the moral law; that the Islamic revelation brought about a radical transformation of the Arabic language and 'set it as the unsurpassable ideal of the art of letters'.[50] After the Qur'ān, the Arabic language could not remain confined to a particular people but became the sacred medium of expression for the entire Ummah for time to come just as the Prophet (ṢAAS) was sent as a mercy to all mankind. Consequently,

> There is nothing more damaging to this identity of Qur'ānization-Arabization than the introduction by the Western enemies of Islam of a meaning to *'urūbah* that is foreign to it, namely, the racist or nationalist meaning differentiating the Arab Muslims from his Muslim brothers belonging to other ethnicities. This so-called Arab ethnocentrism or nationalism is a new *shu'ūbiyyah* designed only to split the Ummah as under . . . and to set the Muslim against his co-religionists in fratricidal conflict and war.[51]

Islamically-conscious Arabs, therefore, refuse to define Arabism in any other terms but Islamic. The luminaries of al-Azhar and the activists of Muslim Brotherhood condemned Arab nationalism, or any other nationalism espoused by Muslims, and called upon Arabs to strive towards Islamic unity resting nationality only on the bonds of faith. Arab nationalism is the product of a Christian and Jewish conspiracy to keep the Ummah divided. It was equally the work of a few marginalised intellectuals having nominal acquaintance with Islam. The latter-day acquiescence of the 'Ulamā' of al-Azhar to the cause of Arab unity was due to political consideration and the threat posed by the state of Israel.[52] Nevertheless, the majority of Muslims denounce nationalism as an imported heresy undermining Muslim unity.

CONCLUSION

The Muslim Ummah, being based on *tawḥīd*, should be organic, comprehensive and universal. Its constituent members are enjoined severally and collectively to enjoin virtue and forbid vice; to witness to the Truth that 'there is no *ilāh* but Allah and Muhammad is His Messenger'. The decay of the Ottoman *khilāfah*, the European colonial penetration and the extension of technologically more advanced European culture all over the world have undermined the unity of Ummah based on the applicability of the Sharī'ah. Nevertheless, the ideal of a one and united universal Ummah has survived the political discords and is manifested not only in matters of rituals but also in a spiritual yearning for an organic oneness such that whenever a convulsion of resentment shakes one part of the Muslim world the tremor is sensed in all other parts. Attempts are under way to give economic and political shape to this renewed emphasis on the trans-national identity and solidarity of the Ummah and is reflected in such organisations as the Organization of the Islamic Conference (OIC), the Islamic Development Bank, and International Islamic Universities.

6 *Khilāfah*: The Islamic Political Order

The integral relationship of religion to politics, law, and society in Islam is reflected in its emphasis on the vocation of a Muslim, as *khalīfah* of Allah (SWT), to shape the world according to the divine pattern through establishing and spreading an Islamic order. Islam and the political order are certainly not equivalents, yet the political order has been regarded as the agent of religion.[1] It is an instrument for the divinely-ordained Islamic principles that are to govern all aspects of a believer's life. The *fuqahā'* were, therefore, compelled, contrary to Rosenthal's assertion, 'to ask whether and why there must be a state'.[2] They argued the case for the construction of an Islamic political order by referring to explicit Qur'ānic instructions and numerous prophetic traditions in respect to the needs of the Ummah, and to Islamic universalism. The advent of European colonialism and consequent political and economic domination of the Muslim land had somewhat restricted the juristic, political and philosophical discourse pertaining to the political order. The anti-colonial independence movements, in which Islam served as a unifying force, and the emergence of various Muslim states raised the question of the Islamic political order. A significant body of literature has emerged since then which analyses and ponders the Islamic state, yet there remains considerable vagueness as to its precise nature and form, confusing it at times with the Western notion of a nation-state.

THE STATE

A systematic treatment of the nature of the state began with the Greek philosophers. Man, Aristotle remarked, 'is by nature a political being; it is his nature to live in a *polis*' wherein alone he could attain his highest moral nature.[3] The state, for Plato as for Aristotle, existed for the purpose of seeking common good and moral perfection. To them, the state was not merely a political association but it simultaneously served as a religious community and a socialising agency – generally concerned with cultivating the mind and the soul of the individual.

They viewed the individual as a creature tending naturally towards virtue and hence their emphasis was on the moral dimension of man. They stressed the sense of community found in the *polis*, that is, the common agreement on moral beliefs.

Beginning with Niccolō Machiavelli (1469–1527 CE), the emphasis and assumptions changed.[4] Theorists now viewed the man as a self-interested creature who has a 'perpetual and restless desire for power after power that ceases only in death'.[5] Consequently, the focus has shifted from morality and virtue to power and authority. This is true as much of Karl Marx (1818–83 CE) as of Max Weber (1864–1920 CE) to whom the contemporary theorists of state owe a great deal. Both Marx and Weber assumed population, territory, government and sovereignty as self-evident features of the state needing no elaboration. Hence they proceeded to a class or group analysis of the state and its behaviour. Both based their theories on the conceptions of the self-interested man as a member of the group. Both see the state in terms of power, violence, domination and the material conditions of administration. The two differ, however, in terms of their emphasis, the goal and the means used to achieve desired objectives.

Karl Marx on the state

For Marx, the state is the product of class contradictions and class struggle and is controlled by the economically dominant class. The bourgeois state is an instrument of control and coercion at the disposal of the class that owns the means of production in order to exercise power over the exploited classes in a society. The government acts as the 'executive committee' of the ruling class, co-ordinating the behaviour and operation of its members to further the long-term class interests. The bourgeois state, admittedly, has relative autonomy and an appearance of impartiality. It may be democratic in form, but its political system is highly structured so as to ensure the continued dominance of the minority bourgeoisie. Marx contends, however, that since the state is class-based, and since class involves opposition, the bourgeois state shows contradictory tendencies. The high level of productivity secured by the capitalist system, Marx argues, was made possible by the poverty of the many; yet only a few shared in this wealth. This system is bound to give way to the communist society which would ensure economic abundance and satisfy everyone's needs. In such a classless situation, there will be no opposition and hence no need for the repressive apparatus of the state. The state will wither away.[6]

Max Weber on the state

Max Weber agrees with Marxist analysis of the state on many points but would consider the classless society as Utopian. He would reject Marxist critique of the capitalist system and would see little difference between the socialist society in which the bureaucratic elite dominates and the capitalist system where bourgeoisie dominates. To him, the state 'is a relation of men dominating men, a relation supported by means of violence'.[7] Weber considers this relation as analytic, as necessary, since property supplies the material means for domination, be it administrative or coercive. His task, therefore, is to explain how domination can be legitimised. The absence of a social institution 'which knew the use of violence', argues Weber, would lead to 'anarchy' in the specific sense of the word.[8] The state is defined as a 'human community that [successfully] claims the monopoly of the legitimate use of physical violence in a given territory'.[9] Monopoly of violence is rational in that it reduces the possibility of conflict. The rationality of domination, however, centres on the probability of compliance with legitimate commands.

Dahl's *Who Governs?*, considered a seminal study of pluralist politics, is based upon the Weberian conception of the state.[10] Dahl views the state as a collection of individuals occupying role positions (those of governing authority) and acting as a group to govern. The political universe is characterised by different social groups who have different objectives and political resources. Public policy is the outcome of the resolution of vectors resulting from interests and resources.

The conceptualisation of the state from socialist and capitalist perspectives shows several common features. They added group dynamics or class-analysis to the traditional analysis of the state in terms of population, territory, government and sovereignty, in explaining the state behaviour. The class which controls the economy controls the political power in the state. Just as the capitalist system assigns a significant role to the majority of the have-nots, so the 'dictatorship of the proletariat' permits the persistence of some bourgeois structures during the socialist transition. In both the systems, the interest of the class and nation is above the interest of the individual members of the community. Finally, both the systems reject the collective responsibility of the community for the spiritual and even the material welfare of its individual members.

THE NOTION OF STATE COMPARED WITH THE ISLAMIC SYSTEM

The Western models of the state cannot be appropriated by Muslims. The order Islam prescribes is bound neither to a land nor to a person. To be sure, land and people are required but these are only the mechanical steps in the formation of a world order. Islam desires not a small piece of land but aims at subjecting the whole earth to the will of the One and Only Creator. Islam is universal and hence cannot be restricted to a defined piece of real estate. Similarly, it seeks not a particular race or group but the whole of mankind. Unlike the nation-state, Islamic political order is an open society willing to accept anyone who decides to adopt it. Admittedly, patriotism and defence of one's homeland are accepted and encouraged in Islam. This patriotism is encouraged, however, for the protection of the Islamic stronghold. Sovereignty which vests absolute authority in the hands of the representatives of the people to make final legal decisions is likewise alien to Islam and cannot be equated with *bay'ah* or *shūrā*. The legislative bodies in Islamic politics are guided by Sharī'ah and the legislation is aimed at realising the values and principles enshrined in the Qur'ān and the Sunnah. The Islamic political order is an ideological concept. It comprises the community of believers and is concerned with implementing the will of Allah (SWT), preserving order against internal and external threats and striving positively for the achievement of social justice, promotion of good and eradication of evil. Unlike the West, the Islamic perspective assumes a single interest, i.e., promoting the cause of Islam, and does not allow groups and individuals to promote their own, autonomously defined self-interests. The preference of the rulers and the ruled alike are constrained by the Sharī'ah and the enduring belief in *tawḥīd*. Islam does not subscribe to the myth common in the Western notion of the state that legitimacy derives from the consensus of a political community in which sovereignty belongs to the people. The legitimacy of authority in an Islamic Order rests on the implementation of the Sharī'ah through the procedure it prescribes for the realisation of the Divine Will.

The Islamic political order is not an end in itself, only a means to the most paramount design of Islam – the creation of a universal moral order for the temporal and spiritual welfare of all. It is a normative order and is based upon certain eternal spiritual and ethical values of Islam. The system of norms identifies the source of political authority and governs the individual's relationship with the polity and the latter's relationship with the society as a whole. It also lays down principles for institutions and procedures through which Islamic ideals could be realised.

THE CONCEPT OF 'STATE' IN ISLAM

The concept of the nation-state, or its Arabic equivalent *dawlah*, is a relatively recent development in Europe, as is the concept of sovereignty (*siyādah*). The nation-state system is generally linked to the Treaty of Westphalia in 1648, while the concept of sovereignty was first systematically enunciated by Jean Bodin (1530–96 CE) in 1576 CE. It is natural therefore, that the concept of state is neither used in the Qur'ān nor was it in vogue at the time of the Prophet (ṢAAS).[11] The early *fuqahā'* used the terms *khilāfah* or *imāmah* to denote the idea of a political order. The term *dawlah* gained currency in the early seventh century AH, and was employed with reference to the Muslim dynasties owing nominal allegiance to the powerless caliph.[12] Another eight centuries had to elapse for the idea of an Islamic state to gain currency 'as an alternative to the caliphate'.[13] The shift was occasioned by various factors including the abolition of the caliphate in 1924. However, the very term 'Islamic state' is a misnomer and is better replaced with 'Islamic polity' or 'Islamic Political Order'.

Although the terms 'state' or 'polity', do not occur in the Qur'ān, the essential elements that constitute a political order were referred to in the Qur'ān which clearly indicate that the concept, if not the term, was meant in the Qur'ān.[14] For instance, the Qur'ān refers to a set of principles or functions that either imply the existence of a socio-political order, or in some cases, the use of an organised authority for their realisation. They include things like *'ahd* (contract), *amānah* (trust) *iṭā'ah* (obedience) and *ḥukm* (adjudication).[15] There are also general laws or directives, pertaining to the waging of war and the making of peace. The subjects of these laws or directives are 'the justly balanced Muslim community' distinguishable from others by virtue of their possessing special characteristic – a self-sufficient political society. More importantly, there are certain religious obligations such as the collection of *zakāh*, the punishment of criminals, the organisation of *jihād* and so on, which may not be effectively accomplished without the formal intervention of political authority.

Table 6.1 Essential principles of the Islamic political system

Principles	*Meaning*	*Some related Qurānic verses*
Tawḥīd	Indivisible, inalienable divinity of Allah (SWT).	1:2; 3:154; 5:38–40; 6:102, 164; 7:3, 54; 10:31; 12:40; 13:37; 15:36; 42:10; 48:4; 57:2–3; 112:1–4
Sharī'ah	'The way to the water-hole.' It is the Islamic law based on the Qur'ān and the Sunnah.	5:48; 7:163; 42:13; 21; 45:18
'Adālah	To establish justice.	4:58, 135; 5:3, 9, 45; 7:29; 16:90, 152; 42:15; 55:9
Freedom *(hurrīyqah)*	The right to do what one wants, within the confines of the Sharī'ah, to achieve the maximum degree of self and collective realisation.	2:286; 4:80; 10:99; 18:29; 74:39, 56; 76:29; 81:28
Equality *(Musawah)*	Equal opportunity of each individual to articulate his/her potential to the maximum limit.	2:30; 4:1; 6:104, 151; 12:40; 17:33
Shūrā	Consultation.	2:233; 3:159; 42:38

ESSENTIAL PRINCIPLES OF AN ISLAMIC POLITICAL ORDER

The Qur'ān provides a number of important principles (see Table 6.1) pertaining to the Islamic political order. The first is *tawḥīd,* meaning the indivisible, inalienable divinity of Allah (SWT). This principle denies anyone, be it a human agency as with a Hobbesian monarch, or a legal fiction in the form of a state, as in John Austin, the right to order others in his own right to do or not to do certain things. For, as the Qur'ān declares, 'The command rests with none but Allah' (6:57) 'Who is the Lord of the universe' (1:1) and 'grants guidance' (87:3).

Allah's commands and directives have been bequeathed to mankind in two forms. One, the Qur'ān, the divinely-revealed book from which all principles and ordinances of Islam are drawn. Two, the ideal conduct of the last Prophet (ṢAAS), the Sunnah, which clarifies, explains and exemplifies the Qur'ān. The two taken together constitutes, as discussed in Chapter 4, the Sharī'ah which is the ultimate source of authority. It means that all acts, procedures, dispositions and final decisions of the public authorities at any level cannot be valid and legally binding upon the people unless it is in conformity with the law. The Qur'ān categorically enjoins the believers to 'judge between them by that which Allah has revealed' (5:49) and condemns the defaulters as 'unbelievers', 'wrongdoers' and 'rebels' (5:44, 45, 47). By upholding the Sharī'ah, Islam affirms the necessity of government on the basis of norms and well-defined guidelines, rather than personal preferences.

The next principle is *'adālah*, to establish justice for all 'even as against yourselves, or your parents or your kins, whether it be against the rich or poor' (Al-Qur'ān 4:55; 4:135). The believers are commanded to be just for 'justice is next to piety' (5:8). They are enjoined to observe the law and obey the representatives of Allah (SWT) who are appointed 'to judge among men with justice' (38:24). The prophets came with 'the Book and the Balance (of Rights and Wrong) that men may stand forth in justice' (57:25). The Prophet (ṢAAS) was commanded to rule in accordance with the 'truth' and the 'path of Allah' (2:24), the terms most commentators equate with 'righteousness' and 'justice' respectively. The Qur'ān uses multiple words like *sunnat Allāh* (the way or tradition of Allah), *mīzān* (scale), *qist* and *'adl* (both meaning justice), perhaps to impress the significance of justice.

The Qur'ān is emphatic on individuals carrying out their obligations of doing good and liberality to kith and kin, of eschewing shameful deeds, injustice and rebellion, and of abstaining from harming others out of ill will or malice. The Qur'ānic justice not merely protects the weak and the oppressed but also warns of harsh punishments for those who blatantly transgress their rights and cause confusion in the society. The Qur'ān demands of an individual a high moral standard so that he may stand as a witness even against himself. A just political order manifests itself in having upright and capable public officials managing the public policy in a just way and distributing wealth and opportunities in an equitable manner.

'Adālah postulates two fundamental principles of *freedom* and equality. It is an essential condition and consequence of the establishment of justice that the people should be in possession of freedom 'to act

according to one's own moral convictions, to make ideological or intellectual choices, and to take decisions on the basis of these convictions and choices'.[16] The Qur'ānic dictum *lā ikrāha fī al-dīn* (2:256), meaning there is no coercion in *al-dīn*, refers not merely to matters of faith but to every conceivable area of human life and negates all attempts at regimentation of individual life. The freedom espoused by Islam is not confined to believers but extends to minorities and non-Muslim citizens of the Islamic polity. The non-Muslim subjects have the freedom of preserving and practising their languages, religious practices and cultural traditions in an Islamic society. This freedom, it should be noted, is not absolute but relative and proportionate to man's capacity and responsibility. Advocating absolute freedom is irresponsible as its complete denial is erroneous.

This freedom presupposes equality of all – equality in rights, liberties, opportunities and public duties. These are to be enjoyed by all irrespective of race, language and creed. There is no room for privilege under a system which subjects all equally to the identical law. The Qur'ān recognises no grounds for the superiority of individuals or nations to one another except that of moral rectitude and *taqwā* (49:13). 'The aristocracy of yore is trampled under my feet', said the Prophet (ṢAAS) in his farewell sermon. All people are, according to a *ḥadīth*, 'as equal as the teeth of a comb' as they are alike the children of Adam. The sole lawgiver is Allah (SWT); all human beings are equal in their subjection to His ordinances. These principles are stressed in the Qur'ān and *ḥadīth* and has always been recognised as undeniable principles in the Sharī'ah. According to Muhammad Asad, 'it is in these principles and in these alone, that the concept of Islamic polity finds its meaning and justification'.[17]

Finally, the Qur'ān lays down the principle of *shūrā* (consultation) guiding the decision-making process of the political system.[18] The Qur'ān directs Prophet Muhammad (ṢAAS) to 'consult them in the conduct of affairs' (3:159) and refers to the believers as those who conduct 'their affairs by mutual consultation' (42:38). The system of *shūrā*, explains 'AbdulḤamīd AbuSulaymān:

> provides the procedure whereby Muslims sit together and deliberate upon important matters to arrive at and bound by conclusions in the light of the philosophical concept of justice. If the issue under consideration does not concern justice but a case of preferring one to the other, there is no harm in adopting measures such as voting, abiding by the point of view of the minority, etc. The same measure

could be resorted to if the discussion reached a deadlock in the absence of an authentic analogy. But even here, no decision should be taken until everybody has had the chance to express their opinion and cite relevant evidence.[19]

The Qur'ān mentions *shūrā* on the same footing as establishing prayer and paying *zakāh*. According to the text and context of the Qur'ān and the Sunnah, *shūrā* means a decisive participation of the people in governing themselves. It is based on the conviction that matters of fundamental importance are best left to the collective intelligence of the people provided they are guided by the Sharī'ah. The assumption being that, given the freedom of every man to exert himself to understand the spirit of the law and form his opinion accordingly, all considered opinions will eventually gravitate towards the truth. *Shūrā* ensures not merely the participation of the people in public affairs but it acts as a check against tyrannical rule as well. *Shūrā* can be operationalised only if there prevails the two fundamental principles of freedom and equality.[20] The essential feature of an Islamic political order, then, is that in it the government governs not merely by the law, but it reckons in all its decision with the wishes of the governed. Following Iqbāl, it is possible to say that the Islamic political order 'is an endeavour to transform' the principles of *tawḥīd*, *'adl*, equality, *shūrā* and freedom 'into space–time references, an aspiration to realise them in a definite human organisation'.[21]

ISLAMIC POLITY UNDER THE PROPHET (SAAS)

The order referred to in the Qur'ān took on form and substance in Madinah under the guidance and directives of Prophet Muhammad (ṢAAS). On the eve of his journey to Madinah were revealed fifteen verses of the Qur'ān (17:23–37) which in a sense formed 'the directive principles' to be used in erecting the first Islamic political order.

A few months after arriving at Madinah, the Prophet (ṢAAS) drew up the first written constitution of the world which provided the basis for the incipient Muslim polity.[22] It restructured political life in Madinah according to the Islamic conception of the Ummah (section 2); recognised the Prophet (ṢAAS) as the head of the new commonwealth (sections 23, 42), and defined his role as that of maintaining peace and order, arbitrating among groups in conflict; and of providing security from external attack (sections 37, 39, 40, 44). The document confirmed the principle of equality, rejection of tyranny and equal protection of the law even to the humblest of believers (sections 15, 17). The Jews were integrated into the body politic without depriving them of their religious freedom. As the religious and temporal head, the Prophet (ṢAAS) regulated social relations; enacted laws in the light of the Qur'ān and enforced them; raised armies and commanded them;[23] and when the territory expanded, administered these in consultation with his companions. In fact, all important matters, not covered by divine revelation, were settled by the Prophet (ṢAAS) through the process of consultation. Occasionally, he would convene a public gathering, had the matter fully discussed and would follow the course suggested by the consultative body even if it went against his opinion, as exemplified by the famous consultation during the Battle of Uhud in 3 AH/625 CE.

The Madinan political set-up was unusual in several respects. Its membership was based upon the belief system in which all believers were brothers to one another and, as such, they formed a unity in the service of Allah (SWT). Under this unity, all men were equal with no distinction recognised save that of *taqwā* (piety and deserved goodness). Within that relationship, there can be no power struggle because man is nothing but the creature of Allah (SWT) who alone possesses all power. Man's position on earth is that of a *khalīfah* of Allah (SWT) whose mission in life is to administer the Sharī'ah. As a *khalīfah*, the individual has responsibilities to meet, commitments to fulfil and to strive hard for worthy goals. Consequently, the members of the Madinan political order took active part in the public domain. Decisions were taken in accordance with the dictates of the Qur'ān and in consultation with the members of the Ummah. Within ten years, the Ummah had developed a governing apparatus with a strong potential for further expansion.

The *khulafā' al-Rāshidūn*

The succession crisis resulting from the death of the Prophet (ṢAAS), without a designated successor, was resolved by the Ummah in accordance with their tradition and experience which conformed to the spirit of Islam. They resorted to a two-stage process of instituting a successor: (1) consultation, nomination and selection by the representatives of the Ummah (*al-bay'ah al-khāṣṣah*), and (2), subsequent confirmation by the public through general acclamation or *al-bay'ah al-'āmmah*. The first caliph, Abū Bakr, was selected by the notables and confirmed by the general *bay'ah* in the year 11 AH/632 CE. The second caliph, 'Umar, was nominated by the incumbent in consultation with the leaders of the Ummah and was then referred to the general public for confirmation in 13 AH/634 CE. The third caliph, 'Uthmān, was nominated by an electoral college and subsequently ratified by the Ummah in the year 23 AH/644 CE. On the assassination of the third caliph and the ensuing chaos, the representatives of the Ummah approached 'Alī to assume the leadership position. 'Alī, however, insisted on the approval of the masses and was elected accordingly in the year 35 AH/656 CE.[24] These modes of succession were inspired by the Qur'ānic principle of *shūrā*. These have acquired a special significance and remained a basic principle of the constitutional theory of an Islamic political order.

To be certain, the *khalīfah* was not the Prophet, nor did he enjoy any metaphysical or theocratic privilege. He was responsible for upholding the religion against heretics and was entrusted with the function of the spiritual and material well-being of the Ummah through the application of the Sharī'ah. Obedience to the *khalīfah* was conditional upon his obedience to Allah (SWT) and His Prophet (ṢAAS). Should he deviate from the Sharī'ah, as announced by Abu Bakr in his inaugural speech, he forfeits the right to obedience. It means that the Ummah was to guide the *khalīfah* in all his actions, to watch out for any deviations from Islamic norms, to correct him if he 'goes astray', and to help him administer through good counsel.[25]

The period of *al-Khulafā' al-Rāshidūn* was characterised by the minimal tension between the ideals and realities of the circumstances. The *khalīfah* adhered strictly to the dictates of the Qur'ān and the Sunnah, and administered the affairs of the state in consultation with the people 'without whose advice no decision was ever taken in any important matter'.[26]

The *shūrā* was as the Sharī'ah intended it to be, a right of the governed, not a privilege bestowed by the chief executive. The *khulafā'* did exercise *ijtihād* to apply the Sharī'ah to new situations arising from the spatial expansion of Islam but always in conformity with given principles and in consultation with the members of the *shūrā* council.[27] They ensured the rule of law, established separate judicial institutions and delineated rules of judicial procedure applicable to the governors and the governed alike. The righteous caliphate, in short, was characterised by

> an elected republican constitutional government based on the rule of law (political democracy and Sharī'ah nomocracy); socio-economic egalitarianism (social and economic democracy); and the altruistic

Sharī'ah binding personality of the ruling elites (ethical democracy).[28]

The period of the Prophet (ṢAAS) and his rightly-guided successors in Madinah is regarded as

> the base of the Islamic edifice in history. The achievements of that period were extraordinary on all fronts, in all fields. Muslims in every age looked to them for inspiration and norms.[29]

POLITY UNDER THE UMAYYAD AND ABBASID RULE

With the expansion of the community, explains Ibn Khaldūn, the group feeling (of the Arabs) approached its final goal, royal authority. The restraining influence of religion had weakened.[30] The *khilāfah* was transformed into the *mulk*, a change from *siyāsah dīnīyah to siyāsah 'aqlīyah* supported by *'asabīyah* in seizing power. Mu'awiyah ibn Abī Sufyan, the founder of the Umayyad caliphate (41–142 AH/661–750 CE), introduced hereditary monarchy by appointing his son, Yazīd, as his successor. This act, as suggested by al-Ḥasan al-Baṣrī, had a corrupting influence on the subsequent political life of the Ummah.[31] The egalitarian community headed by its elected, pious caliph had now become an empire ruled by a hereditary caliph who wielded absolute power. The principle of *al-shūrā* was muzzled and an Arab warrior aristocracy assumed the responsibility for the unity and stability of the Umayyad caliphate. 'The progressive centralisation and militarisation of the state resulted in an increasingly autocratic and absolutist government. . . .'[32]

The institution of the caliphate eroded further with the advent of the Abbasid rule (132–646 AH/750–1258 CE). Despite the flowering of a grand civilisation under their patronage, the Abbasid rule was characterised by hereditary succession, ostentatious court ceremonies and central administrative organisations controlling a vast area extending from the Atlantic to central Asia.[33] By the middle of the tenth century, political fragmentation and weakening of the caliphate was setting in and army commanders began asserting their independence as rulers of semi-autonomous states. As the effective power of the caliphs declined, the military commanders became sultans exercising *de facto* rule over the emerging political entities. Finally, in 656 AH/1258 CE, the Mongols, under Hülegü, laid siege to the Abbasid capital, Baghdad, and razed it to the ground.

The termination of the Abbasid caliphate meant, in effect, splintering the unity of the Ummah which was administered by a universal caliphate. The political unity of the caliphate gave way to a burgeoning number of Muslim sultanates that governed an extensively large area.[34] By the sixteenth century, three major Muslim sultanates had emerged: the Ottomans in the Near East and Eastern Europe; the Safavids in Persia; and the Mughals in India. These sultanates had to adjust to regional and local conditions and traditions, but overall, Islamic tradition continued to govern the world of Islam. Religious toleration towards non-Muslim subjects was a remarkable feature of the Islamic spirit of equality and justice to all.[35]

Of the three Muslim sultanates, the Ottoman was perhaps the most powerful entity in the Muslim world and certainly the longest-lived. The Ottoman Sultan was invested with the exalted status of a caliph on the ground, as argued by Ottoman intellectuals, that they did more than others to expand the frontiers of Islam and that they respected the Sharī'ah and patronised the 'Ulamā'.[36] The caliph assumed the role of defenders of faith and guardians of the Sharī'ah. Nevertheless, the Ottoman caliphate resembled Ibn Khaldūn's *mulk,* having a mixed constitution with the Sharī'ah as its foundation supplemented by the ordinances of the king which had secular overtones. The Ottoman law was a mixture of Sharī'ah and *qānūn* (the canons or political and administrative ordinances of the caliph). Gradually, the secular forces gained currency among the intellectuals and, after the defeat of Turkey in the First World War, they led a successful struggle against the caliphate. Under the leadership of Mustafa Kemal (Atatürk), the Grand National Assembly of Turkey decided in 1922 to separate the sultanate from the caliphate and then to replace the former with a republican regime.[37] Later, in 1924, the caliphate was abolished and Atatürk founded a secular Turkish republic. The abolition of the caliphate was, as Hamid Enayat explains, due to:

> incompatibility between Turkish nationalism and Pan-Islamism: The conflict between the concept of a modern Westernised state, based on the will of the people, and the notion of a supra-national Muslim state, resting on the bonds of the religious community and finally, the absurdity of a caliphate deprived of temporal authority.[38]

With the exception of a few scholars, no serious attempt has been made to revive the universal caliphate. Most of Muslim energies were consumed in seeking liberation and emancipation from alien political and social orders imposed on them by superior military might. With the destruction of the European colonial empires and the emergence of numerous independent or semi-independent national states, attention has shifted to the creation in different parts of the Muslim world of Islamic political systems which otherwise resemble the nation-state model.

As it is, the Muslim world is divided into about 52 states. Some of these states are autocracies; half of the constitutions of these states (26 out of 52) proclaim Islam as the official state religion (see Appendix C). Yet, the Sharī'ah in its entirety is not the law of the land in any country.

EARLY MUSLIM JURISTS AND THINKERS

From the various developments outlined above it will be seen that the governing institution has undergone several transformations and has widely diverged from the ideal – the political system of Madinah under the Prophet (ṢAAS) and the first four caliphs. These divergences and controversies surrounding the caliphate are reflected in the works of Muslim jurists and thinkers. The orientalists, in their attempts at magnifying the differences, have glossed over the common grounds which united these thinkers of different historical periods. Muslim scholars were convinced that the Madinah model represented the ideal; that the purpose of political authority is to guarantee the maintenance of Islam and the execution of the Sharī'ah which obligates *shūrā* and *'adl*; that politics should not be separated from ethics and morals; and that there should be no tension between religion and politics. As a matter of fact, politics has been conceived by these jurists and thinkers as a necessary extension of religion and morals.[39]

Historically, the only form Islamic polity assumed after the death of the Prophet (ṢAAS) is the *khilāfah* system. The Muslim thinkers therefore developed an elaborate doctrine concerning the origin of the idea of the caliphate, the qualification of the caliph, the nature and mode of election and the purpose of government. On the question of the necessity of imamate or caliphate, the majority of thinkers including the *Shī'ah*, the *Khawārij* and most of the *Mu'tazilah* believe that the *imāmah* is compulsory because of the functions assigned to it by the revealed law. They, however disagree as to the reason for its necessity. Al-Ash'arī, al-Baghdādī (d. 429 AH/1037 CE), Abu al-Ḥassan al-Māwardī (364–450 AH/974–1058 CE) and Abu Ḥamid Muḥammad al-Ghazālī (450–505 AH/1058–1111 CE), among others, consider that the *imāmah* is demanded by revelation, not by reason.[40]

The *Mu'tazilah*, on the other hand, hold the view that the necessity of *imāmah* is proved by reason and not by revelation. Ibn Taymīyah argues, however, that the administration of the affairs of men is demanded by reason no less than revelation. To this, he adds that there is a natural propensity inherent in man which drives him to cooperate with his fellow creatures for common well-being and happiness. This common welfare cannot be attained without a social order and the latter requires some authority to direct it.[41] This sociological argument has been developed in greater detail by Ibn Khaldūn.

Muslim political thinkers and jurists began their expositions from the assumption that Islamic government is based upon Sharī'ah which does not distinguish between religion and other aspects of life and that there is no area of man's activity and concern to which Sharī'ah does not address itself with specific guidance. The political authority and its internal organisation was defined by referring to this law.

The basis of the political authority was the Ummah, the Islamic social order.[42] The ruler, known in the early literature as *khalīfah*, *imām*, *amīr* etc., is not the sovereign but a *primus inter-pares*, first among the equals. Within the Ummah, the governor and the governed are on an equal footing. There is no distinction of rank but of role and no basis of ranking save that of *taqwā*. The *imām* must administer according to the Sharī'ah, the violation of which absolves the Ummah of its obligation to render obedience to him.[43]

The purpose of government is very clearly spelled out: the defence of Islam and the establishment of conditions in which the believer could fulfil his true destiny. Al-Māwardī explains the purpose of an Islamic political system as continuations of the function of the prophethood in 'the defence of the faith and the administration of the world'.[44] Ibn Taymīyah adds that the greatest goal of the political authority is to make sure that Islam as a religion and a way of life extends to all of life and humanity and that 'Allah's word be supreme'. Ibn Khaldūn explains the relationship between al-Māwardī's 'administration of the world' and Ibn Taymīyah's 'Allah's word being supreme' by saying that the worldly affairs, according to Sharī'ah, are all considered with reference to their benefits in the Hereafter. Ibn Khaldūn, therefore, clarifies the function of the Islamic polity as getting all to follow the intent of the Sharī'ah's position in all their affairs for success in this world and in the Hereafter.

Most of the writings on political or constitutional aspects focus extensively on the office of the chief executive in whom all power and authority were centred and no power was considered valid unless delegated by him. It is generally agreed that the affairs of the people cannot be administered properly without a recognised authority. The appointment of an *imām*, therefore, is considered obligatory and obedience to him incumbent as long as his policies did not contravene the Sharī'ah. This is so, explains al-Ghazālī, because the *imām* maintains order, symbolises collective unity of the Ummah and its historical continuity and finally, he derives his authority from the Sharī'ah.[45] There is disagreement, however, on the method whereby the *imāmah* is established. Al-Māwardī, Abū Ya'la and al-Baghdādī, for instance, speak of election by the notables (Abū Bakr's case), designation by the incumbent ('Umar's case), nomination by an electoral college ('Uthmān), and the direct election by the people ('Alī) as the valid forms of instituting an *imām*. Badr al-Dīn Ibn Jamā'ah (639–733 AH/1244–1333 CE) later on added the forcible acquisition of power as yet another valid form of installing a caliph.

Though the Muslim thinkers are unanimous in demanding the institution of the *khalīfah* and in their inclination towards the election of the caliph, they differ in their attitude to the existence of more than one *imām*. Al-Māwardī, opposing al-Ash'arī, forbids it, perhaps because he thought it was akin to denying the universalism of Islam. Al-Baghdādī, though he did not approve of it, nevertheless permits the existence of two caliphs governing simultaneously provided that their territories were far apart from each other. The *Khawārij*, it should be noted, did not limit the number of *imām*s at any one time. Ibn Taymīyah, sharing the same view, maintains that more than one *imām* might exist simultaneously.

The chief executive must also be endowed with qualities which would enable him to fulfil his responsibilities. Consequently, it is difficult to find a single Muslim scholar of note who has not dwelt at length on the virtues of the chief executive. Al-Māwardī, for instance, lays down seven conditions beginning with justice (*'adālah*), followed by knowledge (*'ilm*), physical and mental fitness (*salāmah*), sound judgement (*ra'y*), courage and determination (*shujā'ah wa najdah*) and descent from the Quraysh (*nasab*). Ibn Khaldūn reduces them to five: *'ilm*, *'adālah*, *kafā'ah*, *salāmah* and *nasab*.[46] Al-Ghazālī enumerates similar qualifications with some modifications. In the list of qualities, the predominant role of justice and its ethical sanctions are quite clear. This vision is diametrically opposed to the one espoused by political realists like Machiavelli who had a great impact upon the development of Western political theory. The just *imām* is described by some of the jurists as the shadow of God upon earth. He implements the Sharī'ah, preserves equality between the people, promotes their welfare and redresses the grievances of the oppressed. In short, a just *imām* would establish conditions in which the right religion and Islamic virtues are practised. Obedience to the just ruler is therefore mandatory and is equated with obedience to Allah (SWT) and His Prophet (ṢAAS).

CONTEMPORARY MUSLIM THOUGHT AND THE STRUCTURES OF GOVERNMENT

The demise and the impossibility of resuscitation of the universal caliphate in 1924 precipitated a vigorous debate among Muslim scholars on the nature and function of the caliphate. These discussions have in many ways been the continuation of Muslim political thinking which took shape during the Abbasid period. In particular, the essential attributes of an Islamic political system remained close to the theoretical idealised view of the caliphate sketched by towering Muslim thinker-jurists like al-Māwardī, al-Ghazālī and al-Baqillānī. What is new under the changed situation is a redefinition of the concept of *khilāfah* and an elaboration of the structure of the Islamic political order. Beginning with Imām Ibn Taymīyah, the new trend is evidenced in the writings of Ḥasan al-Bannā, Sayyid Quṭb, Abul A'lā Mawdūdī, Ḥasan al-Turābī and others. Their ideas have deeply affected the consciousness of Muslims around the world and hence require a brief recapitulation.

To begin with, contemporary Muslim thinkers do not treat *khilāfah* as a historical institution to be replicated in its entirety. They idealise the rule of *Khulafā' al-Rāshidūn* as a paragon of Islamic government and society which, as Ibn Taymīyah argues, cannot be recreated in history. Nor do they subscribe to the indispensability of political universalism or a universal *khilāfah*. Instead, they accept the plurality of the Muslim world as a necessity. They argue that since the Ummah is, by definition, non-territorial and encompasses the whole world, plurality of political units is inevitable. 'There is no imperative, therefore', argues Ibn Taymīyah, 'to press the world of Islam into a political unity or federal state; it can better develop through the principle of cooperation, into a confederation of free sovereign states'.[47] Sayyid Mawdūdī similarly argued for the unity of the Muslim world in 1965.[48] To these thinkers, *khilāfah* denotes a system which aims at the welfare of humanity through the implementation of Islamic values and principles. In short, *khilāfah* may be defined as a socio-political system in accordance with the teachings of Islam. As AbdulḤamīd AbūSulaymān explains:

> Whatever system of government the Ummah chooses for itself in order to realise its spiritual and temporal aspiration is the one that should be understood as the *khilāfah* system, and thus deserving of the Ummah's support.[49]

Khilāfah as a historical institution cannot be denied but, more importantly, it signifies the nature of the political system in Islam.

ORGANISATION OF THE ISLAMIC POLITICAL SYSTEM

The Islamic political system is distinguished by its unique theoretical foundations and structural features. Terms coined by orientalists like 'theocracy' (a state governed by a god or gods) or 'universal monarchy' (a system based on a legal code) are not proper means of identification if applied to the Islamic political system.[50] Some of the Islamic thoughts and practices can be compared with non-Islamic ones but the Islamic system '. . . has a social orientation peculiar to itself, different in many respects from that of the modern West, and can be successfully interpreted only within its own context and in its own terminology'.[51]

Sayyid Abul A'lā Mawdūdī defined the Islamic political system as 'nothing more than a combination of men working together as servants of Allah to carry out His will and purpose'.[52] Muḥammad Asad defines it as a system characterised by 'a conscious application of the socio-political tenets of Islam to the life of the nation, and by an incorporation of those tenets in the basic constitution of the country.[53] Since the system is founded upon the Islamic vision and communal needs, it maintains some dynamism and '. . . has room for scores of models which are compatible with the natural growth of a society and the new needs of the contemporary age as long as the total Islamic idea dominates these models in its expansive external perimeter'.[54]

Constitutional government

The Islamic political system is a constitutional system founded upon the conditions underlined by the Sharī'ah, which is a complete system of life and all-embracing social order.[55] The Sharī'ah, according to Mawdūdī, touches upon such matters as:

> religious rituals, personal character, morals, habits, family relationships,

social and economic affairs, administration, rights and duties of citizens, judicial system, laws of war and peace and international relations.[56]

The Sharī'ah specially recognises the authority of the *shūrā* in arriving at communal decisions and upholds the principles of freedom, justice and equality of all Muslims regardless of their ethno-national and racial distinctions.

The Sharī'ah does not specify the structural and functional features of the political system. This dynamism, inherent in the Sharī'ah, permits the Ummah to evolve any suitable method for the enforcement of Islamic law provided these methods do not contravene Sharī'ah injunctions.[57] Consequently, Muslim scholars, using *ijtihād*, suggest the principle of fusion of powers as the method best suited to realise the will of Allah (SWT). This doctrine, according to Muḥammad Asad, 'constitutes a most important, specifically Islamic contribution to political theory'.[58] The fusion of powers requires overlapping executive, legislative and judicial branches of government which perform mostly shared functions of enacting authoritative rules, mapping out policies, enforcing the rules and settling disputes arising from the rules enacted.

The executive

The executive 'branch is the nucleus of authority and the active force in the government'.[59] It is designated in the Qur'ān and the *hadīth* as *ulū al-amr* and *umarā'* and is headed by the *amīr* (the leader) who will be elected from among the 'most respectable' and 'most pious' persons. The executive, according to the convention of 31 'Ulamā' held in Pakistan in 1951, 'shall always be a male Muslim in whose piety, learning and soundness of judgement the people or their elected representatives have confidence'.[60] 'It is obvious', justifies Muḥammad Asad, 'that only a person who believes in the Divine Origin of that Law – in a word, a Muslim – may be entrusted with the office of head of the state'.[61] The caliph must, in addition to piety, be knowledgeable and a capable administrator. The Ummah's acceptance of the caliph, Quṭb asserted, is contingent upon his enforcement of the Sharī'ah as well as his pursuit of the communal interest.[62] The chief executive is subject to the rule of law in exactly the same way as other members of the community. He can be sued in a court of law, is bereft of any special privileged treatment, and is liable to deposition for gross violation of Sharī'ah injunctions.

In consequence, there are limitations on the powers and actions of the chief executive. The *amīr* does not hold his position in his own right or because of his linkage with a family or a tribe but rather as a trustee of the Sharī'ah and the affairs of the Ummah. Monarchy would then be unacceptable because there is 'no place for kingships in Islam and succession could not be on a hereditary basis'.[63] Although the principle of *shūrā* establishes election for succession to rule, it does not specify the method of election. The Ummah, consequently, is free to determine the method of election – direct, indirect, proportional etc. – provided these methods are consistent with the letter and spirit of the Sharī'ah.

The legislature

The *amīr* works in consultation with the legislature which is considered by contemporary scholars as manifesting the concept of *shūrā*, *ijtihād* and *ijmā'*. The caliphate began, according to Ḥasan al-Turābī, as an 'elected consultative institution. Later it degenerated into a hereditary, or usurpatory, authoritarian government'.[64] This consultative or legislative assembly must be restored and, according to Muḥammad Iqbāl, it must have the right to interpret and apply the law (*ijtihād*) which would then constitute the authoritative consensus of the community (*ijmā'*). 'In this way alone we can stir into activity the dormant spirit of life in our legal system and give it an evolutionary outlook'.[65] Muslim scholars conceived of the legislature in terms of the *ahl al-ḥall wa al-'aqd* ('the people who loose and bind') and *shūrā*. These two institutions, i.e., *shūrā* and *ahl al-ḥall wa al-'aqd* have mostly been two distinct institutions; the former was smaller in size than the latter. The two bodies occasionally merged to perform certain important functions such as electing the caliph.

Most scholars argue that the legislature should be composed of representatives, at least the majority of whom must be elected. It must contain a group of experts in the Sharī'ah as well as modern jurisprudence. The legislature would perform the executive and deliberative functions.[66] In terms of legislation, a distinction has to be made between that part of the Sharī'ah which has a permanent and unalterable character and that which is flexible. The basic constitutional elements, the directive principles and values revealed in the Qur'ān and Sunnah are of permanent character. These can neither be questioned nor tampered with but accepted *in toto*. The flexible part relates to the daily concerns of existence not covered by the Qur'ān and Sunnah. This part is very wide and subject to modification according to the needs and requirements of the changing circumstances. In short, the legislature is to enact the explicit directives of the Sharī'ah and to formulate laws, where basic guidance is not available, in conformity with the Sharī'ah and its terms of freedom, justice and equality.

Conception of the legislature as a consultative body has given rise to an erroneous view that its role is confined merely to rendering advice and that the chief executive is at liberty to disregard the legislature's opinion. Such a view has been categorically rejected by scholars and activists alike. Ḥasan al-Turābī, Sayyid Quṭb, 'Abd al-Qādir 'Audah (d.1375 AH/1955 CE), Muḥammad Asad and others argue to the contrary that *shūrā* is mandatory for the resolution of all important public issues and that the outcome of such a process is binding upon the ruler. Even Sayyid Abul A'lā Mawdūdī, who otherwise preferred the advisory role of the legislature, conceded that lacking the spirit and mentality required to practise *shūrā*, the current situation leaves 'no other alternative but to restrict and to subordinate the executive to the majority decisions of the legislature'.[67]

The judiciary

The judiciary, called *Qaḍā*, is independent of the executive and is to adjudicate in strict accordance with the Sharī'ah. The 'Ulamā' convention stipulated in their suggested constitution that 'the judiciary shall be separate from and independent of the executive so that it may not be influenced by the executive in the discharge of its duties'.[68] Scholars are of the opinion that the appointment of the judges by the executives should not affect the independence and the impartiality of the judiciary. The executive and the judiciary are both bound by the same law; the latter needs no authorisation from any other institution in the implementation of the Sharī'ah. On the contrary, the scope of its adjudicative function is so wide as to include all the organs and functionaries of government. The chief executive, like everybody else, is liable to be called upon to appear in a court of law as a plaintiff or a defendant. As Turābī argues,

> He [the ruler] enjoys no special immunities and can, therefore, be prosecuted or sued for anything he does in his private or public life. This is a fundamental principle of Islamic constitutional law, ensuing from the supremacy of the Sharī'ah.[69]

The function of judiciary includes, *inter alia*, settlement of disputes, prevention of wrongful acts and issuing of declaratory judgements.[70] There is some disagreement about its power of judicial review. Some modernist thinkers would not permit the judiciary to possess the power to judge the constitutionality of the laws. Instead, they would restrict the role of the judiciary to seeing that the laws, as framed, are carried out according to the intentions of the legislature.[71] Ḥasan al-Turābī holds the contrary opinion and considers that 'judges, as the guardians of the Sharī'ah, adjudicate in all matters of law'.[72] This viewpoint is echoed by Muḥammad Asad and elaborated by 'Abdulkadir Kurdī.[73] To Sayyid Mawdūdī, even though the judiciary did not exercise such powers during the period of *khulafā' al-Rāshidūn*, the lack of people of 'a very deep and true insight in the Qur'ān and the Sunnah' makes it imperative 'to give the judiciary power to declare void and *ultra vires* of the constitution all laws and legislations enacted in contravention of the Qur'ān and the Sunnah'.[74] This stand was endorsed by the leading 'Ulamā' of Pakistan, Muhammad Asad, as well as the Anṣārī Commission report.[75]

Form of government

Contemporary scholars are unanimous in their opinion that the Qur'ān and the Sunnah do not prescribe any particular form of government, nor elaborate a constitutional theory. Consequently, it is argued that the Islamic polity can take many forms, 'it is up to the Muslims of every age to find one that suits them'.[76]

Muhammad Asad prefers the presidential form of government, as it corresponds to the idea of the caliph. A strong head of state possessing necessary qualifications to the community should be entrusted with the task of managing the affairs of the Ummah. The ministers should hold office during his pleasure. The judiciary would act as a check on his powers.[77] Sayyid Mawdūdī stresses the need for the Islamic polity to correspond as closely as possible to the *Rāshidūn* caliphate. 'This form of government cannot be identified with any modern form of government'.[78] This is a category by itself – 'a theo-democracy, that is to say a divine democratic government, because under it the Muslims have been given a limited popular sovereignty under the suzerainty of God'.[79]

The Anṣārī Commission discussed the problem in detail and suggested that one person should hold the position of head of state as well as head of government – as is the case in a presidential form of government.

The commission however, refrained from equating the Islamic system with either the American presidential system, the British parliamentary model or the French system. Instead, it calls it the *shūrā* system, which could incorporate some of the healthy features from the existing models.[80] Ḥasan al-Turābī has no objection to 'whatever form the executive may take', provided the leader 'always be subject both to the Sharī'ah and to the *ijmā*' 'formulated under it'.[81] Furthermore, 'no rigid theory of separation of government functions can develop in a comprehensive, coherent system like the Islamic political order, except to provide some necessary checks and balances to safeguard liberty or justice'.[82] The form of government preferred by the majority of Muslim scholars is shown in Figure 6.1. The other variant wherein the chief executive is indirectly elected by the legislature or *majlis al-shūrā* can be seen in Figure 6.2. Both the models reflect the supremacy of the Sharī'ah and the principle of fusion of powers which is peculiar to the Islamic system. The similarity of goals pursued by the three branches, it is assumed, would result in a conflict-free relationship among the various organs of government.

CONCLUSION

The Qur'ān and the Sunnah, though they did not elaborate a constitutional theory, gave a clear outline of a political scheme which can be realised under all circumstances. Muslims generally agree that the Islamic political system is based upon the interrelated concepts of *tawḥīd*, Sharī'ah, *shūrā*, justice, equality and freedom. These principles set the Islamic polity apart from both capitalist and Marxist systems. The Islamic polity is neither territory-bound nor restricted by racial or other considerations. It dismisses the notions of nationalism, popular sovereignty, and radical separation of powers. Instead, Islam advocates universalism, the supremacy of Sharī'ah and the fusion or limited separation of powers.

The responsibility for the administration of government is entrusted to the chief executive – *khalīfah* or *amīr*. Whatever form the executive assumes, the *amīr* is elected and is always subject to the Sharī'ah and to the *ijmā* 'formulated under it. The *amīr* is aided by the body 'which looses and binds'. Elected by the people, this body performs many of the functions entrusted to present-day legislatures. Legislation, however, should be within the limits prescribed by the Sharī'ah. The judiciary is functionally an independent arm of government which,

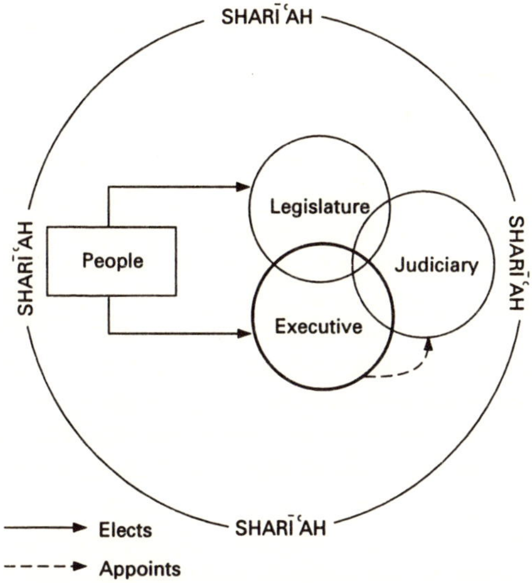

Figure 6.1 The Islamic political system: popularly elected executive

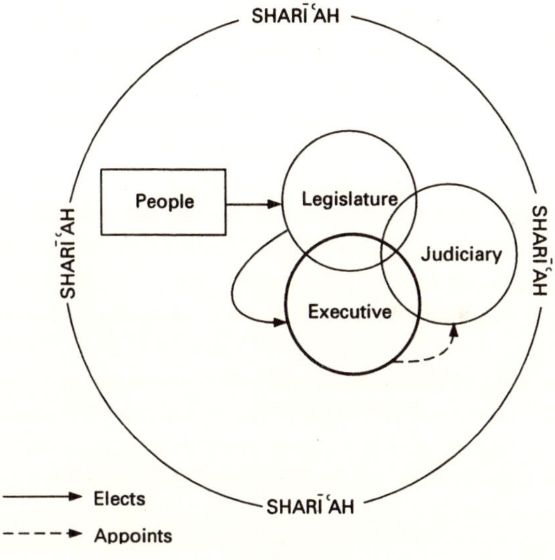

Figure 6.2 The Islamic political system: indirectly elected executive

inter alia, interprets and adjudicates in accordance with the Sharī'ah.

The principles, values and the structural features outlined above make it clear that the Islamic polity can not be categorised as either parliamentary or presidential democracies. The superficial affinities in terms of election, consultation and the rule of law not withstanding, the Islamic way of life is irreconcilable with the Western democratic philosophy. Sharī'ah is not the same as the man-made law, *ijtihād* does not mean complete freedom of independent action, and *shūrā* is not compatible with a liberal democratic structure of authority.

Democracy is the product of the overall evolution of Western civilisation; its secular content is the result of centuries of conflict between the church and the state in which the latter won; its emphasis on suffrage, political freedom and voluntary association is the consequence of the demands made by the rising industrial proletariat in the nineteenth century. In short, democracy is the product of the materialistic philosophy which considers man as the measure of everything whose work is weighed in absolute material terms to the utter neglect of his spiritual aspects. Consequently, the laws in the West lay much emphasis on the individual's right that allows him to do anything he pleases. The separation of politics from religion makes morality a matter of personal discretion. Parties are formed with the expressed purpose of capturing political power and laws are formulated to provide the strong with the right to gratify their interests at the expense of the weak. The principle of justice they profess to uphold is shelved if it does not serve their interests. In the name of justice, Iraq could be demolished to save Kuwait, avowedly to protect their source of petroleum. Bosnia, not being oil rich, could be sacrificed and Serbs allowed to massacre the Bosnian Muslims. Democracy is, as such, antithetical to the Islamic way of life.

The Islamic polity caters for man's welfare in this world as an adjunct to his salvation in the Hereafter. The scope of an Islamic political system is wide and goes beyond the worldly affairs of the people. The key characteristic of an Islamic polity is the continuing responsiveness of the government to the will of Allah (SWT) as well as to the preferences of its citizens as long as these preferences do not violate the principles of the Sharī'ah. In addition to providing peace, order and good government for the healthy existence and development of individuals, the Islamic polity is under obligation, in the words of the Qur'ān, to

> establish the system of *ṣalāh* (worship and prayers) and *zakāh* (purification-tax), enjoin right and virtue and forbid wrong and evil. With Allah rests the end (and decision) of (all) affairs. (22:41)

7 *Muḥāsabah*: Accountability in Islam

The chequered historic practices of Muslim polities and communities have led successive generations of Muslim thinkers to scour relevant literature in search of prescriptions to protect the rights of the individual and to put a check on executive power. They agree on the obligatory nature of installing a government to safeguard the very existence of the community and to implement the Sharī'ah. They also felt the need to subordinate the ruler to the law and the obligation of the ruled to disobey an unjust command. What cannot be discerned in their writings are: (a) the principle of determining the lawfulness of the command as well as of the ruler; and (b) the procedural problem of locating the authority for dealing with a ruler who is found guilty of gross negligence or misconduct. The on-going movement to re-establish an Islamic socio-political order makes it imperative to re-examine these issues and to devise a satisfactory solution to this constitutional problem within the framework of Sharī'ah. It would, however, be instructive to look, first, at the structure and procedures adopted in the West to make the government and its officers responsible to the law and to the people whom they govern.

THE LEGISLATURE: THE REPRESENTATIVE BODY

The organ of government which is given the power of inquiry is the representative assembly or the legislature. This power is generally considered as an essential and appropriate auxiliary to the legislative function. This power of investigation, according to Harold Laski, is 'the main guarantee against dishonesty or inefficient administration'.[1] Also, according to John Stuart Mill:

> the proper office of a representative assembly is to watch and control the government . . . and, if the men who compose the government abuse their trust, or fulfil it in a manner which conflicts with the deliberate sense of the nation, to expel them from the office.[2]

The representative assembly can expel executive officers only through the process of impeachment.

'Impeachment' strictly speaking means a 'charge', an 'accusation'.[3] It is equivalent to indictment by a grand jury. Throughout most of American history, impeachment has been used to remove 'dreary little judges' who were guilty of 'squalid misconduct'.[4] However, impeachment provisions are meant specifically to remove a President for political as well as criminal offences.

Article 1 of the Constitution of the United States of America provides for impeachment and removal of the President from office for 'Treason, Bribery or other high Crimes and Misdemeanours'. The Constitution gives the House of Representatives the power of impeachment, that is, the right to recommend a trial to determine whether the President shall be removed from office. A majority vote for impeachment in the House sends the matter to the Senate. The Senate organises itself into a court of impeachment, composed of all members of the Senate and presided over by the Chief Justice of the United States. The President may appear in person if he so desires but will be excused if he requests it. When both sides have been heard, the Senate votes. Conviction requires a two-thirds vote on any one of the articles of impeachment. So far one president, Andrew Johnson, has been brought before the Senate; he, however, escaped impeachment by one vote. Another president, Richard Nixon, faced with the near-certainty of impeachment and a possible conviction, resigned to avoid this possibility. Conviction on impeachment carries the penalty of removal from office and disqualification from holding any future position of trust and honour in the United States government.

Like any other power, the power of investigation may be used to gain partisan advantage. Impeachment is not designed to force an unpopular President out of office, though it was used in this way in 1868 against Andrew Johnson. This misuse of impeachment procedure illustrates the danger that it could be used for political purposes rather than as a salutary check on the administration.

OBEDIENCE TO AUTHORITY: THE QUR'ĀN AND THE SUNNAH

The authority of governors and the responsibility of the governed is conveyed in Sūrah 4, āyah 59 of the Qur'ān which enjoins the believers to 'Obey Allah and Obey the Messenger and those in authority among you' (*wa ulī al-amr minkum*).[5] By meaningfully omitting the verb 'obey' only in case of those having 'authority', the verse makes obedience to them conditional and subservient to Allah (SWT) and His Prophet (ṢAAS). This condition or requirement is met by 'right belief' and assiduous performance of the prescribed rites and rituals. Additionally, the governors are under obligation to seek the advice of the community and to administer firmly once a policy decision has been made (Al-Qur'ān, 3:159). Declaring the government as a trust, the Qur'ān enjoins the leaders to govern with justice (4:58), to avoid cruelty (3:159), to promote public interest, to take care of the needy, and not to benefit the rich at the expense of the community (59:7).

By issuing commands which run contrary to the Qur'ān and the Sunnah, explains Zamakhsharī, the governor forfeits his claim to obedience from the people.[6] There are several passages in the Qur'ān which categorically forbid obedience to him who follows 'the dictates of his own desires' (18:28) and 'who oversteps the limits set by Allah' (26:15). Indeed, the Qur'ān makes it obligatory upon the believers to rebel against injustice; to defend themselves whenever tyranny afflicts them (13:39) and 'to fight in the cause of Allah and of the utterly helpless men, women and children' who are oppressed (4:75).

The above Qur'ānic attitude is reinforced by several prophetic traditions (*ahādīth*) which urge upon the Muslim to obey those in authority except if he 'orders him to do a sinful act'.[7] In such a case, the obligation lapses automatically, for 'there is no obedience to a Creature, if it involves disobedience to the Creator'.[8] Obedience 'is obligatory only in virtue'.[9] In fact, the Prophet (ṢAAS) has warned of dire consequences if the Muslims refuse to resist a wrongdoer:

> Nay, by Allah, you must enjoin right and forbid wrong, and you must stay the hand of the wrongdoer, bend him to conformity with justice (*al-ḥaqq*) and force him to do justice – or else Allah will set the hearts of you all against one another.[10]

In addition, the entire career of the Prophet (ṢAAS) is characterised by a struggle against misery, tyranny and oppression of one against another. His career presents an ideal role model (*uswah ḥasanah*) which Muslims are required to emulate.

THE *KHULAFĀ' AL-RĀSHIDŪN*

There is general consensus among the Sunni Muslim jurists and thinkers that the *Khulafā' al-Rāshidūn* did adhere strictly to the normative standard found in the Qur'ān and the Sunnah. This era of 'righteous excellence' was characterised by legitimacy and justice. None laid the foundation of a hereditary government nor assumed power by force or trickery.[11] They acceded to the caliphal office by lawful means, i.e., through elections, and they governed through consultation and in accordance with the Sharī'ah. Obedience was made conditional upon their observance of the Sharī'ah provisions as is evidenced from the keynote speech of the first caliph, Abū Bakr:

> O people, I have been entrusted with your affairs, although I am not the best among you. Help me if I do well and straighten me if I do wrong. . . . Obey me as long as I obey Allah and His Prophet. In case I contravene the injunction of Allah and His Prophet, you owe me no obedience.[12]

Similarly, his successor 'Umar declared: 'Verily, I am one among you, I do not desire that you should follow anything out of my caprice'.[13] The third caliph, 'Uthmān, did not merely follow the Qur'ān and the Sunnah, but Muslims bound him further to follow the footsteps of his two illustrious predecessors. He too believed in rule by consultation and upheld the Sharī'ah. It is true that he refused to submit to the insurgent's demand for his resignation. This is because the demand came not from *ahl al-shūrā* but from insurgents and that too at the point of a sword. In fact, one leading member of the *shūrā*, Mu'ādh Ibn Jabal, advised the caliph not to resign so as not to make a precedent for posterity.[14] As for the fourth caliph, 'Alī, he refused to become the *khalīfah* in secret or without the approval of the masses. None of the caliphs believed in the Divine Right of Kings and none solicited unconditional obedience from the masses.

The model caliphate did not long retain its genuine form and popular characteristics. The elective caliphate, as discussed in the previous chapter, soon degenerated into the absolutism of the Umayyad rulers and was further corrupted with the shift of power to the house of 'Abbās in 750 CE. This degeneration of the institution of the caliphate prompted Muslim jurists to deliberate upon its structure.

MUSLIM JURISTS AND THINKERS

The period of *al-Khulafā' al-Rāshidūn* formed an ideal source from which thinkers could draw the blueprint of an Islamic political order. This ideal appears in the writings of Muslim jurists and thinkers from al-Māwardī to Mawdūdī. With the passage of time, the caliphate came to be reduced to a hollow shell of pontifical honours with some local governors seizing their provinces by force while others were not subject to appointment by the caliph. Such an anomalous situation threatened the very existence of the Muslim community. Al-Māwardī tried to regularise the situation by rationalising the seizure of caliphal executive powers by local rulers, provided 'the usurper rules in accordance with the injunctions of the Sharī'ah'.[15] Al-Ghazālī, realising that 'the government in these days is a consequence solely of military power', worked out a new relationship based on the co-operation between the puppet caliph and the *Sulṭān*, the actual ruler.[16] Ibn Jamā'ah, through his concepts of *qahr wa ghalbah* (force and conquest), recognised the military power pure and simple to be the essential constituent of rulership.[17] These and similar other writings helped tone down the principle of disobeying the caliph if he acted contrary to the Sharī'ah, in favour of submission to a ruler, however, oppressive he might be.

The jurists' readiness to revise political thought in the light of prevailing circumstances has been explained by imputing bad motives – arguing that they were high-ranking functionaries in the administration and were thus asserting the authority of their respective caliphs.[18] On the contrary, the jurists' attempts at accommodating both the *de facto* power of the usurper and the *de jure* power of the caliph in the constitutional theory and their doctrine of passive obedience to the ruler was aimed at keeping the usurpers within the framework of the Sharī'ah-based community and to ensure its continuity. They conceived of the institution of the caliphate as representing the sovereignty of the Sharī'ah and the indivisible authority of the Ummah. Though the caliphate was shorn of its power, its continuation nevertheless was necessary to preserve the legitimacy of the application of the law by courts and the contractual relationships and transactions throughout the state. Their recognition of the prevailing status quo does not mean legalisation but a temporary acceptance until the usurper or a tyrant is changed by a legitimate government. Al-Ghazālī conceded that the concessions he made were involuntarily required by 'the necessities of the actual moment'. He gave the analogy of sanctioning the carrion, that is prohibited for Muslims, under dire necessities.[19] This does not make carrion *per se* permissible but only sanctions it, for the time being, under special circumstances. Before him, al-Māwardī admitted that his recognition of an illegal *amīr* and other concessions were 'contrary to the principle of the law' but these were done in the light of 'public interest' which could have been endangered.[20] A revolt against the central authority may result in disastrous anarchy and more injustice and sufferings than the existing tyranny. Hence they advocated the notion of accepting 'the lesser of two evils' on the assumption that challenging the existing institutions poses a greater danger than tolerance for divergencies from a strict application of Islamic rules. There is not a single jurist of significance who gave a verdict (*fatwā*) to the effect that Islam enjoins all believers to render passive obedience to the rulers under all circumstances.

It needs mentioning that despite their condoning of tyranny, the jurists were never tired of laying emphasis on justice as an essential precondition of the rulership; on the dire consequences of injustice; and on service to the cause of Allah (SWT) and welfare of the people. These formulations were put forward by geniuses like al-Ghazālī, Nizām al-Mulk (d.485 AH/1192 CE) and the administrators and writers of the manual of conduct for rulers, 'the Mirror for Princes', as well as in the writings of those who made compromising concessions. Al-Māwardī did not permit even in case of necessity, the lowering of the qualifications of the caliph and was opposed to his claim of undisputed obedience. Imām Abū Hanīfah had earlier decreed that it was obligatory upon the subject to rebel against a ruler who transgressed the limits of Sharī'ah and perpetrated tyranny provided, however, that such rebellion does not 'fizzle out in mere loss of lives and power'.[21] Abū Yusuf's exhortations to the caliph to follow the traditions and footsteps of the *Khulāfā' al-Rāshidūn* was an implicit protest against the modalities of the Sassanian empire pursued by the then rulers.[22] Ibn Jamā'ah, despite according recognition to the men of 'the wielder of force', held the usurper responsible for safeguarding religion, executing legal decisions, collecting Sharī'ah-based dues and protecting the religious endowments.[23] Abū 'Alī Ibn Sīnā (379–428AH/980–1037 CE) roundly condemned usurpation, demanded the death of a tyrant, sanctioned the removal of an incompetent incumbent and advised the people to support the 'worthy rebel' in challenging the disqualified caliph.[24]

Imam Ibn Taymiyyah took even a more drastic stand on the issue. He took Ibn Jamā'ah to task for his views and over his long career carried on such a vitriolic attack against the accommodators and vacillators that he was constantly thrown into prison. He stressed the duty of the citizens to take an active part in public life. Both the Qur'ān and the Sunnah, he pointed out, obligate the believers to do their best with regard to whatever is entrusted to their care.[25] The government is a trust and it requires the joint effort of both the governors and the governed to establish the just political order – an order which runs contrary to personal rule and is based on the principle of equality enjoined for by the Sharī'ah. Obedience to the governor is predicated upon his ordering what is just and lawful. Tyrants and 'those who forsake the Shari'ah even though they might have pronounced the two formulas of the faith (*shahādatān*)' must be fought and disobeyed as a religious duty.[26]

Ibn Taymīyah's formulation was echoed later by Ibn Khaldūn, 'Allāma-Muḥammad Iqbāl (1290–1357 AH/1873–1938 CE), Sayyid Quṭb, Sayyid Abul A'la Mawdūdī and others. It provides the twentieth-century movements with a point of reference for the reassertion of the authority of the Qur'an and the Sunnah.

GROUNDS FOR IMPEACHMENT

In considering the writings of prominent thinkers on the subject of government and authority from al-Māwardī down to the present day, one is struck by the fact that they held on tenaciously to certain fundamental principles even though they knew that these were fully realised in practice only during the period of *al-Khulafā' al-Rāshidūn*. Those principles associated with the executive organ of government can be discussed under the following two broad categories of legality and legitimacy. Contravention of any of the provisions under these categories constitutes a ground for the deposition of an incumbent executive.

Legality

In the enormous expositions written by Muslim scholars about the chief executive, the elective nature of this institution is stressed. They have relied unswervingly on the 'divine guidance of the community and the infallibility of its *ijmā'*.[27] Al-Māwardī argued for an elective process for the choice of the *khalīfah* who, according to Sayyid Quṭb, derives his authority from 'one source, the will of the governed'.[28] This can take place, explains Mawdūdī, only if three principles are observed:

1. the election of the chief executive depends entirely on the will of the

general public with no one having the right to impose himself forcibly as the ruler;
2. no clan or class shall have a monopoly of rulership; and
3. the election shall be free of all coercion.[29]

Such principles of self-government are deduced from the scriptural principle of *shūrā* and from the injunctions to order the good and forbid the evil; and were indeed spontaneously operative during the period of the first four rightly-guided caliphs. Their realisation under the medieval caliphate was unthinkable and hence earlier jurists did not insist on the right of every individual to participate in the election of the *khalīfah*. They, however, never upheld the principle of hereditary government even when vested in republican garb by the practice of *bay'ah*. They considered election as a collective duty which would be performed by those who are best qualified to evaluate the capability of the candidate for the office.

It is essential to note that Islam does not specify any particular method of election. The translation of this principle of election into a workable scheme of government is left to be determined by other considerations. Furthermore, the nomination and succession to the office of the chief executive need not entail any particular procedure such as consecration or ordination.

The simplicity of the procedure, however, should not be mistaken for a laxity in the qualifications of a prospective candidate. Muslim scholars and theologians of different schools (*madhāhib*), with minor variations, have concurred in their views that the candidate for leadership must be a Muslim, male, adult and sane.[30] These merely mark out the formal legal bounds to eligibility for the headship of the Islamic society; far more important are the qualities of:

(a) commitment to Islam, *wara'*;
(b) knowledge of and ability to understand the demands of the Islamic system, *'ilm*;
(c) capacity and competence to carry out the administrative duties, *kafā'ah*; and
(d) a strong resolution to uphold justice, *'adālah*.

In detailing these qualities, contemporary thinkers relied on the expositions of al-Māwardī, al-Ghazālī and other early masters.

They insist that the electors give careful consideration to the merits of the candidate before electing him as the chief executive. Ibn Sīnā went to the extent of saying that 'the electors become unbelievers (*fa-qad kafarū bi-Allāh*), if they are guilty of a wrong choice'.[31] This view, though unjustified, shows the significance attached to the question of a right choice of the head of the polity. In any case, the executive in an Islamic system is constituted by the general will of the Muslims according to certain prescribed qualifications and criteria. The Ummah also has the right to depose the incumbent should he forfeit any of the qualifications or try to accede to power by force or trickery.

Legitimacy

If, as stated, the nature of an Islamic political system is elective, its legitimacy requires the consent and approval of the people as well as the sovereignty of the Sharī'ah.[32] From the very beginning, Islamic political thought conceived of Islam as prescribing that government be by consultation. In this respect, the Qur'ān prescribes that 'the Muslims should manage their affairs by mutual consultation' (12:38) 'and when you have resolved, put your trust in Allah' (3:159).

Throughout the whole range of Muslim political thinking, there is hardly any write-up which does not invoke the two verses cited above. They differ, however, in terms of the scope of consultation. Some would restrict it to the representatives of the people, others would include every Muslim who is capable and qualified to give sound opinion on matters of Islamic law. To most of the thinkers, a decision by consensus does not necessarily mean unanimity, but simply the agreement of the majority of those present. As for the specific method of consultation, it is left for the Muslims to determine. What is important, however, is that the command for consultation can neither be flouted altogether nor can it be assigned a form that would violate its substance by rendering it ineffective. For, as 'Umar ibn al-Khaṭṭāb declared, 'There can be no *khalīfah* except by consultation'.[33]

The validity of consensus depends on its being based on Sharī'ah. The polity exists for the sake of the law and not the other way around. Sharī'ah dominated the mind and conscience of successive generations of Muslims and has been considered the source and highest form of law embodying moral, ethical and religious values. It is 'the epitome of the true Islamic spirit, the most decisive expression of Islamic thought, the essential kernel of Islam'.[34] They are unanimous that Sharī'ah be the law of the land; it is absolute and permits no compromise. The caliph or the *amīr* rules as *primus inter pares* and acts according to the Sharī'ah and the will of the community. He is elected to establish the ordinance of the law, to secure its sanctions, and to ensure compliance with all the matters contained in it. The community backs him to translate the law from the sphere of potentiality into actuality. 'It deposes him and replaces him by another, if he commits any act that would justify his removal from office'.[35]

The caliphate or the Islamic political order, in Islam, is not a right but a function to be performed on behalf of the community. The Sharī'ah rules out usurpation and hereditary succession as grounds for political legitimacy. It abhors personal authority which according to Iqbāl is 'inimical to human individuality'.[36] The *amīrs* forfeit their right to govern if there occurs a change in their moral status: if they become slaves to their passions and flout the prohibitions of Sharī'ah, or if there occurs a change in their physical nature which incapacitates them from performing the leadership function. The best exposition of the people's right to deal with an evil-doer *imām* is provided by Mu'ādh ibn Jabal, one of the companions of the Prophet (ṢAAS):

> Our leader is one of us; if he implements among us the teachings . . . of the Qur'ān and the Sunnah, we shall have him over us. If he goes against it, we shall depose him. If he commits theft, we shall amputate his hand; if he commits adultery, we shall flog him . . . He will not hide himself from us, nor will he be self-conceited . . . He is a person as good as we are.[37]

INSTITUTIONAL APPARATUS FOR IMPEACHMENT

It is clear from the above discussion that an illegal or illegitimate executive forfeits the right to govern and is subject to removal from office. It is not clear, however, as to how he should be removed from office, as no tribunal or method has been proposed by means of which such an action might be brought about. Anticipating the fact of historical evolution, Islam left a vast field of institutional and constitutional developments to individual reasoning and collective wisdom to be shaped according to the broad principles laid down in the Qur'ān and the Sunnah of the Prophet (ṢAAS). Early jurists talked about outright rebellion simply because there was no other way of removing an evil-doer imām. With the relative easing of absolutism and the possibility of removing an executive through peaceful means, efforts are being made to devise a constitutional formula for impeaching the chief executive within the framework of Sharī'ah. Three institutions have been suggested to deal with the impeachment problem: the judiciary, the 'Ulamā' or the leadership Council, and the Consultative Assembly.

The judiciary

It has been argued that an Islamic political order is governed in accordance with Sharī'ah, the Islamic law, which is divine in origin, requiring implementation only. Its application involves interpretation and not legislation in the sense of innovative law-making. The government in accordance with the Sharī'ah, therefore, implies the pre-eminence of the judiciary over the executive and the legislative organs of government.

The *amīr* of an Islamic polity is legitimate in so far as, he ensures the application of the Sharī'ah. That is to say, the *amīr* performs his functions within immutable legal parameters laid down in advance. His performance has to be under constant scrutiny and the body best qualified to fulfil this assignment is the judicial community 'because of its specialisation in Islamic law' and because of extraordinary qualities and exceptional faculties demanded of them before being selected as judges.[38] Consequently, Kurdi and others give wide-ranging powers to the judiciary, including the 'right to issue a declaratory writ to discharge, impeach, or imprison any public officer, executive, or legislator', including the Head of government.[39]

The body which historically exercised judicial as well as supervisory functions over the conduct of the administration is known as *dīwān al-naẓr fī al-maẓālim*. Intended to set right cases of miscarriage of justice and tyrannical behaviour of the members of the ruling elite, the *diwān* served as a court of appeal as well as a court of first instance. Though its origin is traced to the time of the Prophet (ṢAAS), it was the fourth caliph, 'Alī, who personally looked into the cases of misdeeds and injustices suffered by the general public. The Umayyad caliphs, beginning with 'Abd al-Malik ibn Marwān (685–705AH/1286–1305CE), handled such cases personally at specified days each week.[40]

The *dīwān al-maẓālim* had the power to hold public officials, including the chief executive, to strict legal accountability for their acts. Nobody, not even the caliph, could secure or demand any preferential treatment. There are several examples in which the reigning caliph was required to appear in person before the court as a mere defendant. Yet the court was never authorised to depose the caliph. Al-Māwardī is perhaps the first Muslim thinker to deal, systematically and in detail, with the structure and functions of the *dīwān*. He took much pain to enumerate various functions of the *dīwān al-maẓālim* and specified the types of cases to be handled and the personnel involved in each case, none of which include the person of the chief executive as a subject for probing and nowhere did he mention the possibility of impeaching the chief executive through the *dīwān* or any other courts. The fact that the *dīwān* functioned as an instrument of the caliph precluded any possibility of its move to overthrow the caliph.

Historically too, there is not a single instance of a caliph being ousted by the judiciary. First of all, there was no provision for impeaching the caliph. Even if its existence is assumed, it could not be made operative owing to the lack of power to enforce it. The problem of deposition and succession to rule was frequently left to the arbitration of the sword. Most cases, particularly during the Abbasid period, were of forced abdication. The judges of the court were brought in for the sole purpose of attestation to the abdication decision of an incumbent. Once this task was accomplished, the incumbent was brought before the public to declare his own deposition.

The function of the *qāḍī* (judge), therefore, was confined merely to attestation and not to deposition. This position of the judges was clearly understood and accepted by the *qāḍī* of the Abbasid era. This is evident from the abdication incident of the Abbasid caliph, al-Qāhir bi-Allāh (932–934AH/1525–1527CE), whose refusal to consent to his self-deposition made the *qāḍī*, who was sent to attest the document of abdication, ask: 'What use was it to summon us to a man who had not been forced to consent?' To this 'Alī ibn 'Īsā remarked: 'His conduct is notorious and therefore he must be deposed'. The *qāḍī* replied: 'It is not for us to establish dynasties – that is accomplished by the men of swords. We are *only suited and required for attestation*' (emphasis mine).[41] Thus, there is not much of a support for those who advocate authorising the judiciary to impeach an incumbent chief executive.

The leadership council

All the powers that the *maẓālim* court enjoyed are assigned to the supreme judicial council in the Constitution of the Islamic Republic of Iran which was approved by 98.2 per cent of those who voted and it was implemented in 1979. Though the constitution gave the judicial council the power to decide the case should the President violate any of the provisions of the constitution, the power to impeach the President is left outside its jurisdiction.[42] That power is given to the *vilāyet-e-faqīh,* consisting of the Leader of the Leadership Council. Article 5 of the Iranian Constitution of 1979, embodying the Shiite principle of the Islamic polity, states that:

> During the occultation of the *walī al-'aṣr* (may God hasten his re-appearance), the *wilāyah* and leadership of the Ummah devolve upon the just (*'ādil*) and pious (*muttaqī*) *faqīh* who is fully aware of the circumstances of his age; courageous, resourceful, and possessed of administrative ability; and recognised and accepted as Leader by the majority of the people; in the event that no *faqīh* should be so recognised by the majority, the Leader, or the Leadership Council, composed of *fuqahā'* possessing the aforementioned qualifications, will assume the responsibilities of this office in accordance with Article 107.

Specific qualifications of the Leader or members of the Leadership Council, according to Article 109, are:

(a) scholarship and piety, as required for performing the functions of *muftī* and *marji'*;
(b) political and social perspicacity, courage, strength, and the necessary administrative abilities for leadership.

The Constitution conferred on the *vilāyet-e-faqīh*, as per Article 110, the supreme and ultimate authority in the polity, makes the elected offices of the Presidency and the Parliament subordinate to the office of the *faqīh*. With respect to the Presidency, the functions of the Council include, *inter alia*,

(a) signing the decree formalising the election of the President of the Republic by the people;
(b) dismissal of the President of the Republic, with due regard for the interest of the country, after the Supreme Court holds him guilty of the violation of his constitutional duties, or after a vote of the National Consultative Assembly testifying to his political incompetence (Article 110, Sec. 4 and 5).

That these clauses are no hollow words was amply demonstrated by Ayatollah Khomeini (1320–1410AH/1902–1989CE). In 1981, the first elected President, Dr Abū Ḥasan Banī Ṣadr was impeached, duly removed from office and was replaced by another candidate from the Islamic Republican Party.

The Iranian Constitution has operationalised the issue in a Shiite conception of an Islamic state, which is based upon the principle of the imamate of the Prophet's (SAAS) son-in-law and cousin, 'Alī ibn Abī Ṭālib, and through him, 11 of his male descendants. The argument being made is that the mantle of guiding the Muslims after the death of the Prophet (ṢAAS) fell upon the imāms and that after the disappearance of the imām, i.e., after the end of the 'cycle of imamate', the same responsibility has to be assumed by the 'Ulamā' and *mujtahids,* those who are qualified to derive legal norms from the sources of the law.[43] Hence, the Constitution made the institution of the *vilāyat-e-faqīh* responsible for the overall supervision of the government, guaranteeing the conformity of its methods and functioning with Islamic precepts. A political language that finds its roots in the Shiite tradition may be acceptable in Iran which is coextensive with Shiism. The majority Sunni population would find it hard, however, to identify with a similar option. Furthermore, the Sunni 'Ulamā' do not enjoy that religious authority which is bestowed upon their Shiite counterparts. They are neither centrally organised in terms of formal institutional status roles nor are they effective at the level of primary group activity in attaining and maintaining the solidarity of their organisation and their independence of government control.[44] They did participate in public life and, during the Ottoman caliphate, held important administrative and legal positions in the system as *qāḍīs*, judges. But it was the state that held the reins of power. As Hodgson points out, the 'Ulamā' 'exercised an effective – but never decisive – pressure in the realms of public order and government.[45]

The consultative assembly

The essence of the Sunni view of government is that political power derives from two sources, the Sharī'ah and the Ummah, i.e., the divine law and the community of believers. This sharply distinguishes it from the Shiite doctrine of imamate based upon the descent from 'Alī ibn Abī Ṭālib. The Sunni doctrine looks upon the caliphate not as a right bestowed upon the caliph, but a function to be performed on behalf of the community. The assumptions of the equality of all believers, brotherhood, and collective responsibility of the Ummah to enjoin virtue and for bad vice preclude the acceptance of an 'all-wise' absolute ruler, or the emergence of 'religious experts' who arrogate to themselves all powers of decision making to the exclusion of the masses. Hence, the importance of consultation or *shūrā* which includes *inter alia*, the duty of active supervision and moral censure called for by the obligation to enjoin good and forbid evil.

As discussed in the previous chapter, *shūrā* was required of the Prophet (ṢAAS); it was adhered to by *Khulafā' al-Rāshidūn* and is mandatory for every leader of an Islamic polity. The *amīr* should use the *shūrā* not only to 'enlighten himself on various aspects of the issue',[46] but he must, as well, adhere to the conclusions reached through consultation. Muslim jurists and political thinkers, likewise, upheld the view that whoever is entrusted with the task of governing the affairs of the Ummah should discharge his duties in consultation with *ahl al-shūrā*. The caliph is also answerable to the *shūrā* for all his actions.[47] Sayyid Rashīd Riḍā (1282–1354AH/1865–1935CE) convincingly argued that the past authorities have imposed the obligation to resist injustice and oppression on *ahl al-hall wa al-'aqd* and that these are the only people qualified to pass judgement on the conduct of the caliphs and to depose them if they contravene the Sharī'ah.[48]

It would be absurd to look for historical precedence to lend credence to *ahl al-shūrā* exercising power of impeachment. For throughout Muslim history, the deposition of caliphs was performed by the men of swords at the point of the swords. Of the 51 caliphs during the Umayad and Abbasid period, 42 were killed or died, five were forced to abdicate voluntarily, three were blinded and thus disqualified and one was impeached. Caliph Rashīd bi-Allāh (529–30 AH/1135–36CE) was the only one whose impeachment was done after due consultation with *ahl al-shūrā*. Convened by sultān Masud, the *shūrā* council was composed of the '*qāḍīs*, scholars and notables of the community'. They examined the written petition which contained witnesses as to Rashīd's injustices, appropriation of properties, brutal killings and drinking of alcohol; found the caliph guilty, and gave the verdict impeaching the caliph. Abū 'Abdullāh M. Al-Muktafī li-Amr Allāh (530–555AH/1136–60CE) was sworn in as the new caliph.[49]

There is also the case of the attempted impeachment of Aliyu Babba (1258–1296AH/1842–1859CE), the sultān of Sokoto in West Africa. Here six leading members of the *shūrā* charged the sultān that:

> First, he herded all revenues instead of distributing them among the Muslims as required by Sharī'ah. Secondly, he had allowed the walls of Sokoto and the Shehū's (the founder of the Sokoto caliphate) mosque to fall into disrepair. Thirdly, he had never taken part in any *jihād*, and had recently not even gone on any campaigns.[50]

They declared the withdrawal of their allegiance from the sultān and even suggested the names of two qualified candidates as a possible replacement. The incumbent sultān rushed to the capital, appeared before the members, and defended himself against allegations. Agreeing 'that the caliph had acquitted himself of their charges', the *shūrā* members 'renewed their allegiance'.[51] The sultān undertook the campaign and improved his conduct in office.

The cases discussed above exemplify the structural facilities and procedural arrangements that existed and operated to ensure the accountability and responsiveness of those in authority to the representatives of the community in accordance with the supreme authority of the Sharī'ah.

In modern times, contemporary thinkers, like Rashīd Riḍā and others, have suggested replacing the *shūrā* of the early Islamic polity by a representative body (the legislature) of the people elected through a modern ballot system.[52] Sayyid Mawdūdī actually argues that 'the legislature is what in the old terminology of *fiqh* was known as the *ahl al-hall wa al-'aqd*.[53] They also concur in subordinating the executive to the majority decisions of the legislature. They have the support in this respect of modernist Muslim thinkers like Fazlur Rahman, who is of the view that: 'for any major breach of public confidence, the head may be deposed after an overwhelming vote of the Legislature against him on that score'.[54] This view also received forceful recognition in the Report of the Commission set up by President Zia-ul-Haq of Pakistan in July 1983 to examine and recommend an Islamic set-up for the governance of Pakistan.

The 22 member Commission (16 members, three associate members and three honourary members) included leading 'Ulamā', serving and retiring judges, educationists, and members of the Federal Council. It was chaired by a seasoned politician and a veteran of the Pakistan movement, Maulana Zafar Ahmad Ansari. The Committee observed that the Chief executive shall be bound by the decisions of the *majlis al-shūrā* (Consultative Assembly) which will also have the power to impeach him for contravening the Sharī'ah, violating the law, for gross misconduct or for forfeiting any of the qualifications which initially made him eligible for the office. Any member of the *majlis*, with the support of at least one-third of his colleagues in the Assembly, may initiate the process. The incumbent head shall have a period of 10 days from the day the impeachment motion is tabled, to defend himself against the charges levelled. He shall stand impeached if the motion receives the vote of at least a two-thirds majority of the members of the Consultative Assembly.[55]

Realising perhaps that the feasibility and effectiveness of consultation depend upon solid constitutional arrangements, the Islamic Council of Europe produced *A Model of an Islamic Constitution* in December

1983. The model, as claimed by the Secretary General of the Council, was 'the result of prolonged effort by many eminent Muslim scholars, jurists, statesmen and representatives of Islamic movements'.[56] Article 26 of the Model Constitution states that 'the imām is entitled to obedience by all persons even if their views differ from his. There is, however, no obedience if it involves disobedience of Allah and His Prophet' (ṢAAS). Article 31 enunciates that:

> The imām shall assent to legislation passed by the *majlis al-shūrā* and then forward it to the concerned authorities for implementation. He shall not have the right to veto legislation passed by the *majlis*. . . .

Article 33 specifies that:

(a) The imām shall be impeached if he intentionally violates the provisions of the constitution, or for wanton violation of the Shari'ah, by a resolution to that effect by a two-thirds majority of the members of the *majlis al shūrā*, . . .
(b) Rules and procedures to govern the impeachment and removal of the imām shall be determined by law.

The draft constitution produced by the committee appointed by the Islamic Research Academy of al-Azhar states that 'those entitled to give mandate shall have the right to dismiss the imām when reasons exist for so doing and in the manner laid down by the law' (Article 50). However, Article 83 vests the power of 'surveillance over the activities of the executive authority' with the legislature, the *majlis al-shūrā* (see Appendix A). Before taking a decision to impeach the imām, it would be advisable for the *majlis*, however, to appoint a tribunal composed of the best jurists and members of the judiciary to investigate the matter and to recommend appropriate actions in the light of its findings.

CONCLUSION

The famous Qur'ānic verse enjoining the believers to obey Allah, and to obey His Messenger and those in authority provides the basis not only for political obligations in Islam but sets the limits, as well, of obedience to constituted authority. It stresses the need for the subordination of the chief executive to the law and the obligation of the governed to disobey an unlawful command. The Qur'ān and the Sunnah are emphatic about this and the practices during the period of *al-Khulafā' al-Rāshidūn* amply demonstrated its feasibility.

The threat to the community and to the institution of the caliphate caused by the subsequent degeneration of the ideal caliphate into an authoritarian system forced the Muslim jurists and thinkers to recognise the illegal seizure of power under the doctrine of necessity. Never, not once, did they legalise the status quo nor did they uphold the doctrine of passive obedience under all circumstances. They concurred on the need for political leadership to rely on the consent of the community of the faithful and to subscribe to the priority of the Sharī'ah governing the imām and the public alike. The obedience to the imām was made contingent upon his upholding the Sharī'ah and promoting justice. Failure in these respects justified his deposition and, in extreme cases, outright rebellion.

Despite sanctioning the removal of the incompetent or disqualified chief executive, the ground for an articulate procedure to impeach an incumbent head was never fully elaborated by Muslim political thinkers. The lone exception being al-Māwardī, who systematically treated the grounds for the deposition of the imām but was careful not to lay down any procedure by which an imām may be impeached. The scanty information gleaned from the writings of jurists and thinkers and the guidance available from the Qur'ān and the Sunnah, however, suggest several grounds for impeachment, which are classified under two broad categories of legality and legitimacy. The first pertains to the qualifications and the manner of instituting the caliph. It stipulates that the leader must be a Muslim, a male, an adult and sane possessing *wara', 'ilm, kafā'ah* and *'adālah*. His elevation to the highest office must be by the general will of the community expressed through a free and fair election. The legitimacy aspect required the imām to govern through consent and approval of the people and within the confines of the Sharī'ah. An illegal or illegitimate ruler forfeits the right to rule and is subject to deposition.

The Qur'ān and the Sunnah are silent on the procedure for impeaching an executive. Drawing upon the basic principles outlined in the two revelatory sources, Muslim thinkers have suggested the judiciary, the 'Ulamā' council, and the Consultative Assembly as possible organs or agencies for initiating and deciding the cases of impeachment. The Iranian Constitution vests the power of impeachment with the *vilāyet-e-faqīh*. The majority Sunni view is in favour of empowering the *ahl al-shūrā* to deal with the problem of an incompetent or disqualified ruler. The exercise of such authority by the *ahl al-shūrā* has a precedence in Muslim history. It received unanimous approval of the members of the Anṣarī Commission of Pakistan. The Islamic Council of Europe as well as the al-Azhar Committee tried to give the *majlis al-shūrā* a solid constitutional base to enhance the effectiveness and feasibility of consultation and accountability.

To conclude, Islam rejects obligatory passivism and affirms instead the Ummah's obligation to disobey and oppose those leaders who do not comply with the Divine Law. The Qur'ān obligates obedience to those in authority. The same Qur'ān also obligates the leaders to comply with the Sharī'ah and observance of communal interests. Failure in these respects would justify removal of leaders from positions of authority. The legislature or the *majlis al-shūrā* in exercising the power of impeachment should seek assistance from a tribunal constituted to investigate the matter in an impartial and just manner.

8 *Nahḍah*: The Islamic Movement

Islam, as discussed in previous chapters, is at once a religion and a social order which seeks for governance a polity based upon the eternal principles laid down in the Qur'ān and the Sunnah. Meant for practical application, Islam demands of believers to actively participate in the affairs of the world, to display a pious and honest character in all temporal activities and to struggle to establish the supremacy of the righteous moral code in all spheres of life. Consequently, throughout Muslim history there have been movements to purge society of alien or non-Islamic accretions and to establish a viable civilisation, a righteous order guided by the Sharī'ah.

The current Islamic movements all over the Muslim world have their roots deep in the earlier period going back to the time of the Prophet (ṢAAS). The Western observers of Islam term these movements erroneously as fundamentalism and are at a loss to understand and explain their recurrence. The correct approach would be to analyse these movements, 'in the light of their [Muslims'] own perceptions of their role'.[1] Neglecting the variable of the Islamic world view to explain the Islamic movements has resulted not merely in erroneous labelling of these movements but in overlooking their varying and diverse manifestations as well. This chapter examines the term fundamentalism and its appropriateness to characterise Islamic movements; provides an alternative concept and approach for analysing their emergence; and finally attempts an analysis of their diverse manifestations as exemplified by the faith movement of Mawlana Muḥammad Ilyās (1303–1363AH/1885–1947CE), the *Jamā'at-e-Islāmī* of Pakistan led by Sayyid Abul A'la Mawdūdī, and the Revolution in Iran under Ayatollah Ruhullah Khomeini (1321–1409AH/1902–1989CE).

'FUNDAMENTALISM' VERSUS *'NAHḌAH'*

The term "fundamentalism" has been applied to those movements in the Muslim world which aim at establishing Islamic political order in which the Sharī'ah will be publicly recognised and legally enforced.[2] The term originated in America and referred specifically to a movement in American Protestantism whose main objective was to combat 'Modernist' or 'Liberalist' tendencies. Coined early in the twentieth century, Protestant fundamentalism refers to those who 'do battle royal' for the achievement of fundamentals, viz., inerrancy of scripture, the virgin birth of Christ, the substitutionary atonement, the bodily resurrection of Christ, and the authenticity of miracles.[3] The fundamentalists of the 1920s achieved notoriety because of their vigorous campaign against schools of modernist tendencies and against the teaching of Darwinian evolution in public schools. Losing the battle, the fundamentalists retired to a kind of cultural ghetto and resurfaced later in such movements as the Moral Majority.[4]

Despite its Protestant origin, attempts have been made to use 'fundamentalism' and transform it into a term usable in the discourse of the Islamic movement by Muslims and non-Muslims alike.[5] Bruce Lawrence argues that fundamentalism is 'a kind of ideological formation, affirming the modern world not only by opposing it but also by using its means against its purposes'. It is anti-intellectual, anti-modernist and a class or generational struggle.[6] John O. Voll defines it as 'an approach marked by an exclusivist and literalist interpretation of the fundamentals of Islam and by a rigorist pursuit of socio-moral reconstruction'.[7]

Thus understood, all devout Muslims are 'fundamentalists': all devout Muslims must, by definition, believe in the unity and uniqueness of the Creator, accept the Qur'ān as the word of the Divine, and believe in the duty to fulfill certain obligations in accordance with the Qur'ān and the Sunnah. To be sure, the Muslims consider Islam to be an all-inclusive societal order providing answers to all questions of life and beyond. They are not, for that matter, opposed to new legislations and interpretations arrived at through the accepted procedure of *ijtihād*. Muslims or Muslim organisations seldom, if ever, identify themselves as fundamentalists. This term has no equivalent in Arabic or any other language of the major Muslim groups. Those engaged in Islamic movements view themselves simply as Muslims, they talk only of Islam and abhor all attempts at attaching any (Western) 'ism' to it. It should also be noted that the vast majority of those regularly labelled 'fundamentalist' seek to promote the goal of Islam not through violence and bloodshed but by peaceful persuasion and through constitutional means. The frequent association of the term, in the Western media, with terrorism, reactionary fanaticism and medieval mentality reveal more about the people using the term than its referents.

In the judgement of many scholars, the term 'fundamentalism', invented in the Christian context, should not be applied to Islam. The late Ismā'īl al-Fārūqī suggested the Arabic term *'Nahḍah'* which 'agrees with the reality of our situation'.[8] Derived from the Arabic root *nahaḍa*, to rise, it means the actualisation of potentialities latent in the child. This applies to society very well.[9] It is, therefore, proper to say that the Muslim world is undergoing a process of *nahḍah*. The substance, which is Islam, remains the same. Its potentialities and capabilities are receiving increasing recognition by the Ummah such that they are struggling to apply them to their contemporary problems.

THE *NAHḌAH* AND THE ISLAMIC WORLD VIEW

The Islamic movement, irrespective of its form, content or goals, has received considerable attention in the West. The importance of oil-producing Arab countries to Western economies, serious strategic questions raised in 1979 by the triumph of the revolution in Iran, the foreign policy dimension acquired by the Mujāhidīn resistance to Soviet occupation of Afghanistan and similar other considerations provide credence and justification for this concern. Given the failure of the displacement transformation perspective of the modernisation theorists to explain the Muslim *nahḍah*, much reliance came to be placed on the 'dual or hybrid society' perspective.[10] This latter view assumes that there are two primary poles of attraction, that of Islam in whatever form – dynamic, stultified or reformed – and that of the West which is both the object of hostility and the primary cause of the challenge which Muslims have to face, cope, and come to terms with, or transcend. In other words, most studies dealing with the Islamic movement are anchored in what is thought about or reacted to by Muslims in relation to the West both in its liberal or Marxist versions. In this sense, Muslims are reacting people incapable of taking initiative and planned action.

While the linkage between Islamic assertion and Western penetration or challenge may inform the general discussion, it glosses over the fundamental question of the relevance of Islam to these movements. In the specific context of the Middle East, for instance, it is true that Islamic movements have generated considerable support for the Palestinians in their struggle against British imperialism and Zionism and that such support could have been rendered on the basis of common opposition to European penetration. It is equally correct to suggest, however, that Muslim groups rendered that support on the basis of the religious significance of Palestine and because of Islamic affinities. Similarly, the Iranian revolution may be looked upon as a response to the challenges of the West and modernity (Western military and political power and strong intrusion of Western culture) but it is more appropriate to suggest, as did Khomeini, that 'If the Iranian people are now rising up against the Shah, they are doing so as an Islamic duty'.[11]

To understand the on-going *nahḍah* movements, it is essential to remember that the Muslim dwells in a universe where religion occupies the centre stage in the social, economic and political life. Islam is a total comprehensive civilisation. Unlike Christianity, it does not divide corporate functions between Caesar and God. Islam is an all-pervasive phenomenon which entails within itself religion and state, society and culture. The emphasis in Islam is on *tawḥīd*, i.e., the unity of the Creator, the unity of the community of the faithful (Ummah), the unity of life as a totality, the unity of the temporal and the spiritual. According to Muslim belief, every aspect of life is provided for by appropriate regulations.

It is true that Muslims differ in the actual observance of religious practices and rituals with the rich, the Western-oriented and the urbanite more lax in the observance of the rituals than the poor, the illiterate, and the rural masses who live out their lives firm in the conviction of being under the rule and the grace of a sovereign divine power. Despite these differences, a belief in the role of religion constitutes a basic part of the social ideology of the Muslims. The consciousness may be inchoate and vague but there is neither doubt nor hesitation about the rightness of this perception of reality and of man's duty. The Qur'ānic revelation guarantees, and the experiences of the community, during the time of the Prophet (ṢAAS) and the *Khulafā' al-Rāshidūn*, testifies to the absolute rectitude of a way of life in which one may feel certainty and also pride.

The early community, in seeking to carry out its mission, found a civilisation that was crowned with all the evidences of worldly success in addition to bliss in the Hereafter. In addition to sheer power and glory, there was prosperity and cultural creativity of the highest order. All of these in the Muslim's understanding are a manifestation of Islam and the result of the faithful Muslim having accepted their special and Messianic role in the world. Muslims, aware of their glorious past, share in the confident optimism about their destiny which is predicated upon a total commitment to make Allah's way supreme on earth (*jihād*). Sayyid Mawdūdī's reminder to the Muslims that if they followed the strategy chalked out by the Prophet (ṢAAS) for the propagation of Islam, 'the same result will appear' is but one instance of an expression of the Muslim's self-assurance and expectations.[12] The concept of *jihād* and the resultant confidence and optimism provide an in-built mechanism in the Muslim society for a continuous process of *nahḍah*. That Islam carries within it the seeds of continuous *nahḍah* is attested to by the *hadīth* which clearly stipulates that 'there will arise at the turn of every century, people who will call for the revival of Islam'.[13]

Thus understood, *nahḍah* movements across the Muslim world are neither modern nor new; they represent not a response to the challenges of the West but a quest to mould Muslim life after the Prophetic pattern in an imperfect world. This is exemplified by the Salafīyah movement, the Sokoto *Jihād* and the Mahdiyah movement.

The Salafīyah movement

The Salafīyah movement of Muḥammad ibn 'Abd al-Wāhhāb (1115–1207AH/1703–1792CE) provides a striking example of this trend. Ibn 'Abd al-Wahhāb, being a believer in the original purity of Islam, revolted against laxity and corruption among the rulers and the Muslim masses. He preached return to the Qur'ān, the Sunnah and the Sunni legal positions that were worked out in the first three centuries of the Islamic calendar. He and his followers denounced all else as heresy (*bid'ah*), singled out saint veneration for annihilation, attacked *Ṣūfi*sm fiercely and stamped out anything resembling *shirk* (idolatry). Ibn 'Abd al-Wahhāb joined forces with the local leader Muḥammad ibn Sa'ūd (d.1179AH/1765CE) of al-Dirīyah (near modern-day Riyadh) and conceded worldly authority to him. This led to the strong partnership of Saudi royalty and Wahhābī religious sectarianism that dominates the kingdom of Saudi Arabia till today.[14]

The Sokoto *jihād*

The Islamic movement of the early nineteenth century in what is now Nigeria similarly called for a purification of Islamic belief and practice which had been corrupted by un-Islamic customs. This movement accused the leaders of Hausaland and their associates of unbelief:

> [They] worship trees by sacrifices to them, make offerings and daub them with dough. They are unbelievers.[15]

The guiding spirit behind the *jihād* was Shaykh 'Uthmān ibn Muḥammad Fūdī (1168–1233AH/1754–1817CE) known as Shehu (Arabic *Shaykh*) 'Uthman dan Fodio. As discussed in his manifesto, Shehu's *jihād* was aimed at teaching and spreading pristine or true Islam and the establishment of a system of government based upon Sharī'ah. Supported by the Fulani and Hausa peasants, the Shehu succeeded in establishing an Islamic political order governed by the *Sarkin Musulmi* or *Amīr al-Mu'minīn* (commander of the faithful). The administrative set up produced by the *jihād*, is known as the Sokoto caliphate in which Islamic culture and the Sharī'ah were the binding force and the legal code of the polity.

The Mahdīyah movement

The Mahdīyah movement, led by Muḥammad Aḥmad ibn 'Abd Allāh (1250–1303AH/1834–1885CE) also aimed at establishing the universal reign of justice and equity before the final struggle of the false Messiah (*al-Dajjāl*) against God and the Day of Judgement. The Mahdi and his followers had nothing but scorn for Ottoman Egyptian rulers who 'disobeyed the command of His messenger and his prophets . . . altered the Sharī'ah of our master, Muḥammad, and . . . blasphemed against the faith of Allah (SWT)'.[16] They were equally appalled at the widespread corruption of Sudanese Islamic society through prostitution, gambling, alcohol and music. Like the Salafīyah movement, the Mahdists aimed at the purification of Islamic belief and practice and at overthrowing the corrupt and heretical government, to be replaced by a society and polity that would replicate the Madinah model. The Mahdist political system lasted for 14 years till it was defeated in 1899 by Anglo-Egyptian forces.

The Salafīyah movement of Muḥammad ibn 'Abd al-Wahhāb and the Sokoto *Jihād* led by Shaykh 'Uthmān dau Fodio in West Africa were contending with the evident corruption and distortions of the Islamic system *in situ*, and did not view Islamic decline in relation to either the West or to its pressures. Similarly, the Mahdist state in the Sudan emerged in the context of a declining Islamic society which the Mahdi believed was no longer governed systematically and coherently by the Islamic belief system. The challenge of the West were added elements which perhaps intensified the struggle but did not cause it. The contemporary manifestations of the rise of Muslims is better understood and appreciated in the context of the continuation of Muslims striving for the prophetic model. The movements such as, al-Ikhwān al-Muslimūn in the Arab world, the Jamā'at-e-Islamī and the Tablīghī movement in South Asia, the various Islamisation programmes, and the emergence of a somewhat united political front in the form of the Organisation of Islamic Conference are all constituents and continuation of Muslim *nahḍah.*

If this is a reasonable and plausible characterisation of the genesis and motives of Muslim *nahḍah* today, it suggests that the problem it reflects is one which concerns the Muslim society itself – responding to the divine call of 'promoting good and prohibiting evil' and thus to return to pure Islam. The fact that the Islamic aspirations were harnessed in the cause of anti-colonial and anti-imperial struggle does not negate the causative Islamic moorings of the *nahḍah.* The pressures and challenges of the West are added elements solidifying and intensifying the Muslim resolve to search for an Islamic order.

VARIOUS MANIFESTATIONS OF THE MUSLIM *NAHḌAH*

The main streams of Muslim *nahḍah* can be grouped into two broad categories: one, those having primarily religious orientations and, two, those which are dominated by socio-political considerations. The Tablīghī movement initiated by Mawlānā Muḥammad Ilyās can be categorised under the first head, while the Islamic revolution in Iran and the Jamā'at-e-Islāmī movement in Pakistan are examples of the second. It must be pointed out at the outset that all these movements are inspired by the visions of a return to pure Islam. First, they are alike in perceiving Islam, not as a religion composed of certain rituals but as a comprehensive way of life. Second, they believe in the universality of Islam and, as such, emphasise the unity of all Muslims transcending all barriers of race, colour and territory. Third, they reject ideologies like capitalism, socialism, nationalism and secularism as man-made and hence incapable of ensuring happiness for mankind. Muslim societies suffer, according to them, because they follow Western materialism and relegate religion to personal, private life. Fourth, they abhor blind imitation (*taqlīd*) and advocate independent reasoning in matters of legal judgements (*ijtihād*). Finally, they stress the need for continuous, ceaseless struggle to fulfil the divine obligation of founding an Islamic order.

Even though the contemporary *nahḍah* is a continuation of the aspirations of Muslims for an ideal order, there are significant new elements in its latest expression that need to be clearly identified. First, the current *nahḍah* is spatially much wider than was the case in the past. It is not confined to any particular geographic area but extends to the entire Muslim world each with distinct character and organisation. Second, unlike the past wherein the Muslim *nahḍah* was led by the elites of the religious institutions, today it includes leaders of various persuasions capable of mobilising and directly involving the masses. Various *nahḍah* movements have extended their sphere of influence to various organised sectors, for example, the students, the workers, and the armed forces, with the result that it has acquired a mass base that can sustain the pressure from within as well as the hostility from the external forces. Third, the vast majority of the states with a predominant Muslim population have accommodated themselves, willingly, half-heartedly, haphazardly or under extreme pressure, to the Islamic thrust in their social and cultural fabric. Of approximately 52 Muslim majority states, no less than 26 stipulate in their constitutions that Islam is the religion of the state. Such stipulations may simply be viewed as symbolic in nature, but they quite frequently have an important bearing on the conduct of these states. Finally, there is the 1979 revolution in Iran which is 'the most significant and profound event in the entirety of contemporary Islamic history'.[17] The political dynamism and acumen of the traditional leadership, 'Ulamā', in galvanising mass support to successfully remove all traces of the Shah's regime and supplant it with a nascent Islamic polity is something that must be admired. The success of the revolution in the face of opposition from all major super powers and their clients is a testimony to the strength inherent in Islam which must have been a traumatic experience to the forces of *kufr*.

The Tablīghī Jamā'at

The Tablīghī Jamā'at, known also as the 'Faith Movement', originated in and around Delhi, India, during the early 1920s. It was founded by a dedicated missionary, Mawlānā Muḥammad Ilyās, to correct the decaying moral and religious condition of the people of Mewat, a part of the Gangetic plateau in northern India.[18] It is perhaps the largest non-political group devoted to the cause of Islam through what Jansen calls 'moral rearmament'.[19] Divorcing politics from its scheme of activities, it aims at regenerating the benevolent spirit of Islam through purification of intention, strengthening the faith, meticulous observance of prayer, acquisition of knowledge and following the Sharī'ah in all aspects of life and thus bring about a change from within. The overall aim is to bring all activities of life under the aegis of the Sharī'ah. As explained by its founder, 'perfection in political matters can be attained by correcting morals, business and social relations'.[20]

The movement has neither a permanent organisational structure nor a fixed membership and subscription. Participating voluntarily and bearing their own expenses, Jamā'at participants are grouped into small units and send to various places to learn and propagate the faith. They travel far and wide into the remotest corners using local mosques as temporary halting stations. They adopt a door to door, man to man approach in inviting people to troop to the mosque to hear the words of the Lord. They invariably present their message in the form of the following six-point formula: (1) *Shahādah* or the confession of faith, its correct recitation and understanding of its meaning, (2) *ṣalāt* or performing the obligatory five-times prayer regularly as an act of submission to the Will of Allah (SWT), (3) *dhikr* or ceaselessly remembering Allah (SWT) to cultivate piety, (4) *ikrām al-Muslim* or respect for Muslims as a religious obligation and an effective strategy for preaching, (5) *da'wah* or propagating the word of Allah (SWT) in groups and away from home, and (6) *ikhlāṣ* or inculcating honesty and sincerity of purpose in *tablīgh* activities.[21] Being publicity-shy, the Tablīghi movement has not captured the attention of the mass media but it certainly provides the Muslims with a solid foundation for *nahḍah*. The movement proves that Muslim awakening is the result of Islam's in-built mechanism for continuous revival.

The Tablīghī Jamā'at leaders insist on eschewing politics and does not involve itself in any issues of socio-political significance. In private conversations, however, they do concede that Islamic polity is desirable but its establishment should not be the prime concern of Muslims. Such a preoccupation not merely distorts Islam but creates disunity among the Muslims.[22] To them, Islamic revolution, without the true spirit of Islam preceding it, is bound to founder on the moral infirmities of its members. 'Shunning politics' is, therefore, the first step in reviving Islam. Muslim societies, to counter the forces inimical to Islam, should take to preaching activities through implementing the prescriptions laid down in the 'five pillars' of Islam; fostering the link of reverential fear and love with the Lord and, in the last resort, by *hijrah* and *jihād*.[23]

It is difficult to quantify the achievement of the Tablīghī movement, it is worth mentioning, however, that its preaching activities are spread into some 24 countries in the world. The annual gatherings of the Tablīgh in various countries are attended by millions of people from all walks of life. Finally, it has enthused many intellectuals to carry out preaching activities.

The Jamā'at-e-Islāmī

The Jamā'at-e-Islāmī in Pakistan was founded in Lahore by Sayyid Abul A'lā Mawdūdī in 1941 as an ideological movement rather than a political party. He is generally recognised as having the most comprehensive grasp of the theoretical and practical aspects of Islam in Pakistan. The party he found 'have a well defined objective and work for it with single-mindedness of purpose and determination'.[24] Islam, to Mawdūdī, is a universal and comprehensive way of life, it is a well-ordered system, a consistent whole with set answers to all problems. Its fundamental postulate is the unity and sovereignty of Allah (SWT). The scheme of life envisaged by Islam is known as Sharī'ah and is established on the bedrock of faith. It is on that foundation that the edifice of moral, social, political and economic system is created.

The ideal Islamic society, to Mawdūdī, consists of people who, through putting their faith in Islam, have liberated themselves from all allegiances except to Allah (SWT); such a society would be free and 'theo-democratic' and its citizens would be as equal as the teeth of a comb. Muslims belong to the *Ummah Waṣath* (just and balanced community), and, as such, are duty bound to enjoin what is right and forbid what is evil. The Qur'ān, he wrote, is not a book of abstract theories and religious enigmas to be unravelled in monasteries and universities, it is a book of movement and agitation.[25] Consequently, Islam is the religion of revolutionary struggle and utmost exertion (*jihād*) aimed at shattering the myth of the divinity of demi-gods and promoting the cause of Allah (SWT) by establishing the Islamic political order. Mawdūdī defines revolution as 'an alteration in the structure, supporting myth, political institutions and elite personnel in conformity with fundamental principles of Islam'.

To that end, Mawdūdī formed the Jamā'at-e-Islāmī and propounded principles and techniques of organisation by following the footsteps of the Prophet (ṢAAS). First of all, to plunge straight into the revolutionary task with an uncompromising declaration of the unity of Allah (SWT) and to present Islamic beliefs and injunctions in their right perspectives. Second, to identify, select and organise those who respond to the call on one platform and devise a programme of their moral, intellectual and social upliftment. Third, to initiate an all-out campaign for the regeneration and reconstruction of the collective life of the community on Islamic principles. Finally, to change the social, economic, and most importantly the political leadership of the country. The revolutionary movement has no choice but to capture governmental machinery, for without it the pious order which Islam envisages can never be established. The Islamic movement, however, is for the cause of Allah (SWT) and it should be conducted openly and peacefully within the boundaries of the law and existing constitution. As Mawdūdī admits:

> I have never violated even those laws which I have fought hard to oppose. I have tried to change them through lawful and constitutional means and never adopted the path of violation of the law.[26]

The Jamā'at recruited it members from schools, universities and other institutions. It combined religious, commitment and modern learning to produce a new educated elite. Beginning with a membership of 25 in 1941 CE, the Jamā'at's active membership swelled to 3500 in 1978 CE with associated members numbering about half a million in Pakistan. It has affiliated organisations in four other countries. The *Jamaat* has established a number of institution which impart Islamic and modern education. It has produced over 300 books and pamphlets and ran, as far back as 1955–6 CE, some 50 fixed and 11 mobile dispensaries. By the time of his death, Mawdūdī had achieved the visible and auditory support of many thousands including General Zia-ul-Ḥaq, the President of Pakistan. The Zia regime, aided and advised by many front-ranking Jamā'at members, implemented many Islamic principles and was experimenting with several others at the time of his death.

The revolution in Iran

The Iranian revolution can only be understood by viewing it within the framework of Islam and by digging deep into the roots that underlie the thrust of Iranian history which cannot be done here.[27] The leadership of the revolution was provided by Ayatollah Ruhullah Musavi al-Khomeini who first gained fame as a teacher concerned with devotional and mystical matters. As Algar points out, 'the life of Imām Khomeini is a clear indication that the Revolution wrought by Islam necessarily begins in the moral and spiritual realm'.[28] Islam, to Khomeini, is a complete code providing instructions and setting norms for all aspects of life. Islamic law is universal and immutable and must, therefore, be implemented *in toto*. Since the Imāms were appointed by the Prophet (ṢAAS) 'in accordance with the divine will to' perform this task, it becomes obligatory on their followers to establish an Islamic government.[29] During the period of Occultation (*ghaybah*) it is the right of jurists to rule by divine commands: 'the true rulers are *fuqahā'* themselves'.[30]

Khomeini voiced his nostalgia for the initial Madinan period of the *Khulafā' al-Rashidūn* and in particular, of course, 'Alī, the son-in-law of the Prophet (ṢAAS). After this period, *shirk* (polytheism) entered society in the form of economic suppression and exploitation. In Iran, the 'Alid form of religion opposed the Ṣafawīd as one which corrupts religion, serves the interests of those in power, and legitimises social injustice. Khomeini's criticism of the Shah's monarchy often centred around the social injustices that were prevalent in Iran. Thus he calls upon the people to launch 'sacred *jihād*':

> Islam is the religion of militant individuals who are committed to truth and justice. It is the religion of those who desire freedom and independence. It is the school of those who struggle against imperialism.[31]

The purpose of *jihād* is the 'establishment of just social order' – a just society that will morally and spiritually nourish refined human beings.

The method Khomeini adopted, for the *jihād*, consisted of: (1) the total and, uncompromising opposition to the tyrannical regimes which, in the Iranian context, was the Pahlavī dynasty: (2) he exposed the regime of the Shah as a puppet of the USA and Israel; (3) he rejected the piecemeal reformist approach; and finally, but most importantly, he mobilised the masses to rise against the regime through his sermons, delivered in exile and recorded on cassettes: 'revolution by cassette'. Thus he exhorts his audience: 'Write and publish books concerning the laws of Islam and their beneficial effects on society. Improve your style and method of preaching and related activity . . . Have confidence in yourselves and know that your are capable of fulfilling this task'.[32]

Khomeini's message appealed to all types of people to rise against political oppression, economic exploitation and foreign servitude. He readily spoke of the right of the masses, the destitute, the workers, the oppressed at home and abroad. The relative ease with which the Shah was toppled in Iran was the most dramatic manifestation of the revolutionary potential of Islam. The Pahlavi regime was replaced by a nascent Islamic polity under the leadership of the Imām. The *vilāyet-e-faqīh*, supreme over government, a post held by Khomeini, need not be from Iran as long as he is a *faqīh* and accepted by the majority. Proclaiming the superiority of Islamic spirit over the national spirit, this is a unique provision of the Iranian constitution which no other system can match. Foundations were laid for new economic institutions directed to the welfare of lower middle and lower classes in the rural areas. For all its manifold problems, the Islamic Republic 'represents a novel phenomena whose scope and importance extend well beyond Iran'.[33]

A COMPARATIVE PERSPECTIVE

The achievements of the Jamā'at-e-Islāmī and the Tablīghī movement pale into insignificance when compared to the process of *nahḍah* in Iran and the victory it gained. The reasons are obvious. Unlike Mawdūdī, who had no tradition to build on, Khomeini inherited and made use of the reformers' ground breaking tools and ideas, which he supplemented with his own personality and knowledge. Furthermore, unlike Sunni Muslims, a strong revolutionary component has been inherent in the Shiite school of thought. They consider only the Imāms and those whom they appointed to be the legitimate holders of authority. All others are illegitimate, and therefore must be resisted. 'This is the root of the matter: Sunni-populated countries believe in obeying their rulers, whereas the Shiis have always believed in rebellion – sometimes they were able to rebel, and at other times they were compelled to keep silent'.[34] Finally, Mawdūdī's efforts were consumed at winning the Western educated Muslims to the Islamic fold, a task which Dr 'Alī Sharī'atī performed successfully for Iran. The masses, in the absence of any meaningful contribution by the 'Ulamā' to the cause of the movement, remained generally untouched and as such the Jamā'at could never win mass support in any election. In the case of Iran, the 'Ulamā' played an important role in galvanising mass support for Imām Khomeini who himself was an *'ālim* of the highest order. To this was added the strength which 'Alī Sharī'atī provided. The gap thus bridged, paved the way for the success of the revolution in Iran.

CONCLUSION

The ongoing process of Muslim reawakening throughout the world has been termed as fundamentalism, Islamic resurgence, renaissance and the like. These terms, originating in the West, indicate prejudice, fear and emotionalism, and are inappropriate. The Arabic term *nahḍah* properly characterises the process and agrees with the reality experienced by Muslims.

What distinguishes the *nahḍah* movement is its Islamic nature and traits. Islam maintains a powerful hold on the masses. Muslims see themselves as belonging to a just and balanced community. It disavows the segregation of religious and secular realms. It denies the separation of church and state. Islam is seen by the believers to have a definite role to play in every aspect of life. As the best community produced for mankind, Muslims are duty bound to establish virtue and prohibit evil wherever it achieves power. This *jihād* was carried out by the Prophet (ṢAAS) and early companions who succeeded in constructing a glorious Muslim civilisation of which Muslims are justifiably proud. The *jihād*, the optimism, and the success are the in-built mechanisms for the continuous process of *nahḍah*. It is this factor which, in conformity with the Prophetic tradition of the emergence of a Mujaddid at the turn of every century, has enthused the Muslims for continuous struggle to return to pure Islam. The *nahḍah* movements can therefore be properly understood only within the framework of Islam. Particular social settings and specific political pressures are other variables which strengthen and intensify the movement.

The *nahḍah* movements have various manifestations. Some are concerned with moral reforms while others are socio-politically motivated. There are subvariations under each category which need to be properly understood. Nevertheless, the goal of all these movements are one and the same, which is to establish a sane, humane world order. The strategies pursued have serious implications as to their final outcome. The success, as the Iranian case exemplifies, is the result of blood, sweat, tears, determination and faith in Allah (SWT). It is a long-drawn out process of political, spiritual and intellectual preparation, of a successful fusion of the elite and mass energies, and a psyche which extols the virtues of resistance and martyrdom.

Glossary

'Adālah (root, *'adl*): moral probity; to act justly; rendering everyone his due. The term is much more comprehensive than 'justice'. *'Adālah* in Islam is not simply legal but pervades every matter in life including oneself. Doing a thing which one ought to do is *'adālah* to oneself or to others.

Adillah (sing. *dalil*); evidence, proofs or indications in deducing a law either from the divine texts or from an established law.

'Adl probity of character; justice; acting in obedience to Allah (SWT).

'Ahd testamentary designation; agreement, covenant.

Aḥkām (sing. *hukm*), statutes, regulations, stipulations; refers to divine commandments and, in a restricted sense, to the body of positive legal rulings.

Aḥkām kullīyah wa far'īyah Rulings of the Sharī'ah that are of general and subsidiary nature, ones that encompass more than one situation and ones that have limited effect.

Ahl al-ḥall wa al-'aqd those who loosen and bind; influential people: the qualified representatives of the Muslim community who act on their behalf in appointing and deposing a ruler (*khalīfah*).

Ahl al-kitāb 'people of the book', meaning especially the Jews and Christians, but also the Zoroastrians.

Ahl al-Shūrā participants in consultations, members of deliberative assembly (legislature or parliament).

Ahl hadhihī al-ṣaḥīfah the people of this document.

'Ālī elevated, high, exalted.

'Ālim (pl. *'ulamā*), scholar, learned; a person who possesses knowledge of the religious sciences.

Amānah trust, trusteeship; it has meaning not only in interpersonal dealings but also in the dealing between man and Allah (SWT), that Allah (SWT) has made man His vicegerent commissioning him with the trusteeship of *khilāfah*; this responsibility of *khilāfah* is called *amānah*.

Amīr commander; prince, emir.

Amīr al-Mu'minīn commander of the faithful; the title was adopted by the second *khalīfah*, 'Umar ibn al-Khattab, and subsequently it was exclusively reserved for the *khalīfah*.

Amr bi al-Ma'rūf wa Nahy 'an al-munkar enjoining virtue and forbidding vice.

Anṣār adherents, sponsors, patrons; 'the helpers': the Madinan followers of the Prophet (ṢAAS) who joined with Meccan Muslim followers in establishing the Ummah.

'Asabīyah group loyalty, community of interests, solidarity of social groups.

A'wān helpers, aides, assistants.

Awliyā' helpers, benefactors, patrons, protectors.

Āyah 'sign' of Allah (SWT) in the created universe; also 'verse' of the Qur'ān.

Āyāt al-aḥkām revealed verses that have legal values and ordinances or revealed verses from which laws and rules could be deduced.

'Ayn al-yaqīn knowledge acquired with certainty by perception and reported perception or observation.

Bay'ah contract, agreement, arrangement, homage; oath of allegiance to a ruler, especially a *khalīfah*.

Bay'ah al-'āmmah general oath of allegiance.

Bay'ah al-khāṣṣah oath of allegiance by leaders representing the Ummah.

Bid'ah innovation, novelty, practice or belief for which there is no precedent in the Sunnah of the Prophet (ṢAAS) and that of the *Khulafā' al-Rashidūn*; heresy in the context of Islamic law and doctrine.

Dār al-ḥarb 'the abode of war'; territory under the jurisdiction of the enemies of Islam.

Dār al-Islām 'the abode of Islam'; territory in which the Sharī'ah prevails.

Ḍarūrīyāt necessary, essentials without which things can not run; applied to a political system which guarantees the necessities of life to its citizens.

Da'wah call, appeal, invitation, missionary activities seeking either to convert non-Muslims or to bring Muslims who have strayed back to the true path.

Dawlah state, government or the domain of politics.

Dayā' wastage, spending one's energy, time, wealth in a manner that guarantees no moral or ethical return.

Dhikr 'mentioning', 'remembering' Allah (SWT). The central Sūfī form of spiritual discipline, with many specific types.

Dīn religion in a wider sense; a system which includes every aspect in human life.

Al-dīn lillāh wa al-waṭan li-jamī' religion is for Allah (SWT) and the fatherland is the concern of all.

Diwān administrative office, bureau, hall; also account book of the treasury.

Diwān al-maẓālim shortened term for *diwān al-naẓr fī al-maẓālim.*

Diwān al-naẓr fī al-maẓālim the body which historically exercised judicial as well as supervisory functions over the conduct of the administration.

Diyah ransom paid as blood money to the relatives of a person killed.

Dūlah to change periodically, alternate, rotate; circulation or making a circuit.

Falāsifah the 'Philosophers'; the medieval Muslim scholars who pursued knowledge allegedly in the Greek (Peripatetic) tradition.

Fa-qad kafarū bi-Allāh they, indeed, denied Allah (SWT).

Faqīh (pl. *fuqahā*)', a specialist in Islamic jurisprudence, a jurisconsult.

Farā'iḍ (sing. *Farḍ*), Injunction, statutory portion, lawful share. Action made obligatory upon Muslims by Allah (SWT).

Farḍ (pl. *farā'iḍ*), obligatory duty, as the five daily prayers, the omission of which will be punished and the performance of which will be rewarded.

Farḍ al-'ayn a duty incumbent upon the individual

Farḍ al-kifāyah a duty incumbent upon the community, the fulfilment of which by a sufficient number of individuals excuses others from fulfilling it.

Fatwā (pl. *fatāwā*), a learned legal opinion of a jurist on a point of law or legal problem. The person who gives a fatwa is a *muftī.*

Fiqh originally, understanding, knowledge, comprehension; technically, it refers to the science of Islamic jurisprudence.

Fuqahā' (sing. *faqīh*) jurists, experts in *fiqh* or in understanding of the law, and therefore jurisprudence.

Ḥadd (pl. *ḥudūd*), edge, borderline, terminal point; punishment laid down for acts forbidden in the Qur'ān.

Ḥadīth report, event, news; a literary form that communicates a Sunnah of the Prophet Muhammad (ṢAAS).

Ḥāfiz guardian, keeper. One who knows the Qur'ān by heart.

Ḥajiyāt things needed but not essential.

Ḥajj pilgrimage to Makkah.

Ḥalāl lawful, permissible as regards food and activities.

Ḥaqq truth.

Ḥaqq al 'ibād individuals' divinely ordained duties and obligations unto themselves, fellow human beings and nature as a collective property of mankind.

Ḥaqq Allāh individuals' divinely ordained duties and obligations unto Allah (SWT).

Ḥaqq al-yaqīn knowledge acquired with certainty by personal experience or intuition. Absolute truth with no possibility of error of judgement or sense perception.

Ḥarām unlawful, prohibited, contrary to halal; can also mean sacred and therefore also forbidden in the sense of taboo.

Ḥijāb cover, curtain, Muslim women's veil, covering the hair or the entire head and face.

Hijrah migration from one place to another, especially the migration of the Prophet (ṢAAS) from Makkah to Madinah in 622 CE. The event marked the beginning of the Islamic calendar.

Ḥisbah the duty of every Muslim to enjoin the good and forbid evil; office for the supervision of moral behaviour and of the markets.

Ḥizb Allāh the party of Allah (SWT); those who follow the ideology prescribed by Allah (SWT).

Ḥudūd (pl. of *ḥadd*), punishments prescribed in the Qur'ān and the Sunnah.

Ḥudūd al-Shar'iyah Islamic legal punishments.

Ḥukm (pl. *aḥkām*), ordinance, rule, authority; a judgement of a *qaḍī*; an act of adjudication; a decree; dispensing of justice.

Al-ḥurmah sanctity, sacredness, sacrosanctity, inviolability.

Al-ḥurrīyah freedom, liberty.

'Ibādah (pl. *'ibadāt*), worship, act of devotion; religious observance; the performance of duties and obligations laid upon Muslims by Allah (SWT), including ritual practices; abiding by the order of Allah (SWT) in each and every step of life, in action, and thought.

Ijmā' consensus; one of the four sources of Islamic law; unanimous agreement of the Ummah on a regulation or of the leading 'Ulamā' of a generation.

Ijtihād exertion, independent legal reasoning; use of logical reasoning in elaborating and interpreting the Sharī'ah or in order to deduce laws from the Qur'ān and the Sunnah. A qualified person who exercises *ijtihād* is a *mujtahid.*

Ikhlāṣ sincerity and faithfulness.

Ikrām al-Muslim respect for the Muslim.

Ilāh deity, god, godhead.

'Illah effective cause of a particular ruling or action.

'Ilm knowledge, science, wisdom; knowledge of the reality in any field.

'Ilm al-kalām dialectical or systematic theology; one of the 'religious sciences' of Islam.

'Ilm al-yaqīn knowledge by reasoning or inference.

Imām leader, master, chief, leader in prayer; synonym of *khalīfah.*

Imāmah imamate; synonym of *khilāfah* (caliphate); the Islamic political system.

Imān faith, a source of religious virtue that is more highly regarded than Islam; 'surrender'.

Inna Yahūd Bani Awf Ummah ma'a al-Mu'minīn the Jews of Banī Awf are Ummah along with the believers.

Istiḥsān approval, consent, discretion; juristic preference, to consider something good; application of discretion in a legal decision to settle the problems of legislation in conformity with the requirements of everyday life; considered as a mode of arriving at a legal opinion.

Istiṣḥāb a juristic principle to the effect that a given judicial situation previously existing is held to continue to exist until it can be proved that it no longer exists or has been modified.

Istiṣlāḥ consideration of public interest; seeking the interest or welfare of the people; considered as a source of law.

Iṭā'ah obedience.

Jāhil ignorant, one who cannot comprehend the values of a civilised life as ordained by revelation.

Jāhilīyah period of ignorance, the pre-Islamic period of Arab history; the meaning has been extended to include the corruptness of Muslim society.

Jamā'ah group, community; synonym for the Ummah, but it has more restricted meanings, too.

Jihād striving, exertion; exertion directed, individually or collectively, towards the attainment of spiritual and religious perfection; military action to defend Islam. One who is actively engaged in *jihād* is a *mujāhid.*

Jihād fi sabīl Allāh striving; utmost exertion in the way of Allah (SWT) to fulfil one's responsibilities, both in outward actions and in inward correction of one's own mistakes; working or fighting in the cause of Allah (SWT).

Ka'bah literally 'cube': the main Islamic sanctuary in Makkah.

Kafā'ah competence, efficiency, fitness.

Kāfir unbeliever, infidel, ungrateful; one who does not believe in or accept the message of Islam.

Kalām speech, discourse, especially on religious matters.

Khalīfah one who comes after, deputy, successor; especially successor to the Prophet (ṢAAS); caliph.

Khilāfah succession, caliphate; the institution of vicegerency and custodianship on earth, equivalent of *imamah.*

Khilāfat al-nubū wah the vicegerency of the Prophet (ṢAAS) a term by which the Madinan caliphate is sometimes known.

Khawārij those who went out, dissenters, Kharijites; those who withdrew from the camp of the fourth caliph, 'Alī, on the occasion of the battle of Ṣiffīn and established themselves as a separate group. They insisted upon the right to depose an *imām* who has deviated and regarded anyone who has committed a moral sin as being an apostate.

Khulafā' al-Rāshidūn the rightly guided successors; refers to the first four caliphs, Abu Bakr, 'Umar, Uthmān and 'Alī, who were the companions of the Prophet (ṢAAS) and were elected by the community. The period of their rule is regarded as an exemplar of Muslim society worthy of emulation.

Kitāb writing, book, scripture.

Kufr unbelief, blasphemy, ingratitude, infidelity.

Lāikrāha fi al-dīn there is no coercion in *al-dīn*.

Madhhab way of acting, adopted procedure; school of jurisprudence; used to denote the four sunni schools: the Ḥanbalīs, the Malikīs, the Ḥanafīs and the Shāfi'īs.

Mahdī guide, leader; messianic figure who will appear to usher in a new order of justice and peace.

Mahdīyah pertaining to Mahdī, Mahdism.

Majlis a consultative body in which issues of public interests are discussed.

Majlis al-Bay'ah National Assembly.

Majlis al-Shūrā consultative body.

Makrūh unpleasant, reprehensible; an action which Muslims are discouraged from doing: they will be rewarded for avoiding it but will not be punished for doing it.

Mandūb recommended, advised to do; an action which Muslims are encouraged to do and will be rewarded for doing, but will not be punished for not doing.

Ma'rifah mystical knowledge, understanding, gnosis.

Ma'rūfāt good, beneficial, fitting. Virtues enjoined upon a Muslim by revelation and/or reason.

Mawālī patrons, clients, friends.

Maẓālim misdeed, wrong, inequity, act of injustice.

Mizān balance, scale, weight; equity, fairness.

Mu'ākhāt virtual brotherhood among the believers inaugurated by the Prophet (ṢAAS) in Madīnah.

Mu'āmalāt treatment, behaviour, conduct toward others; transactions according to the principles of Islamic jurisprudence.

Mubāḥ permissible; an action for which Muslims will be neither rewarded nor punished.

Mubīn clear, manifest, evident; intelligible in time and space so it is suitable for humanity at large.

Muftī jurisconsult, learned in the Qur'ān, the Sunnah and fiqh.

Muḥarramāt forbidden, punishable. Can also mean 'sacred' and hence forbidden in the sense of taboo.

Muḥāsabah accountability, examination of conscience.

Muḥtasib the official in charge of the *ḥisbah*.

Mujaddid renewer or reformer of Islam, one who seeks a regeneration of authentic Islam as a response to perceived deviation from the commands of the Qur'ān and the Sunnah.

Mujāhid one who is actively engaged in *jihād*.

Mujtahid one who is qualified in or exercises *ijtihād*, 'independent legal reasoning'.

Mulk reign, supreme authority, royal dignity, kingship; rule, government, temporal authority.

Munkarāt vices prohibited by revelation and or reason.

Musāwah equality.

Musayṭir watchguard, manager of affairs by force, enforcing one's own will on others against their will.

Mushrikūn polytheists. Those who associate anything with Allah (SWT). This is the one unforgivable sin according to the Qur'ān.

Mustakhlaf custodian.

Mu'tazilah the rationalist school of theology whose name comes from a word that means 'to stand aloof'.

Muttaqī (root *taqwa*) one who is conscious of his Islamic responsibility in relation to Allah (SWT), nature and humankind.

Muwaḥḥid unitarian that is, a believer in tawhid, divine unity and 'making the unity' constant in thoughts and actions.

Nahḍah raising, awakening: actualisation of potentialities latent in the child; refers to Islamic movement.

Nasab lineage, descent; kinship, affinity.

Nīyah determination, will, volition, intention, especially before any ritual act, such as the salah.

Qaḍā the office and function of a *qāḍī*; judiciary; a judgement given by a *qāḍī*.

Qadhf slanderous accusation.

Qāḍī judge; appointed but independent religious authority who adjudicates cases brought before him in accordance with the Shari'ah.

Qahr wa-ghalbah force and constraint.

Qānūn the canon or the political and administrative ordinances of the caliph.

Qasamah division, share, part.

Qawā'id Maxims or general principles.

Qawm tribe, race, people, nation.

Qiblah the direction of Makkah, towards which Muslims turn themselves in prayer.

Qiṣāṣ to avenge, for a harm done to someone.

Qisṭ justice, fairness, equitable.

Qiyās analogical deduction or analogical reasoning, the fourth source of the Sharī'ah. It is in fact a particular technique of *ijtihād*.

Rasūl messenger. A prophet entrusted with a special divine message for humanity at large.

Ra'y personal opinion, especially in legal decisions.

Ribā usury, interest, charging of interest on a loan. Ribā is forbidden in Islam.

Ribāṭ a military outpost or fort on the boundaries of a Muslim country. Has come to mean a Sufi retreat or cloister.

Risālah a divine revelation sent to a particular community through a prophet; also the institution of prophethood.

Salafīyah pertaining to forebears, the worthy successors.

Salāmah blamelessness, flawlessness, soundness, integrity, unimpaired state.

Sha'b community of people held together solely by the ties of kinship.

Shahādah the testimony of faith, the 'bearing witness' to the unity of Allah (SWT) and messengerhood of Prophet Muhammad (ṢAAS); saying the shahādah once in one's life, with belief, makes one a Muslim; also proof or evidence of delivering and fulfilling the assigned mission.

Shahādatān the two formulae of the testimony of faith.

Shara'a to introduce a legal code of conduct based on the revealed sources of Islamic law.

Shar'ī lawful, legitimate, legal.

Sharī'ah Literally, the way to the water hole; the code of conduct for humans in Islam, the Islamic law based on the Qur'ān, the Sunnah, Ijmā', qiyās or ijtihād. It is the totality of the Islamic system.

Shī'ah party, faction, sect; the adherents of 'Alī and his descendants as the rightful caliphs.

Shirk association, especially of anything with Allah (SWT); polytheism, idolatry.

Shūrā consultation, deliberation, taking counsel; a political principle referring to the participation of people in governing themselves; classical theory held that a leader should consult the notables of the community who had a duty to give advice and equate the institution of shura with that of the parliament (*majlis al-shūrā*).

Shu'ūbīyah a movement which refused to recognise the privileged position of the Arabs.

Ṣiḥāḥ refers to the six authentic compilations of *Ḥadīth* (traditions) of Prophet Muhammad (ṢAAS) by Imām al-Bukharī, Imām Muslim, Abū Dā'ūd, al-Nisā'ī, Ibn Mājah and al-Tirmidhī.

Sīrah biography.

Ṣirāṭ al-mustaqīm the straight path, the revealed way.

Siyāsah authority, administrative justice dispensed by the sovereign and his political agents, governmental administration, policy, politics.

Siyāsah 'ādilah just (ideal) government.

Siyāsah 'aqlīyah a rational regime.

Siyāsah dīnīyah a divine system.

Siyāsah shar'īyah a regime based on the Sharī'ah.

Ṣūfī a Muslim mystic, one who practises Islamic mysticism.

Sulṭān power, temporal government; an independent or paramount ruler.

Sunnah custom, usual procedure, a way of acting; the practice of the Prophet (ṢAAS) inclusive of sayings, actions and silent approval, as recorded in the *ḥadīth*. The Sunnah of the Prophet (ṢAAS) is one of the sources of the Sharī'ah.

Sūrah chapter of the Qur'ān.

Tablīgh proclamation, conveyance, transmission, preaching; synonym of *da'wah*.

Ṭāghūt transgressive force, evil force, rebel force against Allah (SWT); an idol, a false god, seducer, tempter (to error).

Taḥsīnīyat beautification, embellishment; perfection which makes things excellent.

Tajdīd Renewal, regeneration, revival. Revival of Islamic teachings in line with their authentic and original sources in time and space (history). One who does *tajdīd* is known as *mujaddid*.

Taqlīd imitation, emulation, reliance on precedence or tradition; acceptance of a legal position of theological assertion on mere authority without independent inquiry.

Taqlīd al-a'immah to hold or imitate the opinions expressed by jurists concerning a ruling of Shari'ah.

Taqwā piety, fear of Allah (SWT); it combines faith, piety, loyalty and commitment to Allah (SWT). Contrasted to fear of Allah (SWT) in the sense of being closer to Him and wishful to please Him.

Tashrī' legislation.

Tawḥīd the oneness, unity and uniqueness of Allah (SWT), epitomised in the first half of the profession of faith: There is none worthy of worship save Allah (SWT). This is the essence of the totality of Islam.

Ta'wīl allegorical or symbolic interpretation of a text that is vague or has different connotations.

Ta'zīr deterrence, discretionary penalty determined by the *qadi*.

Ta'zīrāt deterrences, discretionary penalties.

Ukhū wah (root, *akh*, brother); brotherhood, fraternity.

'Ulamā' (sing. *'ālim*) Muslim jurists, scholars, theologians; learned men who are experts in Sharī'ah.

Ulu al-amr rulers, commanders, jurisprudents and those who are knowledgeable.

Umam (pl. of Ummah) communities, peoples.

Umarā' (pl. of Amīr) rulers and commanders.

Ummah community, group, group of people; Muslim community as identified by the integration of its ideology, religion, law, mission and purpose of life and group consciousness, ethics and mores, irrespective of their differences in origin, region, colour, language and so on.

Ummah Muslimah community of faithfuls; the Muslim community, irrespective of race, ethnicity and so on.

Ummah Wāḥidah a single community. The Qur'ān in verse 10:19 refers to the entire human race as a single community.

'Urf mores of society, customs; contemporary practice or laws founded on custom.

'Urūbah Arabism, Arabdom, the Arab character.

Uṣūl al-fiqh science of jurisprudence.

Uswah ḥasanah role model, exemplary character worthy of emulation.

Wājib obligatory but lesser in degree compared to *farḍ*, according to Ḥanafi school.

Wajibāt (pl. of *Wājib*) obligations.

Wakīl authorised representative, agent. One entrusted with an obligation by one or both the parties in a conflict, marriage, mediation and so on.

Waqf a charitable trust dedicated to some pious or socially beneficial purpose; religious endowment.

Wara' fear (of Allah SWT), consciousness of the punishment of Allah (SWT); commitment to Islam.

Wasaṭ the median way.

Wilāyah public function; competence, jurisdiction; the office of government; authority.

Zakāh alms-giving; an obligation on every Muslim to purify his earnings and possessions by giving away a portion to the poor and the needy on the basis of one's wealth. One of the categories of Islamic worship (*'ibādah*).

Zinā adultery.

Ẓulm oppression, tyranny, injustice; not rendering someone his due, contrary to *'adālah*. As used in the Qur'ān, *shirk*, attributing partners to Allah (SWT), is *ẓulm* and infidels are tyrants (*al-kafirūna hum al-ẓalimūn*).

Appendix A: Framework of an Islamic State

Bismillāh al-Raḥmān al-Raḥīm

1 THE ISLAMIC UMMAH

Article 1

(A) Muslims form one single Ummah.
(B) The Sharī'ah is the source of all legislation.

Article 2

There may be several states within the Islamic Ummah with different forms of government.

Article 3

The state may unite with any other Islamic state or states on any form mutually agreed upon.

Article 4

The people shall be watchful of the Imām, his lieutenants and the rest of the functionaries of the state and shall hold them accountable in accordance with the Shari'ah.

2 DUTIES OF THE STATE

Article 5

Mutual cooperation and social security form the basis of society.

Article 6

It shall be the duty of every one to call to virtue and piety, and to forbid from evil, and any one failing to fully discharge this duty despite his ability shall be a sinner.

Article 7

Family is the basic unit of society, the essentials of which are *din* and morality. The state shall guarantee to support family, to protect motherhood and to preserve childhood and shall insure to provide all means for the realisation thereof.

Article 8

Protection of family is a duty of the state to be carried out by encouraging marriage and providing its material means such as housing and other possible aid. Marital life shall be respected and conditions shall be created wherein it is possible for the woman to become a good female partner to her husband, to look after their children and to consider the care of the family as her foremost duty.

Article 9

Protection of the Ummah and the health of its individuals is the duty of the state. It shall be the responsibility of the state to provide free medical services for the protection as well as the cure of citizens.

Article 10

Acquisition of knowledge as an obligation and instruction shall be the duty of the state in accordance with the law.

Article 11

Religious education shall constitute the basis of instruction at all levels.

Article 12

The state shall be bound to teach the Muslims the agreed principle of obligation, and to educate them with the *sīrah* of the Holy Prophet and life of the Orthodox caliphs up to a sufficient level during the course of their academic years.

Article 13

It shall be the duty of the state to arrange for the study and memorising of the Holy Qur'ān by Muslims during their educational periods for different kinds of study. It shall also create special institutes to cater for the needs of the non-regular students to memorise the Holy Qur'ān. It shall publish the Holy scripture and shall facilitate its circulation.

Article 14

Display of one's wealth, riches and official authority is forbidden and to refrain therefrom is obligatory. The state shall issue orders and enforce laws in accordance with the injunctions of the Sharī'ah to insure protection of public character from vulgarity.

Article 15

Arabic shall be the official language and the reference to the *Hijrah* calendar in official writings shall be compulsory.

Article 16

General authority of the government shall be contingent upon the serving of public interests particularly the protection of *din*, sanity, life, property and honour.

Article 17

For the validity of an act it is not sufficient that its end is lawful, but it is necessary that in all circumstances and conditions, the means to achieve a lawful end, should also be lawful.

3 ISLAMIC ECONOMY

Article 18

The economy shall be based on the Sharī'ah. It shall guarantee human honour, social justice and shall make it incumbent on all persons to strive in life intellectually and industriously and shall protect a living earned by *ḥalāl* (lawful) means.

Article 19

Freedom of trade, industry and farming shall be guaranteed within the limits prescribed by the Sharī'ah.

Article 20

The state shall formulate plans for economic development in accordance with the Sharī'ah.

Article 21

The state shall prevent hoarding and monopoly and shall intervene in price stabilisation when necessary.

Article 22

The state shall encourage the development of barren lands and the expansion of cultivable lands.

Article 23

Any transaction involving receipt or payment of *ribā* or any act to hide or disguise a transaction of *ribā* is prohibited.

Article 24

The state shall be the owner of whatever lies beneath the earth of mines, raw materials and other natural wealth.

Article 25

A property without any owner shall be owned by the public exchequer, and shall be disposed of only in the manner prescribed by law.

Article 26

The state shall disburse the *zakāt* paid to it by individuals on the items of expenditure determined by the Sharī'ah.

Article 27

Creation of *waqf* for welfare purposes shall be valid and necessary laws shall be enforced for the organisation thereof from all aspects.

4 INDIVIDUAL RIGHTS AND LIBERTIES

Article 28

Justice and equality are the foundations of government and the inviolable rights of defence and litigation are guaranteed.

Article 29

Religious and intellectual beliefs, freedom to work and express opinion orally, in writing or otherwise, to form associations and unions and to join them, enjoyment of individual freedom, freedom of movement and assembly: all are natural fundamental rights which shall be guaranteed by the state within the limits prescribed by the Sharī'ah.

Article 30

The privacy of houses, correspondence and other personal matters shall be sacred and its violation shall be prohibited. The law shall determine the limits to this sanctity which might be imposed by the state with the permission of a court of law in such cases as crimes of high treason or in a situation of unexpected extraordinary danger.

Article 31

Right of movement in and outside the state's territory shall be permitted. The citizens shall not be prevented from travelling abroad nor shall they be forced to stay at one particular place instead of another except by the order of a court of law wherein the court shall record the reasons of its order. The citizens cannot be exiled.

Article 32

Handing over of political refugees is prohibited but the extradition of normal criminals shall be subject to the agreements with the state concerned.

Article 33

Torturing people is a crime. Liability incurred by this crime shall not be waived off from the person who has committed this crime throughout his life. The criminal and the abettor in crime shall also be financially liable. If the crime is committed with the abetment of an official, his concurrence or his tacit approval, he shall be regarded abettor in the crime and liable to penal and civil punishments, and the government shall be responsible for damages.

Article 34

Any official in whose jurisdiction the crime of torture is committed and he fails to bring it to the notice of the authorities concerned in spite of his knowledge of its commission, such official shall be liable to punishment by way of *ta'zeer*.

Article 35

No bloodshedding can go unchecked and unpunished in Islam. It shall be the duty of the state to compensate for the deceased and such persons are entitled therefore in case the murderer is not known or to pay indemnity in case someone is disabled and the offender is not known or when the murderer, or offender becomes known but fails to pay compensation due to bankruptcy.

Article 36

Every person shall have the right to file a suit in respect of any offence committed against him or against someone else or a suit in respect of any embezzlement or misappropriation of any public property.

Article 37

The right to work, to earn, and to own shall be guaranteed and there shall be no encroachment thereupon unless it is dictated by the injunctions of Islamic Sharī'ah.

Article 38

The women shall have the right to work within the limits provided by the injunctions of the Sharī'ah.

Article 39

The state shall guarantee the freedom of ownership and the rights of ownership and its immunities. There shall be no public confiscation through any device whatsoever. A private confiscation, however, shall be possible by order of a court of law.

Article 40

No one shall be deprived of ownership except in the public interest and after the payment of due compensation in accordance with the law to be promulgated for this purpose.

Article 41

Bringing out of newspapers shall be permissible and the press shall be free subject to the injunctions of the Sharī'ah.

Article 42

The citizens shall have the right to form associations and unions in accordance with the law. But if the activities of any of them are directed against the system of the society or are clandestine in nature with a militant character or in some manner are in violation of the injunctions of the Sharī'ah, such associations or unions shall be liable to be banned.

Article 43

All rights shall be exercised in accordance with the objectives of the Sharī'ah.

5 THE IMĀM

Article 44

The state shall have an Imām whose obedience shall be obligatory even if someone is opposed to his opinion.

Article 45

There can be no obedience to any creature in the event of the disobedience to the Creator; nor can there be any obedience to the Imām in any matter decidedly in contravention of the Sharī'ah.

Article 46

The law shall lay down the procedure of public mandate in the choice of Imām provided that such public mandate is given under the supervision of the judiciary. The mandate shall be with the majority of the votes of all the participants in the process of giving the mandate.

Article 47

It shall be necessary for the contestant for the office of Head of State to fulfil the following conditions:

(a) That he is a Muslim.
(b) That he is a male.
(c) That he is an adult.
(d) That he is sane.
(e) That he is righteous.
(f) That he possesses the knowledge of the injunctions of the Islamic Sharī'ah.

Article 48

The appointment of the Imām shall take place after a general mandate of all the strata of the Ummah in accordance with the law. The women may demand participation in the election when they fulfil its conditions whereupon they shall be allowed such participation.

Article 49

Nothing shall be held against any person who expresses his opinion in the general mandate for the Imām before it is completed.

Article 50

Those entitled to give mandate shall have the right to dismiss the Imām when reasons exist for so doing and in the manner laid down by the law.

Article 51

The Imām shall submit to the judiciary and he may appear before it through his agent.

Article 52

The Head of the State shall enjoy all such rights as are enjoyed by the citizens and similarly he shall have all those obligations as they have. In financial matters he shall follow such rules and regulations as are laid down by the law.

Article 53

There can be made no will in favour of the Imām nor any *waqf* can be created for him or his relations up to the fourth degree except if it is a will of a person from whom the Imām inherits. Furthermore, the Imām shall not be entitled to purchase, hire or sell any of the state's properties to the state.

Article 54

Gifts presented to the Imām are shackles and they have to be deposited in the public exchequer.

Article 55

The Imām should be a model for the people in justice, acts of piety and virtue and he should dedicate himself, in cooperation with other *aimmah* of the Muslims, to all that concerns the Islamic Ummah. He should also send *ḥajj* missions every year whereby participation may be made in all formal and informal meetings of the Muslims.

Article 56

The Imām shall be responsible for the command of his army in *jihād* against the enemy, to protect the frontiers, to defend the soil, to establish *ḥudūd* and to conclude treaties and to ratify them.

Article 57

The Imām shall be responsible for enabling the people individually and collectively to call unto virtue and to forbid from evil and to perform the obligatory duties.

Article 58

The Imām shall appoint the State functionaries. The law may delegate to someone else the powers to appoint officials other than those in the key positions.

Article 59

There can be no pardon for crimes save by laws. The Imām shall have the power to pardon the punishments of crimes in special circumstances with the exception of punishment of *ḥudūd* and high treason.

Article 60

The Imām shall have the power to take extraordinary measures specified in the law when disturbances take place or the conditions exist which may lead to the eruption of disturbances or threaten the very existence of the state or of a civil war or war with any other state may break out, provided that such measures are submitted to the Assembly of Deputies within one week of their adoption. If the new Assembly has not already been elected then the former Assembly shall be convened for the purpose. If this procedure is not followed then such measures shall be deemed to have been null and void. A law shall be enacted to regulate these extraordinary measures and their legal consequences and to determine which authorities shall be empowered to take such measures and the mode of dealing with their consequences in case they are not specified.

6 JUDICIARY

Article 61

Members of the judiciary shall administer justice in accordance with the injunctions of the Sharī'ah.

Article 62

The people shall be equal before the judiciary and there shall be no discrimination of any individual or group through special courts.

Article 63

Establishment of special courts shall be prohibited and no litigant shall be deprived of his normal adjudicator.

Article 64

The judiciary shall not be prevented from the hearing of cases against the Imām or the ruler.

Article 65

Decisions shall be made and enforced in the name of Allah, the Most Compassionate, the Most Merciful and the judges in the discharge of their judicial functions shall not be subject to any law other than the Sharī'ah.

Article 66

Implementation of the Court's decision shall be the duty of the state and any slackness in it or failure to implement them shall be a crime liable to punishment.

Article 67

The state shall guarantee independence of judiciary and any encroachment upon its freedom shall be a crime.

Article 68

The state shall choose for judiciary the best qualified men and shall facilitate the discharge of judicial functions.

Article 69

It shall be incumbent in the crimes of *ḥudūd* that the accused appears in the trial attended by a defence counsel of his own choice or, if he doesn't choose one, another to be deputed by the state.

Article 70

The proceedings of the courts shall be open and the public shall have the right to attend them. They shall not be made secret unless it is required by the Sharī'ah.

Article 71

The punishments of *ḥudūd al-Shar'īyah* shall be awarded in the crimes of *zina. qàzf*, theft, highway robbery (*ḥirābah*), drinking and apostasy.

Article 72

The law shall specify the punishment awarded by courts by way of *ta'zir* in crimes other than those of *ḥudūd*.

Article 73

The law shall lay down the provision of *qasamah* and no civil liability shall exceed the scales of *diyat*.

Article 74

The law shall lay down the conditions for the acceptance of repentance and provisions related thereto.

Article 75 (not mentioned)

Article 76 (not mentioned)

Article 77

Diyah in respect of a woman may be equal to a man.

Article 78

A complete equalisation and full certainty on the part of the court are preconditions for the enforcement of *wiṣāṣ*.

Article 79

Whipping is the basic punishment in *ta'zirāt*; and imprisonment is prohibited except in a few cases and for limited periods to be determined by the Court.

Article 80

Any act which humiliates, oppresses or offends the dignity of the prisoner shall be prohibited.

Article 81

There shall be established a supreme constitutional Court which shall be competent to give its decision as to what extent the laws and regulations enforced from time to time as well as the provisions of this constitution are in conformity with the injunctions of the Sharī'ah; the law shall also determine any other powers to be enjoyed by the said Court.

Article 82

There shall be established a *diwān al-maẓālim*, and the law shall prescribe its constitution, jurisdiction and the emoluments of its members.

7 SHURA, SURVEILLANCE AND LEGISLATION

Article 83

The state shall have a *majlis al-shūrā* which shall exercise the following powers:

(1) To legislate in accordance with the injunctions of the Sharī'ah.
(2) To approve the annual budget of the state and to review its final accounts.
(3) To exercise surveillance over the activities of the executive authority.
(4) To determine the duties of the Cabinet and to withhold its confidence therefrom when required.

Article 84

The law shall lay down the provisions relating to its election, the procedure relating to its election, the procedure of holding it and the qualifications for its membership. These provisions shall be based on the principle of *shūrā* so as to guarantee the participation of every adult and sane person of good reputation in giving opinion. The law shall also lay down the rules governing the financial matters of the members. The *majlis* shall adopt its internal rules of business and procedure.

8 THE GOVERNMENT

Article 85

The government shall be responsible for running all the governmental affairs and for the achievement of all interests recognised by the Sharī'ah and shall be responsible to the Imām (This clause shall be deleted in States having a *majlis al-shūrā*).

Article 86

The law shall prescribe the conditions of the appointment of ministers, the acts prohibited for them during the period of holding office, and the procedure of their trial for any omission or commission during the discharge of their functions.

9 GENERAL AND INTERIM PROVISIONS

Article 87

The city of . . . . shall be the capital of the country.

Article 88

The law shall specify the state's flag and its emblem and shall lay down the rules and regulations relating to each of them.

Article 89

The laws shall come into force from their dates of promulgation and shall not be enforceable with retrospective effect unless specifically provided therein in which case it shall be necessary to get the approval of two-thirds of the members of the Assembly of Deputies, provided no retrospective effect shall be given to any legislation in criminal matters.

Article 90

All the laws shall be published in the official gazette within two weeks of their promulgation and they shall come into force after one month from the day following their publication except when some other period is fixed for this purpose.

Article 91

Both the Imām and the Assembly of Deputies shall have the right to demand amendment in any article or articles of the Constitution. It shall be necessary to specify in the demand, the articles sought to be amended and to give the reasons for such amendment. If such demand is made by the Assembly of Deputies, it shall have to be signed by two-thirds of the members of the Assembly of Deputies. Initially the Assembly shall, in all circumstances, debate the proposed amendment and shall give its decision with a majority of two-thirds of its members. In case the demand is rejected, amendment in the same articles shall not be demanded before the passage of one year from its rejection.

If the Assembly of Deputies initially approves the amendment, it shall debate the articles required to be amended after two months from such approval; if two-thirds of the members of the Assembly approve the amendment, it shall be submitted before the Ummah for referendum.

If approval is given, it shall be deemed to have come into force from the date of the announcement of the result of referendum.

Article 92

All the laws and rules and regulations in force prior to the enforcement of this Constitution shall continue to be valid and in force. However, they may be annulled or amended in accordance with the provisions and procedures laid down in the Constitution. If they are repugnant to the injunctions of the Shari'ah, it shall be incumbent to annul them to the extent of this repugnance or to replace them with other legislation.

Article 93

This Constitution shall come into force from the day when the approval of the Ummah in the referendum shall be announced.

Source: The Muslim World League Journal, 9 (6) April 1982, pp. 29–34.

Appendix B: Model of an Islamic Constitution

PREAMBLE

WHEREAS Islam is a complete code of life suitable for all people and all times, and Allah's mandate is universal and eternal and applies to every sphere of human conduct and life;

WHEREAS every individual has his own personal dignity;

WHEREAS all capabilities, individual and collective, and all power are a trust to be discharged within the terms laid down by the Sharī'ah, to qualify for fulfilment of the Divine promise of a life from want and oppression, and blessed with harmony, plenitude, security, health and fulfilment;

ACKNOWLEDGING that the setting up of a society based on Islam and its principles requires the complete application of the Sharī'ah in the constitution and in the law, and that every individual under this order is able to undertake and fulfil his duty to himself, to his country and to all humanity;

We, the people of ...., commit ourselves to make the following the prime values of our socio-political order:

(a) submission to Allah alone;
(b) freedom governed by responsibility and discipline;
(c) justice tempered with mercy;
(d) equality strengthened by brotherhood;
(e) *shūrā* as the method of governance.

We, the people of ...., therefore, hereby, by mean of a referendum[1] held for this purpose on ...., assent to adopt this constitution, committing ourselves to the above principles and to a covenant to do our utmost to faithfully discharge our duties in accordance with them. And Allah is our witness.

FOUNDATION OF AUTHORITY AND BASIS OF SOCIETY

Article I

(a) Sovereignty belongs to Allah alone, and the Sharī'ah is paramount.
(b) The Sharī'ah – comprising the Qur'an and the Sunnah – is the source of legislation and policy.
(c) Authority is a trust which the people exercise in accordance with the Sharī'ah.

Article 2

.... is part of the Muslim world and the Muslim people of .... are an integral part of Muslim Ummah.

Article 3

The state and society are based on the following principles:

(a) The supremacy of the Sharī'ah and its rules in all walks of life;
(b) *Shūrā* as the method of governance;
(c) The belief that everything in the universe belongs to Allah and is a blessing from Him to mankind, and that everyone is entitled to a just share in this Divine bounty;
(d) The belief that all natural resources are a trust (*amānah*) from Allah and that man is individually and collectively custodian (*mustakhlaf*) of these resources. Man's economic effort and its reward are determined within the framework of this trust;
(e) Inviolability of the Islamic code of human rights and obligation to support and defend the oppressed anywhere in the world;
(f) The paramount importance of inculcating an Islamic personality in the individual and in society, through Islamic education, cultural programmes, the media, and other means;
(g) Provision of opportunities for work to all able-bodied members of society and guarantee of the provision of the necessities of life for the disabled, the sick and the old;
(h) Provision of public services for all: health, education, cultural and social;
(i) Unity of the Ummah and unceasing efforts for its realisation;
(j) Obligation to engage in *da'wah islamiah*.

OBLIGATIONS AND RIGHTS

Article 4

(a) Human life, body, honour and freedom are sacred and inviolable. No one shall be exposed to injury or death, except under the authority of the Sharī'ah.

(b) As in life, so also after death, the sanctity of a person's body and honour is inviolable.

Article 5

(a) No person shall be exposed to torture of body, mind or threat of degradation or injury either to himself or to anyone related to him or otherwise held dear by him; nor shall he be made to confess to the commission of a crime, or forced to act or consent to an act which is injurious to his or another person's interests.
(b) Torture is a crime and shall be punishable irrespective of the passage of time.

Article 6

(a) Every person is entitled to the protection of his privacy.
(b) The right to privacy of home, correspondence and communication is guaranteed and cannot be violated except through the judicial process.

Article 7

Every person has the right to food, housing, clothing, education and medical care. The state is to take all necessary steps to provide the same to the extent of resources available.

Article 8

Every person has the right to his thoughts, opinions and beliefs. He also has the right to express them so long as he remains within the limits prescribed by law.[2]

Article 9

(a) All persons are equal before the law and are entitled to equal protection of the law.
(b) All persons of equal merit are entitled to equal opportunity, and to equal wages for equal work. No person may be discriminated against or denied the opportunity to work by reason of religious beliefs, colour, race, origin or language.

Article 10

(a) Every person shall be treated in accordance with the law and only in accordance with the law.
(b) All penal laws shall apply prospectively and shall not have retrospective effect.

Article 11

(a) No act shall be considered a crime and no punishment awarded therefore unless it is stipulated as such in the clear wording of the law.
(b) Every individual is responsible for his actions. Responsibility for a crime cannot be vicariously extended to other members of his family or group, who are not otherwise directly or indirectly involved in the commission of the crime in question.
(c) Every person is presumed to be innocent until finally adjudged guilty by a court of law.
(d) No person shall be adjudged guilty except after a fair trial and after reasonable opportunity for defence has been provided to him.

Article 12

(a) Every person has the right to protection against harassment or victimisation by official agencies. No one is liable to account for himself except for making a defence to charges made against him or where he is found in a situation wherein a question regarding suspicion of his involvement in a crime could be reasonably raised.
(b) No person shall be subjected to any form of harassment while he is seeking to defend personal or public rights.

Article 13

(a) Every Muslim is entitled to found a family through marriage and to bring up children in conformity with the Sharīʻah.
(b) Every husband is obliged to maintain his wife and children according to his means.
(c) Motherhood is entitled to special respect, care and assistance on the part of the family and the organs of state and society.
(d) Every child has the right to be maintained and properly brought up by his parents.
(e) Child labour is forbidden.

Article 14

(a) Citizenship shall be determined by law.
(b) Every Muslim has a right to seek citizenship of the state. This may be granted in accordance with law.

Article 15

Without any restriction unless imposed by law, every citizen has the right to freedom of movement to and from and within the country, and to stay within the country. No citizen shall be expelled from the country or prevented from returning to it.

Article 16

(a) There is no compulsion in religion.
(b) Non-Muslim minorities have the right to practise their religion.
(c) In matters of personal law the minorities shall be governed by their own laws and traditions, except if they themselves opt to be governed by the Sharī'ah. In cases of conflict between parties, the Sharī'ah shall apply.

Article 17

Every citizen over the age of. . . . years has an obligation and a right to participate in the public affairs of the state.

Article 18

(a) Citizens have a right to assemble and to form groups, organisations and associations – political, cultural, scientific, social, and other – as long as their programmes and activities are consistent with the provisions of the Sharī'ah.
(b) The formation and activities of such groups, organisations and associations shall be regulated by law.

Article 19

The state shall grant asylum to persons who seek it, in accordance with the law. The state shall extend security, protection and hospitality wherever necessary to those given asylum and the facility of safe passage if requested.

MAJLIS AL-SHŪRĀ

Article 20

(a) There shall be a *majlis al-shūrā* consisting of ..... members directly elected by the people.
(b) The term of the *majlis* shall be ..... years.
(c) The qualifications for membership to the *majlis* shall be established by law.

Article 21

The functions of the *majlis al-shūrā* shall be:

(a) To legislate promoting the objectives of the Sharī'ah, seeking the opinion of the Council of Ulamā' as necessary.
(b) To enact laws proposed by the government and by members of the *majlis al-shūrā*;
(c) To approve the financial programmes and budgets and accounts of the government and public bodies receiving or using state funds;

(d) To review policies of the government and its different departments, by questioning and interpellation of the respective ministers; and to investigate or authorise investigation of departments and institutions established under law;
(e) To authorise the declaration of war or peace or national emergency;
(f) To approve treaties and international agreements and undertakings.

Article 22

Members of the *majlis al-shūrā* are free to express their views during the execution of their duties, and may not be arrested, prosecuted, harassed or removed from membership of the *majlis al-shūrā* for so doing.

THE IMĀM

Article 23

(a) The Imām shall be the chief executive of the state, who shall be elected by an absolute majority of the country's voters for a term of ..... years, commencing from the date the *bay'ah* is offered to him by the *majlis al bay'ah*.
(b) The Imām shall be accountable to the people and to the *majlis al-shura*, as stipulated by the law.

Article 24

A person qualified for election to the office of Imām shall be:

(a) A Muslim not under ..... years of age;
(b) Of unblemished character;
(c) Known to be following the injunctions of the Qur'ān and the Sunnah, committed to Islam and knowledgeable in the Sharī'ah;
(d) Physically, mentally and emotionally fit to discharge the obligations of the office;
(e) Of courteous bearing and balanced behaviour.

Article 25

Before taking office, the Imām shall make a decision of commitment, before a National Assembly (*majlis al bay'ah*) consisting of members of the *majlis al-shūrā*, the Council of ulamā', the Supreme Constitutional Council, the higher judiciary, the Election Commission, and the Heads of the Armed Forces, to follow the Sharī'ah in letter and in spirit, to uphold the message of Islam at all costs, to obey the mandate of the constitution and to defend the territorial, ideological, political and economic independence of the state, and the rights to the people, and to ensure justice to all members of the society without discrimination, and without fear or favour, and be available to them directly or through appropriate agencies for the redress of their grievances. On his making this commitment, all the participants shall offer him *bay'ah* on the above terms on their own behalf and on behalf of the people.

Article 26

The Imām is entitled to obedience by all persons even if their views differ from his. There is, however, no obedience if it involves disobedience of Allah and His Prophet (Peace be upon Him).

Article 27

The Imām shall enjoy the same rights as other citizens. He is subject to all the obligations of law, without any special immunity or executive privilege.

Article 28

(a) The Imām shall not purchase or hire any state property, nor shall he rent or sell his own property to the state, nor shall he engage himself in any business within the country or outside.
(b) Gifts presented to the Imām and his family or to other officials of the state in their official capacity shall be treated as public property.

Article 29

The Imām shall have no power to overrule the decision of a court, or to change or annul or delay the punishment a court has resolved against anyone guilty of the *ḥudūd*, *qiṣāṣ* or *diyah*. He may, however, exercise his power of clemency in all other cases.

Article 30

The Imām or his duly authorised representative shall enter into pacts, conventions, treaties and other agreements negotiated by them with other governments and with international organisations.

Article 31

The Imām shall assent to legislation passed by the *majlis al-shura* and then forward it to the concerned authorities for implementation. He shall not have the right to veto legislation passed by the *majlis*; however, he may refer it back to the *majlis* only once, within 30 days from the date of receipt, for reconsideration with his arguments. On return of the legislation after reconsideration, if passed by a two-thirds majority of the members of the *majlis al-shūrā*, he shall assent to the legislation.

Article 32

The Imām shall appoint advisers, ministers, ambassadors and the heads of the Armed Forces.

Article 33

(a) The Imām shall be impeached if he intentionally violates the provisions of the constitution, or for wanton violation of the Sharī'ah, by a resolution to that effect by a two-thirds majority of the members of the *Majlis al-Shūrā*, and, if it is found that he has violated the *bay'ah*, the *bay'ah* would be annulled by approval of a two-thirds majority of the *Majlis al-Bay'ah.*
(b) Rules and procedures to govern the impeachment and removal of the Imām shall be determined by law.

Article 34

(a) The Imām may resign his office under his own signature by submitting his resignation to the *Majlis al-Shūrā.*
(b) In case of vacancy of the office of the Imām, the Speaker of the *majlis al-Shūrā* shall act as Imām until elections for filling the vacancy are held, within a maximum period of.... days from the date of vacancy.
(c) In case of disability of the Imām, the Speaker of the *Majlis al-Shūrā* shall act as Imām until the Imām resumes his duties within ... days. Otherwise, the office of the Imām shall be considered vacant.

JUDICIARY

Article 35

Everyone shall have the right to present a case before the courts.

Article 36

(a) The judiciary is independent and free from all influence of the executive and is responsible for the administration of justice and the protection of the rights and obligations of the people.
(b) The judges are independent and there is no authority above them except the authority of the law.

Article 37

Dispensation of justice shall be free and the law shall protect this dispensation from misuse.

Article 38

All court proceedings shall be in public and not in camera except when sanctioned by the court for protection of personal secrets or honour or out of consideration of national security or public decency.

Article 39

(a) The establishment of special courts or tribunals is not permitted.
(b) However, military courts shall be established to try members of the Armed Forces for acts which constitute offences only under military law. They shall be tried in the civil courts for all other offences.

Article 40

Implementation of court decisions is the duty of every concerned person exercising public authority, and slackness or failure to implement them is an offence liable to punishment, according to law.

Article 41

In consonance with the principles contained in this constitution, the organisational structure of the judiciary, qualifications of the judges and procedures for their appointment, transfer, and removal, relationships with the executive and legislature and related matters, shall be established by law.

Article 42

There shall be an establishment of *ḥisbah* for:

(a) The promotion and protection of Islamic values with a view to establishing what is right and forbidding what is wrong.
(b) The investigation of complaints by individuals against the state and its organs;
(c) The protection of individual rights;
(d) The review of the work of officials of the state, and rectification of cases of maladministration, neglect or dereliction of duty on their part;
(e) Monitoring and examining the legality of administrative decisions.

Article 43

There shall be a *muḥtasib ʻām* as the head of the organisation of *ḥisbah* in the country assisted by *muḥtasibs* at provincial and lower levels, and the rules and procedures relating to this office shall be established by law.

Article 44

The *muḥtasibs* shall be able to act on their own initiative or on application or information received from others. They shall have the power to obtain relevant information and records from any government department or public agency, and officials shall be obliged to respond promptly and affirmatively to their demands.

Article 45

If the *muḥtasib 'ām* considers a law or regulation oppressive or unreasonable, in that it causes difficulty or undue hardship in obedience, or if it appears to be unconstitutional, he shall have the power to refer the law or regulation in question to the appropriate judicial authority for its annulment or amendment.

Article 46

A *muhtasib* shall not take cognisance of a case of which cognisance has already been taken, or is being taken, by a court of competent jurisdiction.

ECONOMIC ORDER

Article 47

The economic order shall be based on the Islamic principles of justice, equity, human dignity, freedom of enterprise, balanced relationship and prevention of extravagant spending. It shall seek to mobilise and develop the human and material resources of society, in a planned and harmonious manner, to satisfy the spiritual, material and social needs of all members of the community.

Article 48

It is the duty of the state to develop all sources of energy and wealth and to put them to optimum use, and to ensure that they are not hoarded, wasted or kept idle. Individuals shall be permitted to participate in this process within the limits prescribed by law.

Article 49

(a) All natural and energy resources belong originally to society as do enterprises and institutions established through the public exchequer.
(b) Private ownership of wealth is lawful and protected provided that it is acquired by means that are held legitimate and is retained and used for purposes allowed by the Sharī'ah.
(c) No publically-owned property or interest can be liquidated except in cases of necessity to the interests of the society; and no privately-owned property or interest can be expropriated by the Senate except in cases of necessity in the public interest and on prompt payment of fair and adequate compensation.

Article 50

(a) Freedom of enterprise is guaranteed within the limits prescribed by law.
(b) All kinds of profit or spending contrary to the Sharī'ah are forbidden.

(c) Confiscation of any legally and legitimately gained profit or entitlement is forbidden.

Article 51

Money being a medium of exchange and a measure of value, no monetary or fiscal policy is legitimate which destabilises the value of money or contributes to its erosion.

Article 52

All wealth and property not owned by private individuals or organisations shall vest in the state.

Article 53

Ribā, monopoly, hoarding, profiteering and exploitation, and other such anti-social practices are forbidden.

Article 54

The state shall take all such measures as may be necessary to terminate and prevent foreign economic domination.

Article 55

There shall be an Economic and Social Council consisting of persons specialising in socio-economic affairs and the Sharīʻah, which shall:

(a) participate in the economic decision-making in the country for the realisation of the socio-economic obligations stipulated in this constitution;
(b) advise the government and the *Majlis al-Shūrā* on economic and social planning and budgeting and other socio-economic matters.

Article 56

The composition of the Economic and Social Council, its rules and procedures shall be established by law.

DEFENCE

Article 57

(a) *Jihād* is a perpetual and inalienable duty.
(b) It is incumbent on every Muslim to defend the Land of Islam and the Islamic order.

Article 58

(a) The state shall be responsible for building viable Armed Forces consistent with its resources and capable of fulfilling the demands of *jihād*.
(b) The state shall take all necessary steps to enable the people to perform the duty of *jihād*.
(c) In addition to military training there shall be a programme of Islamic education and training to inculcate in Armed Forces the concept of *jihād*.

Article 59

(a) The Imām is the Commander-in-Chief of the Armed Forces.
(b) He is empowered to declare war or peace or a national emergency on authorisation from the *Majlis al-Shūrā*.

Article 60

A Supreme *Jihād* Council shall be established to formulate the strategy for war and peace. The composition of the Council, its rules and procedures shall be established by law.

SUPREME CONSTITUTIONAL COUNCIL

Article 61

There shall be a Supreme Constitutional Council – an independent judicial body – which shall be the guardian of the constitution and of the Islamic character of the state.

Article 62

The Council's functions shall include:

(a) Ruling on any question which arises of a law being repugnant to the Sharī'ah.
(b) Interpretation of the constitution and the law.
(c) Deciding cases of conflict in jurisdiction.
(d) Hearing and ruling on complaints against the Election Commission.

Article 63

(a) Rules and procedures for the composition of the Supreme Constitution Council, qualifications of its members, terms of their appointment, removal or retirement, and related matters, and the mode of operation of the Council shall be established by law.
(b) The afore-mentioned law shall be established by a two-thirds majority of the members of the *Majlis al-Shūrā*.

COUNCIL OF 'ULAMĀ'

Article 64

The Council of 'Ulamā' shall comprise persons well-versed in the Sharī'ah, who are known for their piety, God-consciousness and depth of knowledge and who have deep insight into contemporary issues and challenges.

Article 65

The functions of the Council of 'Ulamā' shall be:

(a) the application of juridical *ijtihād*;
(b) to explain the stand of the Sharī'ah on various legislative proposals before the *Majlis al-Shūrā*;
(c) To fulfil the Islamic obligation of declaring the truth and pronouncing judgement without procrastination on issues affecting the Muslim Ummah.

Article 66

Rules for the formation of the Council of 'Ulamā', its composition, qualifications of its members and other relevant matters shall be determined by law.

ELECTION COMMISSION

Article 67

There shall be an independent permanent Election Commission consisting of . . . members.

Article 68

The functions of the Commission shall be:

(a) to organise, supervise and hold elections to the office of the Imām and to the membership of the *Majlis al-Shūrā* and other offices in accordance with the law;
(b) to organise, supervise and hold referenda;
(c) to ensure that candidates for elective offices fulfil the conditions stipulated by law.

Article 69

(a) Members of the Commission shall be appointed from amongst the sitting members of the senior judiciary of the state.
(b) Any person while a member of the Election Commission shall be ineligible for any other post.

Article 70

The rules and procedures concerning appointment of the Election Commission and other allied matters shall be provided by law. This law, while making provisions for organising, supervising and holding elections, shall: determine the qualifications of the electors and assure fair delineation of constituencies, filing and determining of nominations, voting procedures, declaration of election results and assure secrecy of ballots.

Article 71

All public authorities and public servants shall act in aid of the Election Commission to enable it to discharge its constitutional obligations, and obey its commands directly and promptly without leave or consent of any other authority.

UNITY OF UMMAH AND INTERNATIONAL RELATIONS

Article 72

It is the duty of the state to strive by all possible means to seek the unity and the solidarity of the Muslim Ummah.

Article 73

The foreign policy of the state and the conduct of its international relations shall be based on the principles of freedom, justice and peace in the world and shall strive to attain the welfare and well-being of mankind.

Article 74

The state is opposed to all actions, policies and programmes based on inequality, and is committed to strive actively against them to the best of its capabilities.

Article 75

In addition to the above, the state is duty-bound to fulfil the following obligations deriving from the principles and injunctions of Islam:

(a) to protect the freedom of man throughout the world;
(b) to struggle and to strive to end oppression and persecution of the people wherever and whenever it occurs in the world;
(c) to protect and observe the sanctity of all places of God's worship.

Article 76

(a) The state is obliged to refrain from engaging in wars on grounds of difference in religious belief, or for the exploitation of other people's resources and to control their economies.
(b) War is permitted to defend the faith, the territorial and ideological integrity of the state, to defend the oppressed and persecuted of the world, to protect the honour, dignity and freedom of man, and to preserve peace in the world.

Article 77

The state shall oppose power blocs and groups seeking the exploitation and domination of weaker nations.

Article 78

The state shall not allow the establishment of foreign military bases or the provision of military facilities to foreign powers which might in any way impinge on the sovereignty of the state or be prejudicial to its interests or to the interests of other Muslim states.

Article 79

The state shall honour and implement international treaties, pacts, agreements and obligations in letter and spirit.

THE MASS MEDIA AND PUBLICATIONS

Article 80

The mass media and publications have full freedom of expression and presentation of information so long as they respect and adhere to facts and to the norms and values of Islam. The freedom to publish newspapers and journals shall be permitted within these limits and the closing or censuring of the news media shall be through judicial procedure, except in times of war.

Article 81

The mass media and publications are obliged to:

(a) expose and protest against oppression, injustice and tyranny, regardless of whoever is guilty of such acts;
(b) respect the privacy of individuals and refrain from prying into their personal affairs;
(c) refrain from inventing and circulating slander, calumny and rumour;
(d) express the truth and scrupulously avoid spreading falsehood or mixing

the truth with falsehood or knowingly concealing the truth or distorting it;

(e) use decent and dignified language;
(f) promote the right conduct and ethical values in society;
(g) strictly refrain from the dissemination of indecency, obscenity and immorality;
(h) avoid condoning or glorifying crimes or acts repugnant to Islam;
(i) avoid becoming instruments of corruption of any kind.

Article 82

The executive organs of the state shall have no authority to take any administrative action against or to penalise the media or publications in any way except to prosecute violations in a court of law. Similarly, media and publications' personnel are protected in the performance of their professional duties.

GENERAL AND TRANSNATIONAL PROVISIONS

Article 83

Hijrah is the official calendar of the state and the official language is .... If Arabic is not the official language, it shall be the second official language.

Article 84

(a) The Imām or the *Majlis al-Shūrā* may propose amendments to this constitution. Amendments may only be made if approved by a two-thirds majority of the members of the *Majlis al-Shūrā*.
(b) Any amendment which might endanger the Islamic character of the state, or which violates the tenets of the Sharī'ah, would be void.

Article 85

(a) The legislative, executive and judicial authorities and all bodies, institutions and organisations existing at the time of the coming into effect of this constitution shall continue to exercise their functions and activities until the establishment of substitutes in accordance with the provisions of the constitution and the assumption of functions by such substitutes.
(b) All laws, regulations and decrees in operation at the time of the coming into effect of this constitution shall continue to be in operation until annulled or amended in accordance with the provisions set out in this constitution.
(c) After the adoption of this constitution, and in keeping with the provisions of this constitution, the existing legislative authority shall, through an appropriate law, take necessary steps to establish the first *Majlis al-Shūrā*, the first Election Commission and the first Supreme Constitutional Council.

Article 86

There is an imperative obligation on everyone concerned to ensure that the provisions of this constitution are implemented effectively and without delay so that the constitution becomes effective in its entirely as soon as possible after its adoption.

Article 87

This constitution is applicable from ...., the date on which the results of the referendum were published (if adopted by means of a referendum) or the date it was adopted by the country's constitutional body.

Notes

1. Or by a resolution of a parliament or other competent body.
2. It is forbidden according to this constitution for any law to be contrary to the Sharī'ah. Thus, wherever reference is made to 'law' it means the Sharī'ah, or that which is permitted by the Sharī'ah.

Source: Islamic Council, *A Model of an Islamic Constitution* (London: Islamic Council, 1983).

Appendix C: Profile of the Muslim World

Table c.1 Gazetteer of states in the Muslim world

Country	*Area (sq. km)*	*Population (1992)*	*GDP (US $)*	*Per capita (US $)*	*def. exp. (US $)*	*Armed forces (1991)*	*Def. as % GDP*	*Govt. type*	*Foreign debt (US$)*	*Official religion*
AFGHANISTAN	652,225	21,453, 741	3b('91)	200	NA	3,989,232	–	Transitional	2.3b('91)	Islam
ALBANIA	28,750	3,285,224	2.7b('91)	820	1.0b('91)	48,000	–	Democracy	500m('91)	None
ALGERIA	2,381,740	26,666,921	5.4b('90)	2,130	867m('92)	125,000	1.8	Limited Presidential Republic	26.4b('91)	Islam
AZERBAIJAN	86,600	7,450,787	NA	NA	NA	NA	NA		NA	None
BAHRAIN	693,15	551,513	4.0b('91)	7,500	194m('90)	105,587	6	Absolute Monarchy	1.1('89)	Islam
BANGLADESH	144,000	119,411,711	23.1b('91)	200	339m('92)	106,500	1.5	Parliamentary democracy	11.1('91)	Islam
BENIN	112,620	4,997,599	2.0b('91)	410	29m('88)	12,000	1.7	Republic	–	None
BOSNIA	51,233	4,364,000	14b('91)	NA	NA	NA	NA	Democracy	NA	None
BRUNEI	5,770	269,319	3.5b('90)	8,800	233.1m('88)	4,250	7.1	Absolute monarchy	NONE	Islam
BURKINA FASO	274,200	9,653,672	2.9b('91)	320	55m('88)	8,700	2.7	Military	962m('90)	None
CAMEROON	475,440	12,658,439	11.5b('90)	1,040	219m('90)	6,600	1.7	Presidential republic	4.9b('89)	–
CHAD	1,284,000	5,238,908	1.0b('89)	205	39m('88)	17,200	4.3	Republic	530m('90)	None
COMOROS	2,170	493,853	260m('91)	540	NA	NA	–	Republic	1.96m('91)	Islam
DJIBOUTI	22,000	390,906	340m('89)	1,000	29.9m('86)	2,770	NA	Republic	355m('90)	–
EGYPT	1,001,450	56,368,950	39.2b('91)	720	2.5m('91)	420,000	6.4	Limited presidential executive	38b('91)	Islam

ERITREA	93,679	2,614,699	NA	NA	NA	NA	NA	NA	NA	NA
GAMBIA	11,300	902,089	207m('91)	235	1.04m('90)	900	0.7	Republic	336m('90)	None
GUINEA	245,860	7,783,926	3.0b('90)	410	29m('88)	9,700	1.2	Republic	336m('90)	None
GUINEA BISAU	36,120	1,047,137	162m('89)	160	9.3m('87)	7,200	5.6	One-party republic	462m('90)	None
INDONESIA	1,919,440	195,683,531	122b('91)	630	1.7b('91)	278,000	2.0	Limited presidential executive	58.5b('90)	
IRAN	1,648,000	61,183,138	90b('91)	1,500	13b('91)	528,000	14–15	Limited presidential executive	10b('90)	Islam
IRAQ	436,245	18,445,847	35B('91)	1,940	NA	382,000	NA	Unlimited presidential executive	45b('89)	Islam
JORDAN	91,880	3,557,304	3.6b('91)	1,100	404m('90)	101,300	9.5	Absolute Monarchy	9b('91)	Islam
KAZAKHSTAN	2,717,300	17,103,927	NA	NA	NA	NA	NA	Republic	NA	None
KUWAIT	17,820	1,378,613	8.75b('91)	6,200	9.17b('92)	8,200	20.4	Absolute monarchy	9.2b('89)	Islam
KYRGHYZSTAN	198,500	4,567,875	NA	NA	NA	NA	NA	Republic	NA	None
LEBANON	10,400	3,439,115	NA	1,400	271m('92)	18,800	8.2	Republic	900m('87)	None
LIBYA	1,759,540	4,484,795	28.9b('90)	6,800	1.7b('89)	85,000	NA	Unlimited presidential executive	3.5b('91)	Islam
MALAYSIA	329,750	18,410,920	48b('91)	2,670	2.4b('92)	127,900	5	Parl. Democ.	21.3b(91)	Islam
MALDIVES	300	234,371	174m('90)	770	1.8m('84)	NA	NA	Limited presidential executive	70m('89)	Islam
MALI	1,240,000	8,641,178	2.2b('90)	265	41m('89)	7,300	2	Republic	2.2b('89)	None
MAURITANIA	1,030,700	2,059,187	1.1b('91)	535	40m('91)	11,100	4.2	Republic	1.9b('90)	Islam
MOROCCO	710,850	26,708,587	27.3b('91)	1.060	1.1b('92)	195,500	4.2	Dual executive	20b('91)	Islam
NIGER	1,267,000	8,052,945	2.4b('91)	300	27m('89)	3,200	1.3	Military executive	1.8b('90)	None

Table c.1 *continued*

Country	*Area (sq. km)*	*Population (1992)*	*GDP (US $)*	*Per capita (US $)*	*def. exp. (US $)*	*Armed forces (1991)*	*Def. as % GDP*	*Govt. type*	*Foreign debt (US$)*	*Official religion*
NIGERIA	923,770	126,274,589	30b('91)	250	300m('90)	94,500	1	Military	32b('91)	None
OMAN	212,460	1,587,581	10.6b('89)	6,925	1.73b('92)	30,400	16	Absolute monarchy	3.1b('89)	Islam
PAKISTAN	803,940	121,664,539	45.4b('91)	380	2.9b('92)	565,000	6	Parliamentary executive	20.1b('90)	Islam
QATAR	11,000	484,387	7.4b('90)	15,000	NA	7,500	NA	Absolute monarchy	1.1b('89)	Islam
SAUDI ARABIA	2,240,000*	17,050,934	104b('90)	5,800	14.5b('92)	76,500	13	Absolute monarchy	18.9b('89)	Islam
SENEGAL	196,190	8,205,058	5b('91)	615	100m('91)	9,700	2	Unlimited presidential executive	2.9b('90)	None
SIERRA LEONE	7,740	4,456,737	1.4b('91)	330	6m('88)	3,150	0.7	Military	5.72m('90)	None
SOMALIA	637,660	7,235,226	1.7b('88)	210	NA	64,500	NA	–	1.9b('89)	Islam
SUDAN	2,505,810	28,305,046	12.1b('91)	450	610M('89)	71,500	7.2	Military civilian	14.6b('91)	Islam
SYRIA	185,180	13,730,436	30b('91)	2,300	2.5b('89)	404,000	8	Unlimited presidential executive	14.6b('91)	Islam
TAJIKISTAN	143,100	5,680,242	NA	NA	NA	NA	NA	Republic	NA	None
TANZANIA	945,090	27,791,552	6.9b('91)	260	119m('89)	46,800	2	Republic	5.2b('91)	None
TUNISIA	163,610	8,445,656	10.9b('91)	1,320	520m('92)	35,000	5	Limited presidential executive	8.6b('91)	Islam
TURKEY	780,580	59,640,143	198b('91)	3,400	5.2b('92)	579,200	3.4	Limited presidential executive	49.0b('90)	None
TURKMENISIAN	488,100	3,838,108	NA	NA	NA	NA	NA	Republic	NA	None
U.A. EMIRATES	83,600	2,527,315	33.7b('89)	14,100	1.47b('89)	44,000	5.3	Monarchy	11.9b('89)	Islam

UZBEKISTAN	447,400	21,626,784	NA	NA	NA	NA	NA	Republic	2b('91)	None
YEMEN	527,970	10,394,749	5.3b('90)	545	1.06b('91)	65,000	20	Republic	5.75b('89)	Islam

Note: Figures in parenthesis refer to the year.
Sources: Derived from Central Intelligence Agency, *The World Factbook 1993–94* (New York: Brassey's (US), 1993); *The Europa World Book 1992*, 2 vols (London: Europa Publications Ltd, 1992).

Notes

1 Islam, Secularism and the Muslim World

1. The word secularism is derived from Latin *seaculum*, meaning age or generation, but in Christian Latin it came to mean the temporal world. The word 'laicism' is derived from Greek *Laos* (the people) and *laikos* (the lay). For a comprehensive account of secularism, see Eric S. Waterhouse, 'Secularism', in James Hasting (ed.), *Encyclopedia of Religion and Ethics* (Edinburgh: T.&T. Clark, 1954), Vol. xi, pp. 347–50.
2. Owen Chadwick, *The Secularization of the European Mind* (Cambridge: Cambridge University Press, 1975).
3. Irving M. Zeitlin, *Ideology and the Development of Sociological Theory* (New Jersey: Prentice-Hall Inc., 1968), pp. 3–7.
4. John Stuart Mill, *On Liberty*, cited in Chadwick, *The Secularization of the European Mind*, p. 27.
5. *Ibid.*
6. Altaf Gauhar, 'Islam and Secularism', in Altaf Gauhar (ed.) *The Challenge of Islam* (London: Islamic Council of Europe, 1978), p. 302.
7. *Encyclopedia Britannica*, 1974, Vol. 9, p. 523 cited in *Ibid.*, p. 300.
8. W.C. Smith, *Pakistan As An Islamic State* (Lahore: Ashraf, 1954), p. 49.
9. Carl Becker, *The Heavenly City of the Eighteenth Century Philosophers* (New Haven: Yale University Press, 1932), p. 31.
10. Karl Marx and Frederick Engels, *Manifesto of the Communist Party* (New York: International Publishers, 1948), p. 11.
11. Chadwick, *The Secularization of the European Mind*, p. 66.
12. Marx-Engels, *On Religion* (Moscow: Progress Publishers, 1957), p. 83.
13. Karl Marx and Frederick Engels, *Collected Works*, Vol. II (London: Lawrence and Wishart, 1975), p. 176.
14. Karl R. Popper, *The Open Society and Its Enemies*, Vol. II (London: Routledge and Kegan Paul, 1962), p. 255.
15. Alan Bullock and Oliver Stallybrass (eds), *The Harper Dictionary of Modern Thought* (New York: Harper and Row, 1977), p. 546.
16. P.B. Gajendragadkar, 'The Concept of Secularism', *Secular Democracy* (New Delhi, Weekly), Annual Number, 1970, p. 1.
17. R. Grothuysen, 'Secularism', in Edwin R.A. Seligman (ed.), *Encyclopedia of Social Sciences* (New York: Macmillan, 1954), Vol. XIII, p. 63.
18. *Ibid.*
19. Sir Muḥammad Iqbāl, *The Reconstruction of Religious Thought in Islam* (Lahore: Ashraf, 1971), p. 155.
20. Waterhouse, 'Secularism', p. 349.
21. Iqbāl, *The Reconstruction of Religious Thought in Islam*, p. 154.
22. *Ibid.*
23. See Crane Brinton, *The Shaping of Modern Thought* (New Jersey: Prentice-Hall, 1963).

24. S.M. Naqāb al-'Attās, *Islam, Secularism and the Philosophy of the Future* (London: Mansell, 1985), p. 95.
25. This is the thesis of the Belgian historian, Henri Pirenne, cited in *Ibid.*, fn 103, p. 95.
26. *Questions diplomatique et colonials*, 15 May 1901, p. 588 cited in Marwan R. Bukhary, 'Colonial Scholarship and Muslim Revivalism in 1900', *Arab Studies Quarterly*, Vol. 4, Nos 1 & 2, Spring 1982, p. 5.
27. *Ibid.*, p. 6.
28. See D.K. Hingorani, 'Education in India Before and After Independence,' *Education Forum*, Vol. 19, No. 2, 1977, pp. 218–19.
29. *Ibid.*
30. See W.A.J. Archibold, *Outlines of Indian Constitutional History* (London: Curzon Press, 1924), p. 73.
31. A. Babs Fafunwa, *History of Education in Nigeria* (London: Allen and Unwin, 1974), p. 103.
32. *Ibid.*
33. Jawaharlal Nehru, *Towards Freedom* (New York: John Day, 1941), p. 264.
34. Ismā'īl Rājī al-Farūqī, *Islamization of Knowledge; General Principles and Workplan* (Maryland: International Institute of Islamic Thought, 1982) p. 5.
35. J.N. Roseman (ed.), *International Politics and Foreign Affairs* (London: Collier Macmillan, 1969), p. 27.
36. Gauhar, 'Islam and Secularism', p. 303.

2 Politics in Islam

1. Donald Eugene Smith, *Religion and Political Development* (Boston: Little, Brown, 1970), p. 59.
2. E.E. Schattschneider, *Two Hundred Million Americans in Search of a Government* (New York: Holt, Rinehart and Winston, 1969), p. 8.
3. Bernard Crick, *In Defence of Politics* (London: Pelican Books, 1964), p. 16.
4. Aristotle, *The Ethics*, tr. J.A.K. Thomson (England: Penguin Books, 1953), p. 44.
5. See Ernest Barker, *The Politics of Aristotle* (New York: Oxford University Press, 1958), pp. 154–6.
6. Julius Gould and William L. Kolb (eds), *A Dictionary of Social Science* (New York: Free Press, 1965), p. 4.
7. William T. Bluhm, *Theories of the Political System* (Englewood Cliffs, N.J.: Prentice-Hall, 1978), p. 4.
8. Robert A. Dahl, *Modern Political Analysis* (Englewood Cliffs, N.J.: Prentice-Hall, 1970), p. 6.
9. David Easton, *The Political System* (New York: Alfred A. Knopf, 1953), p. 134.
10. Alan C. Isaak, *Scope and Methods of Political Science: An Introduction to the Methodology of Political Inquiry* (Homewood, Illinois: The Dorsey Press, 1975), p. 21.
11. See Harold Lasswell, *Politics: Who Gets What, When, How* (Cleveland: World Publishing Company, 1958).

12. Alan Bullock and Oliver Stallybrass (eds), *The Harper Dictionary of Modern Thought* (New York: Harper and Row, 1977), p. 490.
13. See Bertrand de Jouvenal, *Power: The Natural History of Its Growth*, tr. J.F. Huntington (London: Hutchinson, 1948).
14. Quoted in Bernard Crick, *In Defence of Politics*, p. 16.
15. Hamid Enayat, *Modern Islamic Political Thought* (London: Macmillan, 1982), p. 2.
16. Abul A'lā Mawdūdī, *Towards Understanding Islam*, tr. Khurshid Aḥmad (London: The Islamic Foundation, 1980), p. 88.
17. Yūsuf ibn 'Abd al-Barr al-Qurtubī, *Jami' Bayan al-Ilm wa Fadluh* (Madinah: al-Maktabah al-'Ilmīyah, n.d.), Vol. I, p. 62.
18. Ibn Qutaybah, *'Uyūn al-Akhbār*, Vol. I in Bernard Lewis (ed.), *Islam: From the Prophet Muhammad to the Capture of Constantinople* (London: The Macmillan Press, Ltd., 1976), Vol. I, p. 184.
19. G.H. Jansen, *Militant Islam* (London: Pan Books, 1979), p. 17.
20. Sir Muḥammad Iqbāl, *The Reconstruction of Religious Thought in Islam* (Lahore: Sh. Muḥammad Ashraf, 1971), p. 154.
21. See Marshall Hodgson, *The Venture of Islam: Conscience and History in A World Civilization* (Chicago: University of Chicago Press, 1974), Vol. I.
22. For a discussion of the transformation of the ideal caliphate into the dynastic rule see Mawdūdī, *Khilāfat wa Mulūkiyat* (Lahore: Idārah Tarjumān al-Qur'ān, 1975).
23. S.D.B. Goitein, *Studies in Islamic Religious and Political Institutions* (Leiden: E.J. Brill, 1968), pp. 205–6.
24. Manfred Halpern, *The Politics and Social Change in the Middle East and North Africa* (Princeton, N.J.: Princeton University Press, 1963), p. 11.
25. W.C. Smith, *On Understanding Islam: Selected Studies* (The Hague: Mouton, 1981), p. 202.
26. E.I.J. Rosenthal, *Political Thought in Medieval Islam* (Cambridge: Cambridge University Press, 1968), p. 181.
27. J.J. Saunders, *A History of Medieval Islam* (London: Routledge and Kegan Paul, 1980), p. 171.
28. See Jamīl M. Abū Naṣr, *A History of the Maghreb* (London: Oxford University Press, 1975), pp. 92–103; C.E. Bosworth, *The Islamic Dynasties* (Edinburgh: The University Press, 1967), pp. 28–31.
29. Quoted in Rosenthal, *Political Thought in Medieval Islam*, p. 39.
30. The three-fold classification of Muslim thinkers is suggested by A. K. S. Lambton, 'Islamic Political Thought' in Joseph Schacht with C.E. Bosworth (eds), *The Legacy of Islam* (London: Oxford University Press, 1974), pp. 404–24.
31. H.A.R. Gibb, 'Constitutional Organization' in Majid Khadduri and H.J. Liebesney (eds), *Law in the Middle East: Origin and Development of Islamic Law* (Washington D.C.: The Middle East Institute, 1956), pp. 12–13.
32. Ibn Khaldun, *The Muqaddimah: An Introduction to History*, tr. F. Rosenthal, ed. N.J. Dawood (Princeton, N.J.: Princeton University Press, 1981), p. 155.
33. Khurshīd Aḥmad, 'The Nature of Islamic Resurgence', in John L. Esposito

(ed.), *Voices of Resurgent Islam* (New York: Oxford University Press, 1983) pp. 219–20. *Tajdīd* means renewal, an effort to regenerate the authentic Islamic spirit, to return to the fundamental principles of Islam as found in the Qur'ān and the Sunnah.

34. The acculturationist category includes the modernists, the secularists and Westernisers. Yvonne Yazbeck Haddad, *Contemporary Islam and the Challenges of History* (Albany: State University of New York Press, 1982), pp. 7–11.
35. W.C. Smith, *Islam in Modern History* (Princeton: Princeton University Press, 1957), p. 60.
36. See Seyyed Hossein Naṣr, *Ideals and Realities of Islam* (Boston: Beacon Press, 1972).
37. E.I.J. Rosenthal, *Islam in the Modern National State* (Cambridge: Cambridge University Press, 1965), p. 89.
38. 'Alī 'Abd al-Rāziq, *al-Islām wa Uṣūl al-Ḥukm* (Beirut: al-Ḥayāt Library, 1966), p. 83.
39. *Ibid.*, p. 118.
40. *Ibid.*, p. 143.
41. *Ibid.*, pp. 12–17.
42. *Ibid.*, p. 82.
43. *Ibid.*, p. 201.
44. Enayat, *Modern Islamic Political Thought*, p. 68.
45. *Ibid.*
46. Rosenthal, *Islam in the Modern National State*, p. 100.
47. Malcolm Kerr, *Islamic Reform* (Oxford: Oxford University Press, 1966), p. 208.
48. Haddad, *Contemporary Islam and the Challenge of History*, p. 11. She identifies members of the Muslim Brotherhood as neo-normativists. To this may be added Sayyid Mawdūdī and members of the Jamā'at-e-Islāmi. The late Ismā'īl R. al-Farūqī, Sayyed Hossein Naṣr, Khurshīd Aḥmad, Nawab Ḥaider Naqvi and others also fall in this category.
49. Fazlur Rahman, 'Roots of Islamic Neo-fundamentalism', in Phillip H. Stoddard, David C. Cuthell and Margaret W. Sullivan (eds), *Change and the Muslim World* (Syracuse: Syracuse University Press, 1981), p. 35.
50. Muhammad Iqbāl, 'Presidential Address', in S.A. Vahid (ed.), *Thoughts and Reflections of Iqbal* (Lahore: Sh. Muhammad Ashraf, 1964), p. 167.
51. *Ibid.*, p. 154.
52. Enayat, *Modern Islamic Political Thought*, p. 3.
53. Cited in Rosenthal, *Political Thought in Medieval Islam*, p. 39.

3 Islamic Methodology in Political Science

1. See S.J. Eldersveld, *et al.*, 'Research in Political Behaviour', in S. Sidney Ulmer (ed.), *Introductory Reading in Political Behaviour* (Chicago: Rand McNally & Co., 1961); R.A. Dahl, 'The Behaviourial Approach in Political Science: Epitaph for a Monument to a Successful Protest', *American Political Science Review* 55 (December 1961); David Easton, 'The Current Meaning of Behaviouralism', in J.C. Charlesworth (ed.), *Contemporary Political Analysis* (New York: Free Press, 1967); Austin Ranney

(ed.), *Essays on the Behaviourial Study of Politics* (Urbana, Illinois: University of Illinois Press, 1962).

2. Neil Riemer, *The Revival of Democratic Theory* (New York: Appleton Century-Crofts, 1961), p. 1.
3. David Easton, 'The Decline of Modern Political Theory', in James A. Gould and Vincent V. Thursby (eds), *Contemporary Political Thought* (New York: Holt, Reinhart, and Winston, 1969), p. 308.
4. *Ibid.*
5. Dahl, 'The Behaviourial Approach in Political Science', p. 766.
6. This was realised even by those who earlier advocated behaviourial persuasion in politics. See Michael Haas and Henry S. Kariel (eds), *Approaches to Political Science* (California: Chandler, 1970).
7. See S.H. Naṣr, *Islam and the Plight of Modern Man* (London: Longman, 1975); also *Science and Civilization in Islam* (Cambridge, Mass: Harvard University Press, 1968).
8. See A.H.A. Nadwi, *Religion and Civilization* (Lucknow: Academy of Islamic Research, 1970), pp. 62–70.
9. For their contribution to Muslim philosophy, see M.M. Sharif (ed.), *A History of Muslim Philosophy* (Weisbaden: Otto Hassarowitz, 1963).
10. Erwin I.J. Rosenthal, *Political Thought in Medieval Islam: An Introductory Outline* (Cambridge: Cambridge University Press, 1962), p. 16.
11. al-Māturīdī in M.M. Sharif (ed.), *A History of Muslim Philosophy*, p. 263.
12. Robert Briffault, *The Making of Humanity*, cited in Muḥammad Iqbāl, *The Reconstruction of Religious Thought in Islam* (Lahore: Muhammad Ashraf, 1971), pp. 129–30.
13. Marshall B. Clinard, 'The Sociologist's Quest for Respectability', *The Sociological Quarterly* 7 (1966), pp. 399–412.
14. Irwin Deutscher, 'Words and Deeds: Social Science and Social Policy', *Social Problems* 13 (1966), p. 241.
15. See A. Yusuf 'Alī, *The Holy Qur'an: Text, Translation, Commentary* (Leicester: The Islamic Foundation, 1975), p. 1603.
16. See, for example, Bernard Crick, *In Defence of Politics* (London: Pelican Books, 1964), p. 16.
17. See Yūsuf ibn 'Abd al-Barī'al-Qurṭubī, *Jami' Bayan al'ilm wa Faḍlih* (Madinah: al Maktabah al'ilmīyah, n.d.), p. 62.
18. 'Ali ibn Muḥammad al-Māwardī, *al-Aḥkām al-Sulṭāniyah* (Cairo: 'Isa al-Babi al-Ḥalabī, 1960), p. 5.
19. Cited in Rosenthal, *Political Thought in Medieval Islam*, p. 14.
20. Qamaruddin Khan, *The Political Thought of Ibn Taymiyyah* (Lahore: Islamic Book Foundation, 1983), p. 29.
21. Sayyid Abul A'la Mawdūdī, *The Islamic Law and Constitution* tr. Khurshīd Aḥmad (Lahore: Islamic Publications, 1967), p. 248.
22. M. Iqbāl, *The Reconstruction of Religious Thought in Islam*, p. 155.
23. Ismā'īl Rajī al Farūqī, *Tawḥīd: Its Implications for Thought and Life* (Herndon, Va.: International Institute of Islamic Thought, 1982), p. 153.
24. Cited in *Ibid.*
25. See David Easton, 'The New Revolution in Political Science', *The American Political Science Review*, 63 (December 1969), pp. 1051–61.

26. Christian Bay, 'Politics and Pseudopolitics: A Critical Evaluation of Some Behavioral Literature', in Heinz Eulau (ed.), *Behavioralism in Political Science* (New York: Atherton Press, 1969), p. 117.
27. S.M. Naqīb al-'Aṭṭās, *Islam and Secularism* (Kuala Lumpur: Muslim Youth Movement of Malaysia, 1978), pp. 127–8.
28. See Ziauddin Sardar (ed.), *The Touch of Midas* (Manchester: Manchester University Press, 1984).
29. Sayyid Abul A'lā Mawdūdī, *Towards Understanding Islam*, tr. Khurshid Ahmad (London: The Islamic Foundation, 1980), p. 88.
30. F. Rosenthal, *Knowledge Triumphant* (Leiden: E.J. Brill, 1970). This work is written from an Islamic perspective and contains a mine of information concerning knowledge in Islam and lists 87 definitions as given by various Muslim scholars.
31. See al-Ghazali, *The Book of Knowledge*, tr. Nabih A. Faris (Lahore: Ashraf, 1963).
32. Sayyid Quṭb, *This Religion of Islam* (Gary, Indiana: International Islamic Federation of Student Organisations, n.d.), p. 65.
33. See Muḥsin Mahdī, *Ibn Khaldun's Philosophy of History* (Chicago: The University of Chicago Press, 1964); Franz Rosenthal (ed.), *The Muqaddimah* (Princeton, N.J.: Princeton University Press, 1967).

4 Sharī'ah: The Islamic Legal Order

1. Khurram Murad, *Sharī'ah: The Way to God* (Leicester: The Islamic Foundation, 1981), p. 3.
2. Iredell Jenkins, *Social Order and Limits of Law: A Theoretical Essay* (Princeton, N.J.: Princeton University Press, 1980), p. 35.
3. Anwar Ahmad Qadri, *Islamic Jurisprudence in the Modern World* (Delhi: Taj Company, 1986), p. 32.
4. See 'Abd al-karīm Zai dān, *al-Madkhal li-Dirasāt al-Sharī'ah al-Islamīyah* (Beirut: Muassasah Risālah, 1985), pp. 62–9.
5. Hammudah 'Abd al-'Alī, *The Family Structure in Islam* (Lagos: Islamic Publications Bureau, 1982) pp. 14.
6. S.A. A'lā Mawdūdī, *Tafhīm al Qur'ān* (Lahore: Idarah Tarjumān al-Qur'ān, 1974), Vol. IV, fn 20, pp. 486–7.
7. See Mahmūd Shaltūt, *al-Islām wa al-'Alaqāt al-Duwalīyah fī al-Salam wa al-Ḥarb* (Cairo: Al-Jami'ah al-Aẓhar, 1951), p. 5.
8. S.A. A'lā Mawdūdī, *The Islamic Law & Constitution* tr. & ed. Khurshid Ahmad (Lahore: Islamic Publications Ltd., 1967), p. 53.
9. 'al-Qurṭubī, *al-Jāmi' li-Aḥkām al-Qur'ān* (Beirut: Dar Ihyā al-Turāth al-'Arabi, 1959), Vol. 16, pp. 163–4.
10. Mawdūdī, *Islamic Law and Constitution*, p. 53.
11. See al-Qurṭubī, *Jami' li-Aḥkām al-Qur'ān*, Vol. 2, part 4, p. 43; Abu Ja'far Muḥammad ibn Jarīr al-Ṭabarī, *Jami' al-Bayān fī Tafsīr al-Qur'ān* (Beirut: Dar al-Ma'arifah, 1972), Vols 3–4, part 3, pp. 141–2.
12. S.A. A'lā Mawdūdī, *Four Basic Qur'anic Terms*, tr. Abu Asad (Lahore: Islamic Publications, 1982), pp. 93–103.
13. Fazlur Rahman, *Islam* (Chicago: Univ. of Chicago Press, 1979), p. 117. The word Sharī'ah in its various derivative forms is found in five places

in the Qur'ān, viz., 5:48; 7:163, 42:13; 42:21 and 45:18. The word *dīn* occurs 63 times whereas the word *islām*, without its derivatives, occurs five times in the Qur'ān.

14. H.A.R. Gibb and J. Kramers (eds), *Shorter Encylopaedia of Islam* (Ithaca, N.Y.: Cornell University Press, 1953), p. 524.
15. 'Abd al-Wahhāb al-Khallāf, *'Ilm Uṣūl al-Fiqh* (Kuwait: Dar al-Kuwaitiyyah, 1978) pp. 34–5.
16. Sa'īd Ramaḍān, *Islamic Law: Its Scope and Equity* (Kuala Lumpur: Muslim Youth Movement of Malaysia, 1987) p. 43.
17. G.H. Jansen, *Militant Islam* (New York: Harper & Row, 1979), p. 29.
18. Cited in A. Doi, *Sharī'ah: The Islamic Law* (London: Ṭā Hā Publishers, 1984) p. 7.
19. Jalal al-Din Abd al-Rahman al-Suyūṭī, *al-Itqān fī 'Ulūm al-Qur'ān* (Cairo: Al-Halabi Press, 1951), Vol. I, pp. 39–44.
20. Muḥammad Rashīd Riḍa, *al-Waḥy al-Muḥammadī* (Cairo: Matba'a al-Manār, 1931), p. 225.
21. See Zaydān, *al-Madkhal li-Dirāsāt al-Sharī'ah al-Islamīyah*, pp. 108–18.
22. Ibn Qayyim al-Jawzīyah cited in Ismā'īl R. al-Farūqī, *The Great Asian Religions: An Anthology* (New York: Macmillan, 1969), pp. 337–8.
23. Cited in Mawdūdī, *Islamic Law and Constitution*, p. 191.
24. Muḥammad Iqbāl, *The Reconstruction of Religious Thought in Islam* (Lahore: Muḥammad Ashraf, 1971), p. 148.
25. Khurram Murad, *Sharī'ah: The Way to God*, p. 11.
26. Abdul Ḥamīd Abū Sulaymān, *The Islamic Theory of International Relations: New Directions for Islamic Methodology and Thought* (Herndon, Va.: International Institute of Islamic Thought, 1987) p. 75. Imām ibn al-Munzir has listed 765 matters on which there exist *ijmā'*. See Imām Ibn al-Munzir, *al-ijmā'* (Beirut: Dar al-Kitāb al-'Ilmīyah, 1985).
27. Iqbal, *The Reconstruction of Religious Thought in Islam*, p. 148.
28. Sa'id Ramaḍān, *Islamic Law: Its Scope and Equity*, p. 87.
29. Iqbāl, *The Reconstruction of Religious Thought in Islam*, pp. 149–52.
30. Ismā'īl R. al-Farūqī, *Historical Atlas of the Religions of the World* (New York: Macmillan, 1974), p. 26.
31. See Mawdūdī, *Islamic Law and Constitution*, pp. 80–1.
32. Iqbāl, *The Reconstruction of Religious Thought in Islam*, p. 149.
33. *Ibid.*, pp. 173–4.
34. Ibraheem Sulaiman, 'Islamic Law and Law Reform in Nigeria' (Paper presented to the 19th Annual Conference of the Nigerian Association of Law Teachers, Ahmadu Bello University, Zaria, Nigeria, 7–10 April 1981), p. 4.
35. *Ibid.*, pp. 14–19.
36. The Qur'anic term *ma'rufat* is associated with *adl*, *ihsan* and *itā' dhi al-qurbā* (giving in charity to neighbours and near of kin). The term *munkar* is associated with *fahasha* (abominable acts).
37. Khallāf, *'Ilm Usūl al-Fiqh*, p. 84.
38. S. Parvez Manzoor, 'Quest for the Sharī'a's Past and Future', *Inquiry: Magazine of Events and Ideas*, 3 (1), January 1987, p. 35.
39. Cited in Mona Abul Faḍl, 'Community, Justice and Jihad: Elements of

the Muslim Historical Consciousness', *American Journal of Islamic Social Sciences*, 4 (1), 1987, p. 17.
40. Mawdūdī, *Islam Law and Constitution*, p. 56.
41. Anwar Ahmad Qadri, *Islamic Jurisprudence in the Modern World*, p. 81.1

5 Ummah: The Islamic Social Order

1. The two corresponding Arabic or Qur'ānic terms for community are *sha'b* and *qawm*. The word *sha'b* occurs only once in the Qur'ān and that too in its plural form *shu'ūb*, the term *qawm* has been used extensively to mean a small community or group of persons.
2. R.M. MacIver, *Community: A Sociological Study* (London: Gollanecz, 1936), pp. 22–3, 73.
3. Mabel A. Elliott and Francis E. Merrill, *Social Disorganisation* (New York: The Free Press, 1960), p. 457.
4. The term Ummah occurs in 64 places in the Qur'ān, 53 of which occurs in Makkan verses and the rest in Madinan verses. See Muhammad Fuād 'Abd al-Baqī, *al-Mu'jam al-Mufharas li-Alfāẓ al-Qur'ān al-Karim* (Turkey: Al-Maktabah al-Islamiyyah, 1984), p. 80.
5. Muḥammad Ḥamidullah, *The First Written Constitution in the World* (Lahore: Mohammad Ashraf, 1975).
6. S.D.B. Goitein, *Studies in Islamic History and Institution* (Leiden: E.J. Brill, 1968), p. 128.
7. Articles 1 and 2 of the Document, see the text in Hamidullah, *The First Written Constitution in the World*, p. 55.
8. Article 15, in *Ibid.*, p. 58.
9. Article 20b, see *Ibid.*, p. 59.
10. W. Montgomery Watt, *Muhammad at Medina* (Oxford: Clarendon Press, 1956), pp. 223, 226.
11. E.I.J. Rosenthal, *Political Thought in Medieval Islam: An Introductory Outline* (London: Cambridge University Press, 1968), p. 25.
12. Ismā'īl Rajī al-Farūqī, *Tawḥīd: Its Implications for Thought and Culture* (Herndon, Va: International Institute of Islamic Thought, 1982a), pp. 120–21.
13. Abu Ja'far Muḥammad Ibn Jarir al-Tabari, *Jami' al-Bayān fī Tafsīr al-Qur'ān*, (Beirut: Dar al-Maarifah, 1972), Vols 9–10, part 10, p. 123.
14. Abū 'Abd Allah Muḥammad ibn Aḥmad al-Qurṭubi, *Al-Jami' li-Aḥkām al-Qur'ān* (Beirut: Dar Ihya al-Turath al-Arabi, 1959), Vol. 4, part 8, p. 203.
15. *Ibid.*, Vol. 8, part 16, pp. 322–3.
16. The *hadith* is in al-Bukhāri and Muslim on the authority of Abu Mūsa quoted in Muḥammad Asad, *The Principles of State and Government in Islam* (Gibraltar: Dar al-Andalus, 1980), p. 31.
17. al-Bukhari and Muslim on the authority of Jarir ibn 'Abd Allah quoted in *Ibid.*, p. 89.
18. al-Bukhari and Muslim on the authority of 'Abd Allah ibn 'Umar quoted in *Ibid.*, p. 31.
19. Al-Farūqī, *Tawḥīd*, p. 172. The distinction between the Ummah and the political order, however, must be clearly noted; the latter is the political

dimension of the Ummah and the geographical boundaries of the two need not coincide.

20. Sayyid Abul A'lā Mawdūdī, *Witness Unto Mankind: The Purpose and Duty of the Muslim Ummah*, ed. & tr. Khurram Murad (Leicester: the Islamic Foundation, 1986), p. 27.
21. *Ibid.*, p. 29.
22. *Ibid.*, pp. 31–2.
23. al-Ṭabarī, *Jami' al-Bayān fī Tafsīr al-Qur'ān*, Vol. 2, part I, p. 6.
24. Sayid Abul A'lā Mawdūdī, *The Islamic Law and Constitution*, ed. & tr. Khurshid Ahmad (Lahore: Islamic Publications, 1967), p. 154.
25. A. Yusuf 'Alī, *The Holy Qur'ān: Text, Translation and Commentary* (Leicester: The Islamic Foundation, 1975), fn 434, p. 151.
26. Qamaruddin Khan, *The Political Thought of Ibn Taymiyyah* (Lahore: Islamic Book Foundation, 1983), pp. 123–4.
27. The migration to Madinah was preceded by two pledges or *bay'ahs* of al-'Aqabah. In the first, the Prophet (ṢAAS) met with 12 men who pledged to believe in *tawḥīd* and to adhere to standards of morality. The second *bay'ah* took place a year later with 73 men and two women. This pledge included a belief in *tawḥīd*, adherence to morality, obedience to the authority of the Prophet (ṢAAS), and obligation of the two parties for mutual support and protection as members of a single unit and total obedience in righteousness as a commitment to declare the truth. It should be noted that another *bay'ah* with six people had preceded the two mentioned above. See 'Abd al-Malik ibn Hishām, *Sīrat Sayyid al-Anām Muḥammad* (Beirut: Al-Khayat, 1967), pp. 63–8.
28. See Zakaria Basheer, *Hijra: Story and Significance* (Leicester: the Islamic Foundation, 1983), pp. 101–3.
29. Henry Siegman, 'The State and the Individual in Sunni Islam', *Muslim World*, Vol. 54 (January 1964).
30. Quoted in Muhammad Husein Haykal, *The Life of Muhammad*, tr. Ismā'īl Ragī al-Farūqī (Kuala Lumpur: Islamic Book Trust, 1993), pp. 486–7.
31. Albert Hourani, *Arabic Thought in the Liberal Age* (London: Oxford University Press, 1970), p. 5.
32. Syed Ameer 'Alī, *A Short History of The Saracens* (London, 1934), p. 403.
33. Qamaruddin Khan, *The Political Thought of Ibn Taymīyah*, p. 130.
34. E.I.J. Rosenthal, *Studia Semitica* (Cambridge: The University Press, 1971), Vol. II, p. 209.
35. Al-Farūqī, *Tawḥīd*, p. 143.
36. M.G.S. Hodgson, *The Venture of Islam: Conscience and History in a World Civilization* (Chicago: University of Chicago Press, 1974), Vol. I, pp. 75–8.
37. Hamid Enayat, *Modern Islamic Political Thought* (London: Macmillan Press, 1982), p. 112. See also Abdullah al-Ahsan, *Ummah or Nation: Identity Crisis in Contemporary Muslim Society* (Leicester: The Islamic Foundation, 1992)
38. Carlton J. Hayes, *The Historical Evolution of Nationalism* (New York: Macmillan, 1931), p. 37; Boyd C.Shafer, *Nationalism: Myth and Reality* (New York: Macmillan, 1955), p. 1; Hans Kohn, *Nationalism: Its Meaning and History* (Princeton, N.J.: Princeton University Press 1955), p. 34.

39. See Jawaharlal Nehru, *Toward Freedom* (New York: John Day, 1941).
40. See Carlton J. Hayes, *Nationalism: A Religion* (New York: Macmillan, 1960).
41. Shamloo (ed.), *Speeches and Statements of Iqbal* (Lahore: Muhammad Ashraf, 1948), p. 224.
42. Hamid Enayat, *Modern Islamic Political Thought*, p. 116.
43. Abū Dawūd, cited in Muḥammad Asad, *The Principles of State and Government in Islam*, p. 32.
44. 'Abd Allāh ibn Yazīd al-Qazwīnī ibn Majah, *Sunan ibn Majah*. Researched by Muḥammad Fuād 'Abd al-Baqī (Beirut: Dar al-Fikr wa al-Nashr, n.d.), tr. 4899/3/1373.
45. al-Farūqī, *Tawḥīd*, p. 125.
46. Sayyid Abul A'lā Mawdūdī, *Process of Islamic Revolution* (Delhi: Maktaba Jamaat-e-Islami, 1970), p. 22.
47. Hamid Enayat, *Modern Islamic Political Thought*, p. 115.
48. 'Abd al-Rahman al-Bazzāz, *Min Waḥy al-'Urūbah* (Cairo: n.d.), p. 199 cited in *ibid.*, p. 113.
49. See Sāti'al-Ḥuṣrī, *Ma hiya al-Qawmīyah?* (Beirut: Dar al-'ilm lil-Malāyīn, 1963), p. 195. See also Bassam Tibi, *Arab Nationalism: A Critical Enquiry* (New York: St. Martins Press, 1981).
50. Ismā'īl R. Al-Farūqī, 'Islam as Culture and Civilization' in *Islam and Contemporary Society* (ed.) Salem Azzam (London: Longman, 1982), pp. 143–6.
51. *Ibid.*, p. 146.
52. Hamid Enayat, *Modern Islamic Political Thought*, pp. 117–20.

6 *Khilāfah*: The Islamic Political Order

1. The reader will encounter the terms like 'political order', 'political system' and 'polity' throughout the book. These terms are used interchangeably to mean a politically organised society, a society with some kind of government. These terms replace the term 'state' which has territorial and other connotations at variance with the Islamic perspective.
2. E.I.J. Rosenthal, *Political Thought in Medieval Islam: An Introductory Outline* (Cambridge: Cambridge University Press, 1968), p. 24.
3. Aristotle, *The Politics*, tr. J.A. Sinclair (Harmondsworth, England: Penguin Books, 1962), p. 28.
4. According to one Muslim scholar, 'the dubious honour of pointing men down this road belongs (ironically in our case) to the Muslim thinker Ibn Khaldun. See Abdelwahab Al-Affendi, *Who Needs an Islamic State?* (London: Grey Seal, 1991), p. 5.
5. T. Hobbes, *Leviathan*, ed. C.B. Macpherson (Harmondsworth, England: Penguin Books, 1968), p. 161.
6. For Marxist ideas on the state, see F. Engels, *Origin of the Family, Private Property and the State* (Moscow: Progress Publishers, 1971); Karl Marx, *The 18th Brumaire* (Moscow: Progress Publishers, 1969).
7. Max Weber, 'Politics as a Vocation', in H.H. Gerth and C. Wright Mills (eds), *From Max Weber* (London: Routledge and Kegan Paul, 1970), p. 78.
8. *Ibid.*

9. *Ibid.*
10. Robert Dahl, *Who Governs?: Democracy and Power in an American City* (New Haven: Yale University Press, 1961).
11. The word *dūlah* occurs in the Qur'ān (59:7) but is used in the sense of 'circulation or making a circuit' where it is stated that wealth should not circulate among the rich only. This usage is unrelated to the word state except perhaps figuratively to imply rotation (of political authority). Ahmet Davutoğlu argues that the semantic transformation from the root *dwl* to *dawlah* occurred in three stages. First, it was used to denote the change of political power, next to denote continuity and for the ultimate political authority and, finally as nation-state. See Ahmet Davutoğlu, *Alternative Paradigms : The Impact of Islamic and Western Weltanschauung on Political Theory* (Lauhani, Maryland: University Press of America, 1994), p. 190
12. Abū Ja'far Muḥammad ibn Jarīr al-Ṭabarī, *Tarikh al-Ṭabarī*, ed. M.J. De Goeje (Leiden: E.J. Brill, 1991), Vol.1, pp. 85–115.
13. Hamid Enayat, *Modern Islamic Political Thought* (London: Macmillan Press, 1982), p. 69.
14. Majid Khadduri, 'The Nature of the Islamic State', *Islamic Culture*, Vol. 21, 1947, p. 327.
15. These concepts are defined in a legalistic format in Manzooruddin Ahmed, *Islamic Political System in the Modern Age: Theory and Practice* (Karachi: Saad, 1983), pp. 27–43.
16. 'AbdulHamid A. AbūSulaymān, *Crisis in the Muslim Mind,* tr. Yusuf Talal DeLorenzo (Herndon Va: International Institute of Islamic Thought, 1993), p. 89.
17. Muḥammad Asad, *The Principles of State and Government in Islam* (Gibraltar: Dar al-Andalus, 1980), p. 33.
18. The term *shūrā* occurs in three places in the Qur'ān in 2:233; 3:159; 42:38. Derived from *shawara, shawir* means to consult, to advice, beckon, suggest and *shūrā* refers to consultation. Both al-Ṭabarī and al-Qurṭubī are of the opinion that consultation is a bliss and favour from Allah (SWT) and that consultation is due 'in matters not revealed'. See Abū 'Abdūllāh Muḥammad ibn Aḥmad al-Qurṭubī, *Al-Jami li-Aḥkām al-Qur'an* (Beirut: Dar Ihyā al-Turāth al-'Arabī, 1958), Vol. 2, part 4, p. 249, and al-Ṭabarī, *Tafsīr*, Vol. 3–4, p. 100. It may be noted that shura was thoroughly implemented during the time of the Prophet(ṢAAS) and those of Abū Bakr and 'Umar ibn al-Khaṭṭāb. This period may act as a reference point for the correct Islamic system. The *shūrā* lost its original form during most of the period of Islamic history. Currently, *shūrā* is receiving increasing attention but not much application.
19. 'AbdulḤamīd AbūSulaymān, 'Islamization of Knowledge with Special Reference to Political Science', *American Journal of Islamic Social Sciences*, Vol. 2, No. 2, 1985, p. 285.
20. Ahmet Davutoğlu, *Alternative Paradigms*, p. 132.
21. Muḥammad Iqbāl, *The Reconstruction of Religious Thought in Islam* (Lahore: Muḥammad Ashraf, 1971), p. 155.
22. See Muhammad Hamidullah, *The First Written Constitution in the World* (Lahore: Mohammad Ashraf, 1975).

23. The Prophet (ṢAAS) commanded forces on 25 occasions although the actual fighting took place on nine occasions. See Maulanā Gauhar Raḥmān, *Islāmi Siyāsat* (Lahore: Al-Manar Book Centre, 1982), pp. 189–3.
24. For details, see al-Ṭabarī, *Tarikh al-Rusūl wa al-Mulūk* (Cairo: Dar al'Ma'ārif al-Islamīyah, 1962), Vols 3–5; S. Abul A'lā Mawdūdī, *The Islamic Law and Constitution*, ed. Khurshid Ahmad (Lahore: Islamic Publications, 1967), pp. 249–52.
25. See Al-Baqillānī, Al-Tauhid in Ibish Yusuf (ed.), *Nuṣūs al-Fikr al-Siyāsī al-Islāmī* (Beirut: Ḥayāt Press, 1966), p. 56; also Taqī al-Dīn ibn Taymīyah, *al-Siyāsah al-Shar'īyah fī Iṣlāh al-Ra'y wa al-ra'īyah* (Egypt: Dar al-Kitāb al-'Arabī, n.d).
26. Mawdūdī, *The Islamic Law and Constitution*, p. 255.
27. Two cases (of Usāmah's expedition and *ridda* or apostasy war) have often been cited of Abū Bakr having defied the 'unanimous opinion of his advisers (Mawdūdī, *Islamic Law and Constitution*, p. 246). In the case of Usamah's expedition, Abu Bakr was acting according to the established principle that the *shūrā* is not required or binding on things for which clear injunctions exist either in the Qur'ān or in the Sunnah. In permitting Usamah to proceed on his military campaign, the caliph was simply carrying out the decision of the Prophet (ṢAAS) who organised the expedition and appointed Usāmah as its commander. Abu Bakr could not, in his own words, 'fold up the flag unfurled by the Prophet himself', nor could 'dismiss a man (Usāmah) appointed by the Messenger of Allah' (cited by Dr. Majid Ali Khan, *The Pious Caliphs* (London: Diwan Press, n.d.), pp. 32–3). As for Abū Bakr's determination to fight those who apostatised and refused to pay *zakāh* in the public treasury, he did not defy the opinion of the *shūrā*. Rather he, with the help of 'Umar b. al-Khaṭṭāb who was convinced of the soundness of the caliph's stand, argued the case and won the hearts of the members of the *shūrā* and 'afterwards to his fighting the apostates.' (Muḥammad S. El-Awā, *On the Political System of the Islamic State*, Indiana: American Trust Publications, 1980, p. 5). Even Mawdudi agrees that the companions had 'ungrudgingly accepted' the caliph's decision not because of 'the right of veto of the Caliph' which, contrary to Mawdūdī's contention, he certainly did not have, but because of their 'absolute faith in his deep Islamic insight and wisdom (Mawdūdī, *Islamic Law and Constitution*, p. 246).
28. S. Waqar Ahmad Hussaini, 'Principles of Environmental Engineering Systems Planning in Islamic Culture' (Ph.D. Thesis, Faculty of Engineering, Stanford University, 1971), p. 138.
29. 'AbdulḤamīd AbūSulaymān, 'The Ummah and Its Civilizational Crisis', in I.R. Al-Farūqūi and A.O. Naseef (eds), *Social and Natural Sciences* (Jeddah: King Abdul Aziz University, 1981), p. 103.
30. Ibn Khaldūn, *The Muqaddimah: An Introduction to History*, ed. N.J. Dawood (Princeton, N.J: Princeton University Press, 1981), p. 166.
31. Jalal al-Din 'Abd al-Rahman ibn Abū Bakr al-Suyuṭī, *Tarīkh al-khulāfā* (Beirut: Dar al-Thaqafah, n.d.), p. 224.
32. John L. Esposito, *Islam and Politics* (New York: Syracuse University Press, 1991), pp. 14–15.

33. *Ibid.*, pp. 17–25.
34. *Ibid.*, p. 25.
35. Marshall G.S. Hodgson, *The Venture of Islam* (Chicago: University of Chicago Press, 1974) Vol. 3, pp. 14–15.
36. See I. Metin Kunt, 'The Latter Muslim Empires' in Marjorie Kelly (ed.), *Islam: The Religious and Political Life of a World Community* (New York: Praeger, 1984), p. 127.
37. For details of the process of disintegration of the Ottoman caliphate, see Alan R. Taylor, *The Islamic Question in Middle East Politics* (Boulder: Westview Press, 1988), pp. 23–5. For the step-wise abolition of the caliphate, see Hamid Enayat, *Modern Islamic Political Thought* (London: Macmillan Press, 1982), pp. 52–5.
38. Enayat, *Modern Islamic Political Thought*, p. 55.
39. *Ibid.*, pp. 2–4.
40. See 'Abd al-Qādir al-Baghdādī, *al-Farq bayn al-firāq* (Beirut: Dar al-Fikr, 1973); Abu Hasan Ali ibn Muhammad Al-Mawardi, *al-Aḥkām al-Sulṭānīyah* (Cairo: Matba' al-Musṭafā Babī al-Ḥalabī, 1973).
41. See Ibn Taymīyah, *Al-Siyāsah al-Shar'īyah.*
42. See Chapter 5 for details of Ummah.
43. See Chapter 7 for a discussion on the limits of obligation to the chief executive.
44. al-Mawardi, *al-Aḥkām al-Sulṭānīyah*, p. 6; also E.I.J. Rosenthal, *Political Thought in Medieval Islam*, p. 28.
45. Leonard Binder, 'Al-Ghazali's Theory of Government', *The Muslim World*, Vol. 45, No. 3 (1955), p. 236.
46. See Rosenthal, *Political Thought in Medieval Islam*, pp. 29, 40, 236.
47. Qamaruddin Khan, *The Political Thought of Ibn Taymiyyah* (Islamabad: Islamic Book Foundation, 1983), p. 184.
48. See Abul A'lā Mawdūdī, *Unity of the Muslim World* (Lahore: Islamic Publications, 1967).
49. 'AbdulḤamīd AbūSulaymān, *Crisis in the Muslim Mind*, p. 139.
50. See C. Ryder Smith, 'Theory', in *Encyclopedia of Religion and Ethics* (New York: Charles Scribner's, 1924); T.W. Arnold, *The Proceeding of Islam* (London: Constable, 1935).
51. Asad, *The Principles of State and Government in Islam*, p. 21.
52. Sayyid Abul A'lā Mawdūdī, *The Process of Islamic Revolution* (Delhi: Markazi Maktabah Jamaat-e-Islami, Hind, 1970), p. 9.
53. Asad, *The Principles of State and Government in Islam*, p. 1.
54. Sayyid Quṭb, *Ma'rakat al-Islām wa al-Rasmalīyah* (Beirut: Dār al-Shurūq, 1975), p. 66. Quoted in Yvonne Y. Haddad, 'Sayyid Qutb: Ideologues of Islamic Revival', in John L. Esposito (ed.), *Voices of Resurgent Islam* (New York: Oxford University Press, 1983), p. 71
55. The idea of a written constitution for the Islamic political system has its origin in the constitution of Madinah enacted by the Prophet (ṢAAS). In general, the Muslim rulers did not introduce written constitutions and ruled through decrees and executive orders. Contemporary scholars like Rashīd Riḍā, Mawdūdī and others advocated for a written constitution. See Mohammad Hashim Kamālī, 'Characterisitics of the Islamic State', *Islamic Studies*, Vol.32, No.1, Spring 1993, pp. 26–7.

56. Mawdūdī, *Islamic Law and Constitution*, pp. 217–19.
57. Justice Javed Iqbal, 'The Concept of State in Islam' in Mumtaz Ahmad (ed.), *State, Politics and Islam* (Indianapolis: American Trust Publications, 1986), p. 47.
58. Asad, *The Principles of State and Government in Islam*, p. 52.
59. 'Abdulrahman 'Abdulkadir Kurdī, *The Islamic State: A Study Based on the Islamic Holy Constitution* (London: Mansell, 1984), p. 90.
60. Cited in Mawdūdī, *Islamic Law and Constitution*, p. 334. See also *Niẓām-e-Ḥukūmat ke Bare Me Anṣāri kamishan Ki Report* (Islamabad: Printing Corporation of Pakistan Press, 1984), p. 16.
61. Asad, *The Principles of State and Government in Islam*, p. 40.
62. Sayyid Quṭb, *Ma'rakāt al-Islām wa al-Ra'smālīyah*, pp. 73–4.
63. See Godfrey H. Jansen, *Militant Islam* (New York: Harper and Row, 1979), p. 173.
64. Ḥasan al-Turabī, 'The Islamic State' in John L. Esposito (ed.), *Voices of Resurgent Islam* (New York: Oxford University Press, 1983), p. 243.
65. Muḥammad Iqbāl, *The Reconstruction of Religious Thought in Islam*, p. 243.
66. See Kurdī, *The Islamic State*, pp. 77–9.
67. Mawdūdī, *The Islamic Law and Constitution*, p. 230.
68. *Ibid.*, p. 334.
69. Ḥasan al-Turabī, 'The Islamic State', pp. 248–9.
70. See Kurdī, *The Islamic State*, pp. 85–7 for details.
71. Kamal A. Faruki, *The Evolution of Islamic Constitutional Theory and Practice* (Karachi: National Publishing House, 1971), pp. 72–3.
72. Ḥasan al-Turabī, 'The Islamic State', p. 249.
73. Kurdī, The Islamic State, pp. 86–7.
74. Mawdūdī, *The Islamic Law and Constitution*, p. 228.
75. *Ibid.*, pp. 347–8; *Ansari Commission Ki Report*, p. 51.
76. Asad, *The Principle of State and Government in Islam*, p. 23.
77. *Ibid.*, pp. 65–7.
78. Mawdūdī, *The Islamic Law and Constitution*, p. 241.
79. *Ibid.*, pp. 139–40.
80. *Anṣarī Kamishan Kī Report*, pp. 12–15.
81. Ḥasan al-Turabī, 'The Islamic State', p. 248.
82. *Ibid.*, p. 249.

7 *Muḥāsabah*: Accountability in Islam

1. Harold, J. Laski, *The American Democracy: A Commentary and an Interpretation* (New York: The Viking Press, 1943), p. 89.
2. R.B. McCallum (ed.), *On Liberty and Considerations on Representative Government* (Oxford: Basil Blackwell, 1948), p. 172.
3. Raoul Berger, *Impeachment: The Constitutional Problems* (Cambridge, Mass.: Harvard University Press, 1973), p. 3.
4. *Ibid.*, pp. 91, 118.
5. There are two references to the term '*ulū al-amr*' in the Qur'ān in 4:59 and 4:83. According to Ibn Manẓūr, the term refers to chiefs as well as to the knowledgeable. See Ibn Manzur, *Lisān al-'Arab*, (Cairo: Al-Muassasah

al-Miṣrīyah al-'Āmmah lil-Ta'lif wa al-Nasho, 1965) *al-'Arab*, Vol. 4, p. 31. al-Ṭabarī, al-Qurṭubī, Ibn Kathīr and others agree that the term refers to rulers, commanders as well as to the jurisprudence and knowledgeable. However, al-Qurṭubī's inclination is to use the term *'al-umarā'* for rulers and commanders reserving the term *'al-'ulamā'* for the knowledgeable in religion. He points out that 'to consult *al-'ulamā'* is a duty and complying with their counsel is an obligation'. Abu 'Abd Allah Muḥammad ibn Aḥmad al-Qurṭubī, *al-Jami' li-Aḥkām al-Qur'ān* (Beirut: Dar Iḥyā al-Turāth al-'Arabī, 1959), Vol. 3, part 5, p. 260.

6. Abū al-Qāsim Maḥmud ibn 'Umar Zamakhsharī, *al-Kashshāf* (Beirut: Dar al-Ma'arifah, n.d.) Vol. I, p. 290.
7. *Ṣahīh Muslim* (tr.), Abdul Ḥamīd Ṣiddiqī (Beirut: Dar al-'Arabī, 1971?) Vol. III, No. 4533, p. 1022.
8. *Mishkāt al-Maṣābīh* cited in A.A Mawdūdī, *Islamic Law and Constitution*, tr. & ed. Khurshid Ahmad (Lahore: Islamic Publications, 1967), p. 257. Another *ḥadīth* cited by Mawdūdī reads: 'There is no obedience for those who disobey Allah', *Ibid.*
9. *Ṣahīh Muslim*, Vol.III, No. 4634, p. 1022.
10. Cited in Muḥammad Asad, *The Principles of State and Government in Islam* (Gibraltar: Dar al-Andalus, 1981), pp. 81–2.
11. Abul A'lā Mawdūdī, 'Political Thought in Early Islam' in M. M. Sharif (ed.), *A History of Muslim Philosophy* (Weisbaden: Otto Harrasowitz, 1963), Vol. 1, p. 659.
12. Abū Muḥammad 'Abd al-Malik ibn Hishām, *al-Sīrah al-Nabawīyah*, M. al-Saqqā, I. al-Ahyari and 'Abd al-Hafiz Shalabi (eds) (Cairo: Mustafa al-Babi al-Halabi, 1375AH/1955CE), Vol. II, p. 661.
13. Ya'qūb ibn Ibrahīm Abū Yusuf, *Kitāb al-Kharāj* (Cairo: Salafīyah Press, 1352 AH), p. 14.
14. See Muḥammad ibn Sa'd, *Al-Ṭabaqāt al-Kubrā* (Beirut: Dar al-Taba'ah, 1957), Vol. II, p. 66 and Vol. III, p. 68.
15. Qamaruddin Khan, 'Al-Māwardī' in M. M. Sharif (ed.), *A History of Muslim Philosophy*, p. 729.
16. See E.I.J. Rosenthal, *Political Thought in Medieval Islam: An Introductory Outline* (Cambridge: Cambridge University Press, 1968), pp. 38–43.
17. *Ibid.*, pp. 43–51; also H.A.R Gibb, 'Constitutional Organization', in Majid Khadduri and H.J. Leibesny (eds), *Law in the Middle East* (Washington D.C.: The Middle East Institute, 1955), Vol. I, p. 45.
18. Hamid Enayat, *Modern Islamic Political Thought* (London: Macmillan Press, 1982), p. 11; also Rosenthal, *Political Thought in Medieval Islam*, p. 27.
19. al-Ghazalī, *al-Iqtiṣād fī al-i'tiqād*, quoted in Reuben Levy, *The Social Structure of Islam* (Cambridge: Cambridge University Press, 1957), p. 291.
20. Gibb, 'Constitutional Organization', p. 19.
21. A.A. Mawdūdī, 'Abū Ḥanīfah and Abū Yūsuf', in M. M. Sharif (ed.), *A History of Muslim Philosophy*, Vol.I, p. 688.
22. Abū Yūsuf, *Kitāb al-Kharāj*, Preface.
23. Ibn Jamā'ah cited in Albert Hourani, *Arabic Thought in the Liberal Age 1798–1939* (London: Oxford University Press, 1970), p. 15.
24. Rosenthal, *Political Thought in Medieval Islam*, p. 153.

25. Ṭaqī al-Dīn ibn Taymīyah, *Al-Siyāsah al-Shar'īyah fī iṣlāh al-ra'y wa al-ra'īyah* (Egypt: Dār al-Kitāb al-'Arabī, n.d.), pp. 8–9.
26. *Ibid.*, p. 127.
27. H.A.R. Gibb, 'Al-Māwārdi's Theory of the Khilāfa', *Islamic Culture*, Vol. II (July 1937), p. 294.
28. Sayyid Quṭb, *Ma'rakāt al-Islām wa al-Ra'smālīyah* (Beirut: Dar al-Shurūq, 1975), p. 73.
29. Mawdūdī, *Islamic Law and Constitution*, p. 252.
30. There exists almost unanimity among the scholars that only males, who are capable and qualified, may be elected as the chief executive. However, the recent emergence of several Muslim women as Prime Minister has given rise to a lively controversy over the eligibility of women for public positions.
31. Rosenthal, *Political Thought in Medieval Islam*, p. 153.
32. Throughout the book the terms caliphate and political order or political system have been used synonymously. I have eschewed using the term state or Islamic state. In this respect al-Faruqi's comment is worth noting:

> While we mean the state when we mention the caliphate, we should bear in mind the radical difference between the Western notion of state and Ummah. The caliphate is therefore, the Ummah as far as the Ummah's vicegerency is concerned. It is also the state as regards the Ummah's exercise of sovereignty which is constitutive, though not exclusively so, of the Ummah's vicegerency.

Ismā'īl Rajī al-Farūqī, *Tawḥīd: Its Implications for Thought and Life* (Herndon, Va: International Institute of Islamic Thought, 1982a), p. 172.
33. Cited in Dr S.A. Q. Hussaini, *Arab Administration* (Lahore: Mohammad Ashraf, 1970), p. 37.
34. W.C. Smith 'The Concept of Shari'a Among Some Mutakallimūn', in George Makdisi (ed.), *Arabic and Islamic Studies in the Honour of H. A. R. Gibb* (Cambridge, Mass.: Harvard University Press, 1965), p. 581.
35. al-Baqillānī, 'Al-Radd' in Ibish Yusuf (ed.), *Nuṣūs al-Fikr al-Siyāsī al-Islāmī* (Beirut: Hayat Press, 1966), p. 56.
36. Jamil-ul-Din Ahmad, *Iqbal's Concept of Islamic Polity* (Karachi, Pakistan Publications, n.d.), p. 21.
37. Cited in Aḥmad Ḥasan, 'The Political Role of Ijmā', *Islamic Studies*, Vol.8, No.2 (1969), p. 138.
38. 'Abdulrahman Abdulkādir Kurdī, *The Islamic State: A Study Based on the Islamic Holy Constitution* (London: Mansell, 1984), pp. 86, 89).
39. *Ibid.*, p. 87.
40. 'Alī A. Manṣūr, *Nuẓūm al-Ḥukm wa al-idārah fī Shariat al-Islamīyah wa al-qawanin al-waḍiyah* (Beirut: Dār al-Fath li al-Taba'ah wa al-Nashr, 1391AH/1971CE), p. 379.
41. Ahmad Ibn Muhammad Miskawayh, *Tajārib al-Umam*, ed. H.F. Amedroz (Baghdad: Al-Muthanna Library, 1914), Vol. II, pp. 290–1.
42. See *Constitution of the Islamic Republic of Iran* (Tehran: Ministry of Islamic Guidance, 1985).

43. Hamid Enayat, *Modern Islamic Political Thought*, p. 5.
44. See Leonard Binder, 'The Proofs of Islam: Religion and Politics in Iran', in *Arabic and Islamic Studies in Honour of Hamilton A.R. Gibb* (London: E.J. Brill, 1965), p. 121.
45. Marshall G.Hodgson, *The Venture of Islam: Conscience and History in a World Civilisation* (Chicago: University of Chicago Press, 1974), Vol. I, p. 238.
46. Maulānā Muftī Moḥammad Shafī, *Islam me Mushāwarah kī Ahmiyat* (Lahore: Idarah Islamiyat, 1976), pp. 128–30.
47. Mawdūdī, *Islamic Law and Constitution*, p. 235.
48. Muḥammad Rashīd Riḍā, *al-Khilāfah aw Al-Imāmah al-'Uzmā* (Cairo: Al-Zahra al-Islām al-'Arabī, 1988), pp. 11–13, 124–5.
49. Jalāl al-Dīn 'Abd al-Rahmān al-Sūyuṭī, *Tarīkh al-Khulafā'* (Egypt: Dār al-Maktabah, 1969), p. 436; Sir William Muir, *The Caliphate: Its Rise, Decline and Fall* (New York: AMS Press, 1975), p. 585.
50. Kyari Tijjani, 'The Force of Religion in the Conduct of Political Affairs and Interpersonal Relations in Borno and Sokoto', in *Studies in the History of Sokoto Caliphate: The Sokoto Seminar Papers* (Zaria: Ahmadu Bello University 1979), p. 271.
51. *Ibid.*
52. Riḍā, *Al-Khilāfāh aw Al-Imāmah al-'Uzmā*, p. 21.
53. Mawdūdī, *Islamic Law and Constitution*, p. 255.
54. Fazlur Rahman, 'Implementation of the Islamic Concept of State in the Pakistan Milieu', *Islamic Studies*, Vol. VI, No.3 (September 1967), p. 213.
55. *Niẓam-e-Ḥukūmat ke Bare me Ansari Kamishan kī Report*, (Islamabad: Printing Corporation of Pakistan, 4 August, 1983), pp. 18–20, 73–5.
56. Islamic Council, *A Model of An Islamic Constitution* (London: Islamic Council, 1983?), 'Introduction', p. iv.

8 *Nahḍah*: The Islamic Movement

1. Khurshid Aḥmad, 'The Nature of the Islamic Resurgence', in John L. Esposito (ed.), *Voices of Resurgent Islam*, (New York: Oxford University Press, 1983), p. 222.
2. The first considered use of the term fundamentalism is by L. Binder in *The Ideological Revolution in the Middle East* (New York: Wiley, 1964).
3. George Marsden, *Fundamentalism and American Culture* (Oxford: Oxford University Press, 1982) p. 117.
4. See William Shepard, 'Fundamentalism: Christian and Islamic', *Religion*, Vol. 17 (1987), p. 356.
5. See, among others, Hamid Enayat, *Modern Islamic Political Thought* (London: Macmillan Press, 1982); Fazlur Rahman, 'Roots of Islamic Neo-Fundamentalism', in Philip H. Stoddard, David C. Cuthell (eds), *Change and the Islamic World*, Syracuse: Syracuse University Press, 1981); Bruce B. Lawrence, *Defenders of God: The Fundamentalist Revolt Against the Modern Age* (San Francisco: Harpersan Francisco, 1989).
6. Bruce B. Lawrence, 'Muslim Fundamentalist Movements: Reflections Towards a New Approach', in Barbara Freyer Stowasser (ed.), *The Islamic*

Impulse (London: Croom Helm, 1987) pp. 32, 31.

7. John O. Voll, 'Fundamentalism in the Sunni Arab World: Egypt and the Sudan', in Martin E. Marty and R. Scott Appleby (eds), *Fundamentalism Observed* (Chicago: University of Chicago Press, 1991), p. 347.
8. Ismā'īl al-Farūqī, 'Islamic Renaissance in Contemporary Society', *Al-Ittiḥād*, 15 (4) (October 1978), p. 15.
9. *Ibid.*, p. 16.
10. For modernisation perspective, see Daniel Lerner, *The Passing of Traditional Society: Modernising the Middle East* (Glencoe: The Free Press, 1958); Manfred Halpern, *The Politics of Social Change in the Middle East and North Africa* (Princeton, N.J. Princeton: University Press, 1963); Karl Deutsch, 'Social Mobilization and Political Development', *American Political Science Review*, LV (3) (Sept. 1961). For the latter view see Fouad Ajami, *The Arab Predicament: Arab Political Thought and Practice Since 1967* (New York: Cambridge University Press, 1981). A similar perspective is assumed in Michael Curtis (ed.), *Religion and Politics in the Middle East* (Boulder: Westview Press, 1981).
11. Khomeini, *Islam and Revolution: Writings and Declarations of Imam Khomeini* (ed.), Hamid Algar (Berkeley: Mizan Press, 1981), p. 327.
12. Cited in A. Rashid Moten, 'Pure and Practical Ideology: The Thought of Mawlana Mawdūdī', *Islamic Quarterly*, 18(1984), p. 218.
13. Cited in *Ibid.*
14. See John L. Esposito, *Islam and Politics* (New York: Syracuse University Press, 1984), pp. 102–103.
15. Cited in B.G. Martin, *Muslim Brotherhoods in Nineteenth Century Africa* (Cambridge: Cambridge University Press, 1976), p. 28. See also A. Rashid Moten, 'Political Dynamism of Islam in Nigeria', *Islamic Studies*, 26 (2) (Summer 1987).
16. Quoted in John O.Voll, 'The Sudanese Mahdi: Frontier Fundamentalist', *International Journal of Middle East Studies*, 10 (1979), p. 159.
17. Hamid Algar, *The Roots of the Islamic Revolution* (London: The Open Press, 1983), p. 9.
18. See Sayyid Abul Ḥasan 'Alī Nadwī, *Haḍrat Mawlānā Moḥammad Ilyās awr Unkī Dīnī Da'wat* (Lucknow: Tanweer Press, 1960); M.A. Haq, *The Faith Movement of Mawlana Muhammad Ilyas* (London: George Allen and Unwin, 1972).
19. Godfrey Jansen, 'Islam in Asia Towards an Islamic Society', *The Economist*, 4 September 1982, p. 54.
20. Nadwī, *Haḍrat Mawlana Muhammad Ilyas*. . . . . p. 269.
21. Mohammad Ayub Qadri, *Tablighī Jamā'at Kā Tarīkhī Jā'izah* (Karachi: Maktabah Muawiyah, 1971), pp. 92–3.
22. Maulana Wahiduddin Khan, *Dīn Kya Hai?* (Delhi: Maktabah al-Risalah, n.d.), p. 26.
23. Maulana Wahiduddin Khan, *'Aqliāt-e-Islam* (Delhi: Maktabah al-Risalah, n.d), pp. 4–5.
24. E.I.J. Rosenthal, *Islam in the Modern National State* (Cambridge: Cambridge University Press, 1965), p. 247.
25. A.A. Mawdūdī, *Tafhimul Qur'ān* (Lahore: Idarāh Tarjumanul Qur'an, 1973), Vol. I, p. 33.

26. Quoted in Maryam Jameelah, *Islam in Theory and Practice* (Lahore: Mohammad Yusuf Khan, 1978), p. 334.
27. For the best single-volume study of Iran see Nikkie Keddie, *Roots of Revolution: An Interpretive History of Modern Iran* (New Haven: Yale University Press, 1981).
28. *Imam* Khomeini, *Islam and Revolution. . . .*, p. 14.
29. *Ibid.*, p. 37.
30. *Ibid.*, p. 60.
31. *Ibid.*, p. 28.
32. *Ibid.*, p. 37.
33. Nikki R. Keddie, *Iranian Revolution and Islamic Republic* (U.S: Woodrow Wilson Centre, 1982), p. 13.
34. Khomeini, *Islam and Revolution . . .*, p. 327.

Select Bibliography

'Abdalātī, Ḥammūdah, *The Structure of the Family in Islam*, Indianapolis: American Trust Publications, 1976.

Abdul Rauf, Muhammad, *The Concept of Islamic State: With Particular Reference to Treatment of Non-Muslim Citizens*, Kuala Lumpur: Islamic Affairs Division, Prime Minister's Dept., 1988.

Abū Fāris, Muḥammad Abū al-Qādir, *Al-Niẓām al-Siyāsi Fī al-Islām*, Kuwait: al-Ittihīd al-Islamīyah al-Alamīyah, 1984.

Abul Faḍl, Mona, 'Community, Justice and Jihad: Elements of the Muslim Historical Consciousness', *American Journal of Islamic Social Sciences*, Vol. 4, No.1, 1987.

Abul Faḍl, Mona, *Islam and the Middle East: The Aesthetics of a Political Inquiry*, Herndon, Va: The International Institute of Islamic Thought, 1990.

AbūSulaymān, 'AbdulḤamīd A., *The Islamic Theory of International Relations: New Directions for Islamic Methodology and Thought*, Herndon, Va: The International Institute of Islamic Thought, 1987.

AbūSulaymān, 'AbdulḤamīd A., *Crisis in the Muslim Mind.* Yusuf Talal DeLorenzo. (tr) Herndon, Va: The International Institute of Islamic Thought, 1993.

Abū Yusuf, Ya'zūb ibn Ibrahīm, *Kitāb al-Kharāj*, Cairo: Matba'ah Bulaq, 1302 AH.

al-'Ādah, S. Fawq, *A Dictionary of Diplomacy and International Affairs*, Beirut: Maktabah Lebanon, 1974.

'Afīfī, Muḥammad al-Ṣādiq, *Al-Mujtama' al-Islāmī Wa Uṣūl al-Ḥukm*, Cairo: Dar al-'Itiṣām, 1980.

Ahmad, Aziz, *Islamic Modernism in India and Pakistan, 1857–1964*, London: Oxford University Press, 1967.

Ahmad, Fuad Abd al-Mun'im, *Mabda' al-Musāwah Fī al-Islām Ma'a al-Muqāranah 'bi al-Dimuqrātīyah al-Ḥadithah*, Cairo: Muassasah al-Thaqafah al-Jam'iyyah, 1971.

Ahmad, Jamaluddin. *Speeches and Writings of Mr. Jinnah*, Lahore: Muhammad Ashraf, 1952.

Aḥmad, Khurshīd, *Islam: Its Meaning and Message*, Iran: Centre of Islamic Studies, 1978.

Aḥmad, Khurshīd, *Proportional Representation and the Revival of Democratic Process in Pakistan*, Islamabad: Institute of Policy Studies, 1983.

Aḥmad, Muhammad 'Abd al-Karīm, *Al-Milāl Wa al-Niḥāl*, Cairo: Matba'ah Muṣtafa Babi al-Halabi, 1968.

Ahmad, Mumtaz, (ed.) *State, Politics and Islam*, Indianapolis: American Trust Publication, 1986.

Ahmed, Manzooruddin, 'Islamic Aspects of the New Constitution of Pakistan', *Islamic Studies*, Vol. ii, No. 2, June, 1963.

Ahmed, Manzooruddin, *Pakistan: The Emerging Islamic State*,. Karachi: Allies Book Corporation, 1966.

Ahmed, Manzooruddin, 'The Political Role of the 'Ulama in the Indo-Pakistan Sub-Continent', *Islamic Studies*, Vol. vi, No. 4.
December, 1967.
Ahmed, Manzooruddin, *Islamic Political System in the Modern Age: Theory and Practice*, Karachi: Saad, 1982.
Akhtar, Shabbir, *A Faith for All Seasons: Islam and the Challenge of the Modern World*, Chicago: Ivan R. Dee, 1990.
al-Aḥsan, 'Abdullāh. *The Organisation of the Islamic Conference*, Herndon: The International Institute of Islamic Thought, 1988.
al-Aḥsan, 'Abdullāh, *Ummah or Nation: Identity Crisis in Contemporary Muslim Society*, Leicester: The Islamic Foundation, 1992.
al-Albānā, Naṣir al-Dīn. *Min Silsilah al-Ḍa'ifah Wa al-Mauḍū'ah*, Damascus: Dar al-Qur'an al-Karim, 1384 AH.
al-'Attās S.M. Naqīb, *Islam, Secularism and the Philosophy of the Future*, London: Mansell, 1985.
'Alī, 'Abdullah Yusuf, *The Holy Qur'ān: Text Translation and Commentary*, Leicester: The Islamic Foundation, 1975.
'Alī, Jawād, *Al-Mufaṣṣal Fī al-Tarīkh al-'Arab Qabla al-Islām*, Beirut: Dar al-Fikr, 1970.
Alter, Peter, *Nationalism*, New York: Edward Arnold, 1989.
al-Alusi, Shihab al-Dīn Mahmud al-Baghdadī, *Rūḥ al-Ma'āni Fī Tafsīr al-Qur'ān al-'Aẓīm Wa al-Sab'y al-Mathānī*, Cairo: Idarah al-Tiba'ah al-Munīrah, 1965.
al-Andalusi, Ibn Haẓm al-Ẓahirī. *Al-Faṣl Fī al-Milāl Wa Aḥwa' al-Nihāl*, Cairo: Maktabah al-Salām al-'Alamīyah, n.d.
al-Anṣarī, 'Abd al-Ḥamīd Ismā'īl, *Al-Shūrā Wa Atharuhā Fī al-Dīmuqrātīyah*. Beirut: Manshurah al-Maktabah al-Misriyyah, 1980.
al-'Arabīyah, Jama'ah al-Dawal, *Wathā'iq Wa al-Nusūs Dasatīr al-Bilād al'Arabīyah*, Cairo: Ma'had al-Dirāsah al-'Arabīyah al-'Alīyah, 1955.
Arnold, T.W., *The Caliphate*, London: Routledge & Kegan Paul, 1965.
Aristotle, *The Ethics*, Baltimore: Penguin Books, 1973.
Aristotle, *The Politics*, tr. J. A. Sinclair, Baltimore: Penguin Books, 1975 [1962].
Asad Muḥammad, *The Principles of State and Government in Islam*, Gibraltar: Dar al-Andalus, 1980.
'Audah, 'Abd al-Qādir, *Al-Islām Bayna Jahl Abnā'ihi Wa'uz 'Ulamā'ih*, Beirut: Muassasah al-Risalah, n.d.
'Audah, 'Abd al-Qadin, *Al Tashri' al-Jana'i al-Islami*, Alexandria: Mansha'ah al-Ma'arif, 1974.
Ayoob, Mohamed. *The Politics of Islamic Reassertion*, London: Croom Helm, 1981.
Ayubi, Nabih, N.M., *Political Islam: Religion and Politics in the Arab World*, New York: Routledge, 1991.
'Azzām, 'Abd al-Raḥmān, *The Eternal Message of Muhammad*, New York: The Devin Andair Company, 1964.
al-Badawi, Ismā'īl, *Mabda' al-Shūrā Fī al-Sharī'ah al- Islamīyah*, Cairo: Dar al-Fikr al-'Arabi, 1981.
al-Baghdādī, 'Abd al-Qādir ibn Ṭāhir. *Al-Farq Bayn al-Firāq*, Beirut: Dar al-Fikr, 1973.

al-Balādhūrī, Aḥmad ibn Yaḥyā, *Futūḥ al-Buldān*, Beirut: Dar al-Nashr Lil Malāyīn, 1957.

Basheer, Zakaria. *Hijra: Story and Significance*, Leicester: The Islamic Foundation, 1983.

Bay, Christian, 'Politics and Pseudopolitics: A Critical Evaluation of Some Behavioral Literature', in Heinz Eulau (ed.), *Behavioralism in Political Science*, New York: Atherton Press, 1969.

al-Bayātī, Munīr Ḥamīd, *Al-Dawlah al-Qanunīyah Wa al-Niẓām al-Siyāsī al-Islāmī,* Baghdad: Dar al-'Arabīyah Lil-Tiba'ah, 1979.

Bluhm, William. T., *Theories of the Political System*, Englewood Cliffs, N.J.: Prentice-Hall, 1978.

Boyd, C. Shafer, *Faces of Nationalism: New Realities and Old Myths*, New York: Macmillan, 1972.

Burns, J.H., *The Cambridge History of Medieval Political Thought*, Cambridge: Cambridge University Press, 1988.

al-Dabbūsi, Ṣalah al-Dīn, *Al-Khilāfah: Tawliyatuh' Wa 'Azluh*, Cairo: Muassasah al-Thaqafah al-Islamiyyah, 1965.

Dahl, Robert A., *Modern Political Analysis*, Englewood Cliffs N.J.: Prentice Hall, 1970.

Dahl, Brobert A., *Who Governs?: Democracy and Power in an American City*, New Haven: Yale University Press, 1961.

Davutoğlu, Ahmet, *Alternative Paradigms: The Impact of Islamic and Western Weltanschauungs on Political Theory*, Lanham, Maryland: University Press of America, 1994.

De Santillana, David, 'Law and Society', in Sir Thomas Arnold and Alfred Guillaume (eds), *The Legacy of Islam*, London: Oxford University Press, 1968.

Deiranieh, Akran Roslan, *The Classical Concept of State in Islam*, Washington D.C.: Howard University Press, 1975.

Deutsch, Karl W., *Contemporary Political Science: Toward Empirical Theory*, New York: Columbia University Press, 1967.

Ḍiyā al-Dīn, Muḥammad, *Al-Naẓarīyah al-Siyāsīyah al-Islāmīyah*, Cairo: Dār al-Ma'ārif, 1969.

Doi, 'Abdurrahmān, *Sharī'ah: The Islamic Law*, London: Ta Ha Publishers, 1984.

Donahue, John J. and John L. Esposito (eds), *Islam in Transition: Muslim Perspectives*, New York: Oxford University Press, 1982.

al-Dūrī, Gahtan 'Abd al-Raḥmān, *Al-Shūrā Bayn al-Naẓarīyah Wa al-Taṭbīq*, Baghdad: Matba'ah al-Ummah, 1978.

Easton, David, *The Political System*, New York: Alfred A. Knopf, 1953.

El-Awa, Muhammad. S., *On the Political System of the Islamic State*, Indiana: The American Trust Publications, 1980.

Elwan, Shwikar lbrahim, *Constitutional Democracy and Islam: A Comparative Study*, U.S.A: Emory University, 1971.

Embree, Ainslie T., *Utopias in Conflict: Religion and Nationalism in Modern India*, Berkeley: University of California Press, 1990.

Enayat, Hamid, *Modern Islamic Political Thought*, London: Macmillan Press, 1982.

Esposito, John L., *Islam and Politics*, New York: Syracuse University Press, 1991.

Esposito, John L. (ed.), *Voices of Resurgent Islam*, New York: Oxford University Press, 1983.

Fāḍil, Muḥammad Zakī, *Foundations of Arabic-Islamic Political Thought*. Baghdad: Ministry of Culture and Guidance, 1964.

al-Fārābī Abū Naṣr, *Fī Ārā' Ahl al-Madīnah al-Fāḍilah*, Friedrich Dicterici (ed.), Leiden: E.J. Brill, 1982 .

al-Fārabi Abū Naṣr, *Kitāb al-Siyāsah al-Madanīyah*, Hyderabad: n.p., 1346 AH.

Faruki, Kemal A., *The Evolution of Islamic Constitutional Theory and Practice*, Karachi: National Publishing House, 1971.

al-Farūqī, Ismā'īl R., *Tawḥīd: Its Implications for Thought and Life*, Herndon, Va: International Institute of Islamic Thought, 1982a.

al-Farūqī, Ismā'īl R., *Islamization of Knowledge: General Principles and Workplan*, Maryland: International Institute of Islamic Thought, 1982b.

Gibb, H.A.R., 'Constitutional Organization', in Majid Khadduri and H.J. Leibesny (eds), *Law in the Middle East*, Washington D.C.: The Middle East Institute, 1955.

Goitein, S.D.B., *Studies in Islamic Religions and Political Institutions*, Leiden: E.J. Brill, 1968.

Haddad, Yvonne Yazbeck. *Contemporary Islam and the Challenge of History*, Albany: State University of New York Press, 1982.

Halpern, Manfred, *The Politics of Social Change in the Middle East and North Africa*, Princeton, N.J.: Princeton University Press, 1963.

Hamidullah, Muhammad, *al-Wathā'iq al-Siyāsīyah lil-'Ahd al-Nabawīyah Wa al-Khilāfah*, Cairo: Maṭba'ah Lujnah al-Ta'līf Wa al-Tarjamah, 1956.

Hamidullah, Muhammad, *Muslim Conduct of State*, Lahore: Muḥammad Ashraf, 1973.

Hasan, Ibrāhīm Hasan, *Tārīkh al-Islām*, Cairo: Maktabah al-Nahḍah, 1964.

Hitti, Philip K., *Makers of Arab History*, New York: Harper & Row, 1971.

Hodgson, Marshall, S.G., *The Venture of Islam: Conscience and History in a World Civilization*, 3 Vols, Chicago: University of Chicago Press, 1974.

Hourani, Albert, *Arabic Thought in the Liberal Age 1798–1939*, London: Oxford University Press, 1970.

Ibn al-'Arabī, Abū Bakr Muḥammad ibn 'Abd Allah, *Aḥkām al-Qur'ān*, Cairo: Maṭba'ah al-Babī al-Halabī, 1958, Vol. 1.

Ibn Hāshim, 'Abd al-Malik. *Sirah al-Nabawīyah*, Cairo: Maṭba'ah Muṣṭafā Babī al-Halabī, 1936, Vol. 4.

Ibn Isḥāq, *The Life of Muhammad: A Translation of Ishaq's Sīrat Rasūl Allāh*, tr. Alfred Guillaume, London: Oxford University Press, 1967.

Ibn Kathīr, 'Imad al-Din Abu al-Fidā' Ismā'īl, *Tafsīr al-Qur'ān al-'Aẓīm*, Beirut: Dar Iḥyā al-Turāth al-'Arabī, 1968.

Ibn Khaldūn, 'Abd al-Raḥmān, *The Muqaddimah: An Introduction to History*, tr. F. Rosenthal, N.J. Dawood (ed.), Princeton, N.J.: Princeton University Press, 1981.

Ibn Manẓūr, Jamāl al-Dīn Muḥammad ibn Mukarram, *Lisān al-'Arab*, Cairo: Al-Muassasah al-Miṣrīyah al-'Ammah Lil-Ta'līf wa al-Nashr, 1965.

Ibn Taimīyah, Taqī al-Dīn Aḥmad, *Siyāsah al-Shār'īyah Fī Iṣlāḥ al-Rā'ī Wa al- Ra'īyah*, Cairo: Matba'ah Babī al-Halabī, 1958.

Iqbāl, Muḥammad, *The Reconstruction of Religious Thought in Islam*, Lahore: Muḥammad Ashraf, 1971.

Ismael, Tareq Y. and Ismael, Jacqueline S., *Government and Politics in Islam*, New Delhi: CBS Publishers, 1991.
Jansen, G.H., *Militant Islam*, London: Pan Books, 1979.
Jenkins, Iredell, *Social Order and Limits of Law: A Theoretical Essay*, Princeton, N.J.: Princeton University Press, 1980.
Kamāl, Muṣṭafā, *Sharḥ al-Qānūn al-Dustūrī*, Beirut: Dar al-Fikr, 1975.
Kamali, Mohammad Hashim, *Principles of Islamic Jurisprudence*, Cambridge: Islamic Texts Society, 1992.
Kamali, Mohammad Hashim, 'Characteristics of the Islamic State', *Islamic Studies*, Vol. 32, No. 1, Spring, 1993.
Khadduri, Majid, *Law in the Middle East*, Washington D.C.: Middle East Institute, 1955.
Khadduri, Majid, *War and Peace in the Law of Islam*, Baltimore: The Johns Hopkins University Press, 1957.
Khadduri, Majid, *The Islamic Conception of Justice*, Baltimore: The Johns Hopkins University Press, 1984.
al-Khalidī, Maḥmūd, *al-Shūrā*, Oman: Maktabah al-Muhtasib, 1984.
al-Khāliq, 'Abd al-Raḥmān, *al-Shūrā Fī Ẓilli al-Niẓām al-Ḥukm al-Islāmī*, Kuwait: Dar al-Salafīyah, 1975.
al-Khallāf, 'Abd al-Wahhāb, *'Ilm Uṣūl al-Fiqh*, Kuwait: Dar al-Kuwaytīyah, 1978.
Khan, Qamaruddin, *The Political Thought of Ibn Taymīyah*, Lahore: Islamic Book Foundation, 1983.
al-Khātib, Nu'man Aḥmed, 'Islamic Thought and Political Parties', *Islamic Order Quarterly,* September, Vol. 10, No. 1, 1988.
al-Khatib, Zakariya 'Abd al-Mun'im, *Niẓām al-Shūrā Fī al-Islām Wa al-Niẓam al-Dimuqraṭīyah al-Mu'āsirah*, Cairo: Dar al-Fikr al-'Arabī, 1985.
Kohn, Hans, *Nationalism: Its Meaning and History*, Princeton, N.J.: Princeton University Press, 1955.
Kurdi, Abdulrahman Abdulkadir, *The Islamic State: A Study Based on the Islamic Holy Constitution*, London: Mansell, 1984.
Lambton, A.K.S., *State and Government in Medieval Islam*, Oxford: Oxford University Press, 1981.
Lemberg, Eugen, *Nationalism*, Reinbek: Hutchinson, 1964.
Lerche, Charles O., *The Principles of International Politics*, London: Oxford University Press, 1960.
Levy, Reuben, *The Social Structure of Islam*, Cambridge: Cambridge University Press, 1957.
MacDonald, Cameron, *Western Political Theory*, New York: Harcourt, 1968.
al-Māwardī, Abū ibn Muḥammad, *al-Aḥkām al-Sulṭānīyah Wa al-Wilāyah al-Dīnīyah*, Cairo: Matba'ah al-Muṣṭafā Babī al-Ḥalabī, 1973.
Mawdūdī, Abul A'lā, *Human Rights in Islam*, Leicester: The Islamic Foundation, 1979.
Mawdūdī, Abul A'lā, *The Islamic Law and Constitution*, tr. and ed. Kurshid Ahmad, Lahore: Islamic Publications, 1967.
Mawdūdī, Abul A'lā, *Khilāfat wa Mulūkiyat*, Lahore: Idārah Tarjumān al-Quan, 1975.
Mawdūdī, Abul A'lā, *Four Basic Qur'anic Terms*, tr. Abū Asad, Lahore: Islamic Publications, 1982.

Mawdūdī, Abul A'lā, *Witnesses Unto Mankind: The Purpose and Duty of the Muslim Ummah*, tr. and ed. Kurram Murad, Leicester: The Islamic Foundation, 1986.

Muḥammad Naqvī, 'Alī, *Islam and Nationalism*, Tehran: Propagation Organisation, 1984.

al-Munīfī, 'Abd al-Ḥamīd, *The Islamic Constitutional Theory*, Virginia: University of Virginia, 1973.

Murad, Khurram, *Sharī'ah: The Way of Justice*, Leicester: The Islamic Foundation, 1981.

Murad, Khurram, *Sharī'ah: The Way to God*, Leicester: The Islamic Foundation, 1981.

Mutawalli, 'Abd al-Ḥamīd, *Mabādi' al-Ḥukm Fī al-Islām*, Alexandria: Manshaah al-Ma'arif, 1974.

Naṣr, Seyyed Ḥossein, *Ideals and Realities of Islam*, Boston: Beacon Press, 1972.

Naṣr, Seyyed Ḥossein, *Islamic Life and Thought*, Albany, N.Y.: State University of New York Press, 1981.

al-Nawawīyah, Yaḥyā, *Al-Arba'in al-Nawawīyah*, Lagos: Academic Press, 1979.

Pullapilly, Cyriac K. (ed.), *Islam in the Contemporary World*, Notre Dame, Ind.: Cross Roads Books, 1980.

Qadri, Anwar Ahmad, *Islamic Jurisprudence in the Modern World*, Delhi: Taj Company, 1986.

al-Qaraḍāwī, Yusuf, *al-Ḥalāl wa al-Ḥarām fī al-Islām*, Beirut: al-Maktabah al-Islami, 1973.

al-Qasimī, Ẓafar, *Niẓām al-Ḥukm fī al-Sharī'ah wa al-Tarīkh*, Beirut: Dar al-Nafa'is, 1974.

al-Qurṭubī, Abū 'AbdAllah Muḥammad ibn Aḥmad, *Al-Jami' li-Aḥkām al-Qur'ān*, Beirut: Dar Ihya al-Turath al-Arabi, 1959.

Quṭb, Sayyid, *Social Justice in Islam*, tr. John Hardice, New York: Octagon Press, 1974.

Quṭb, Sayyid, *Ma'rakāt al-Islām wa al-Ra'smālīyah*, Beirut: Dar al-Shurūq, 1975.

Quṭb, Sayyid, *Fī Ẓilāl al-Qur'ān*, Beirut: Dar al-Shurūq, 1979.

Rahman, Fazlur, *Islam*, Chicago: University of Chicago Press, 1979.

Rahman, Fazlur, *Islam in Modernity: The Transformation of an Intellectual Tradition*, Chicago: University of Chicago Press, 1982.

Raḥmān, Maulana Gauhar, *Islāmī Siyāsat*, Lahore: Al-Manār Book Centre, 1982.

Ramaḍān, Sa'īd, *Islamic Law: Its Scope and Equity*, Kuala Lumpur: Muslim Youth Movement of Malaysia, 1987.

al-Rāziq, 'Alī 'Abd, *al-Islām wa Uṣūl al-Ḥukm*, Beirut: Al-Hayat Library, 1966.

Rida, Muḥammad Rashīd, *al-Wahy al Muḥammadī*, Cairo: Matba'ah al-Manār, 1931.

Rosenthal, E.I.J., *Islam in the Modern National State*, Cambridge: Cambridge University Press, 1965.

Rosenthal. E.I.J., *Political Thought in Medieval Islam: An Introductory Outline*, Cambridge: Cambridge University Press, 1968.

al-Ṣa'īdī, 'Abd al-Muta'āl, *Min Ayna Nabda'*, Cairo: Matba'ah al-Khānjī, 1966.

al-Ṣa'īdī, Ḥazīm A., *al-Naẓarīyah al-Islamīyah fī al-Dawlah*, Cairo: Dar al-Nahdah al-Arabiyyah, 1977.

Sardar, Ziauddin, *Islamic Futures: The Shape of Ideas to Come*, New York: Mansell, 1985.

Smith, Donald Eugène, *Religion and Political Development*, Boston: Little Brown, 1970.

Smith, Wilfred C., *Islam in Modern History*, Princeton, N.J.: Princeton University Press, 1957.

Sharif, M. Mohammed (ed), *A History of Muslim Philosophy*, Weisbaden: Otto Hassarowitz, 1963.

Suleiman, Ibraheem, 'The Sharī'ah and the Challenge of Our Time, in 'Abdullah Omar Naseef (ed.), *Today's Problems, Tomorrow's Solutions*, London: Mansell, 1988.

al-Ṣuyūtī, Jalāl al-Dīn 'Abd al-Raḥmān ibn Abū Bakr, *al-Itqān fī 'Ulūm al-Qur'ān*, Cairo: Al-Halabī Press, 1951.

al-Ṭabarī, Abū Ja'far Muḥammad ibn Jarīr, *Tarīkh al-Rusūl wa al-Mulūk*, Cairo: Dar al-Ma'arif al-Islamīyah, 1962.

al-Ṭabarī, Abū Ja'far Muḥammad ibn Jarīr, *Jami' al-Bayān fī Tafsīr al-Qur'ān*, Beirut: Dar al-Ma'arifah, 1972.

Voll, John Obert, *Islam: Continuity and Change in the Modern World*, Boulder, Co.: Westview Press, 1982.

Watt, William Montgomery, *Muhammad at Medina*, London: Oxford University Press, 1956.

Watt, William Montgomery, *The Formative Period of Islamic Thought*, Edinburgh: Edinburgh University Press, 1973.

Weiner, Myron and La Palombara, Joseph, *Political Parties and Political Development*, Princeton, N.J.: Princeton University Press, 1972.

Yūsuf, Ibish (ed.), *Nusus al-Fikr al-Siyasi al-Islami*, Beirut: Hayat Press, 1966.

Yūsuf, Yaqub ibn Ibrāhīm Abū, *Kitāb al-Kharāj*, Cairo: Salafīyah Press, 1352 AH.

Zaydān, 'Abd al-Karīm, *Aḥkām al-Dhimmīyīn wa al-Musta'manīn fī al-Dār al-Islām*, Baghdad: Matba'ah al-Sha'b, 1982.

Zaydāh, 'Abd al-Karīm, *Role of State and Individual in Islam*, Delhi: Hindustan Publications, 1983.

Zaydān, 'Abd al-Karīm, *Al-Madkhal li Dirāsāt al-Sharī'ah al-Islāmīyah*, Beirut: Muassasah Risalah, 1985.

Index

Note: Arabic names that begin with the definite article *al-* are alphabetised under the part of the name following the article.

'Abbasīds 22, 60, 75, 93, 110, 118, 121
'Abd al-Malik ibn Marwān 117
'Abd al-Rāziq, Alī 25–6, 27–8
'Abduh, Muḥammad 25, 27
Abū Bakr 72, 91–2, 97, 110
Abū Ḥanīfah 55, 112
Abū Sulaymān, 'AbdulḤamīd 89–90, 98–9
Abū Ya'lā 97
Abū Yusuf 112
Accountability 107
  see also Caliphs, qualifications and requirements of; Impeachment
Acculturationism, *see* Muslims, westernised; Westernisation
'Adalah, *see* Justice
Afghanī, Jamal al-Din 25
Afghanistan 36, 37, 128
Africa 11, 12, 14, 130–1
Ahl al-ḥall wa-al-'aqd 101, 121–2, 141
Ahl al-Kitāb 65, 141
  see also Jews
Aḥmad, Khurshid 25
Algar, Hamid 136
Algeria 13, 16
Alī, Ameer 75
Alī, A. Yūsuf 70
'Alī ibn Abī Ṭālib 71–2, 92, 97, 110, 117, 119–20, 137
'Alī ibn 'Īsā 118
Aliyu Baba 121–2
Allah 6, 19–20, 28, 40–1
  party of 68
Almohads, *see* Muwaḥḥidūn
Almoravids, *see* Murabitun
Amīr, *see* Caliphs; Imām
Anas ibn Malik 23
Anṣari kamishan 103, 122
Arab countries 14, 128, 132
Arab nationalism 79–81
Aristotle 17, 82–3
Army government 13
Asad, Muhammad 89, 99–100, 102–103
Ash'arī, abū al-Ḥasan, 'Alī al- 34, 95, 97
Atatürk, Mustafa Kemal 3, 94
'Aṭṭās, Sayyid Muḥammad Naqīb al- 40
Augustine, Saint 3
Austin, John 47, 60, 87
Authority 36–7, 38, 95, 108–9, 111–3, 123
  see also Legitimacy
Avicenna, *see* Ibn Sina
'Awdah, 'Abd al-Qādir 102
Azhar, al- 26, 80, 81, 123, 125

Baghdadī 95, 97
Bangladesh 6
Bani Ṣadr, Abū al-Ḥasan 119
Banna, Haṣan al- 79, 98
Baqillānī 98
Bay'ah 85, 91–2, 114
Bazzāz, 'Abd al-Rahman al 79
Bhutto, Zulfikar Ali 30
Bodin, Jean 86
Bosnia 106
Bourgiba, Habib 3
British imperialism 10–11, 128
Brunei 30

Caliphate
  abolition (in 1924), 86, 94, 98
  denied by 'Abd al-Rāziq 26

fragmentation 75–6
Islamic political theory 95–9
substitute for the Prophet 24, 74
see also Khilāfah; Ottoman Caliphate
Caliphs 22, 29, 43, 54, 59–60, 75, 91–4, 121, 129, 137
qualifications and requirements of 97, 100–1, 103, 108–10, 112–16, 124
Carra de Vaux, Baron 9
Central Asia 16, 93
China 5
Christianity,
Islam and 9, 69, 129
secularism and 3, 8–9, 44
Church and state 1, 2, 8, 138
Civil liberties 14, 87–9
Colonialism
political effects of 82
secularization 9–11, 77, 78
Constitution, Islamic 118–20, 122–3
see also Government, Islamic; Madinah, constitution
Consultative assembly, *see Majlis al-shūrā*
Crusades 46

Dahl, Robert A. 18, 84
Dār al-Islām and *dār al-ḥarb* 72, 75, 76, 142
Da'wah 134
Democracy,
Christianity and 3
Islam and 106
values and 40
Deutscher, Irwin 35
Dīn 50
Dīwan al-maẓālim 117–18

Easton, David 18, 38
Economics
Islamic 39
state and 2
Education
colonial 10–11
Islamic 10
Elections 2, 12–13, 101, 104–5, 110, 113–14, 115
Enayat, Hamid 27, 94
Environmental destruction 42
Epistemology, *see* Knowledge
Equality 89, 91
Evil, *see* Good and evil
Executive, Chief, *see* Caliphs; Imām

Faith 41, 127, 139, 145
Family 38
Farūqi, Ismā'īl al- 37–8, 66, 76, 128
Fascism 19
Fiqh 48–9, 61, 143
Force, *see* Power
Framework of an Islamic state (document) 155–67
Freedom, *see* Civil liberties
Fulani, *see* Sokoto; Nigeria
Fundamentalism, Christian 127
Islamic 28, 30, 79, 113, 129–30, 132–3, 138–9 terminology discussed 126–8
Fuqahā', see 'Ulamā'

Gejendragadkar, P. B. 5
Ghazālī, Abū Hamīd al- 24, 31, 34, 95, 97, 111–12, 114
God, *see* Allah
Good and evil
Islamic political theory 19–20, 37, 42
see also Qur'ān, enjoining good and forbidding evil
Western political theory 17–19
Government
branches of 2, 13, 100–3
Islamic 61, 99–106, 155–67
see also Caliphate; Caliphs, qualifications and requirements of; Imām; Qur'ān, political teachings
military 13, 111

Haddad, Yvonne 25
Ḥadith, *see* Sunnah
Ḥajj 19, 68, 72
Ḥalāl and *ḥarām* 42, 45, 57, 58–9

Halpern, Manfred 23
Ḥamīdullah, Muhammad 65
Harūn al-Rashīd 75
Hasan al-Basri, al- 93
Hausaland, *see* Nigeria; Sokoto
Head of state, *see* Caliphs; Imām
Hijrah 20, 21, 63, 90, 134
Hobbes, Thomas 47
Hodgson, Marshall 76, 120
Holyoake, Jacob 1
Ḥusrī, Abū Khaldūn Satī'al- 80

'Ibādah 40, 41, 45
Ibn Ḥanbal, Ahmad 36, 55
Ibn Jamā'ah 97, 111 112
Ibn Khaldūn 24, 29, 34, 44, 70, 94, 96, 97, 113
Ibn Qayyim al-Jawzīyah 52
Ibn Qutaybah 20
Ibn Sīna 27, 112, 114–15
Ibn Taymīyah 37, 70–1, 76, 96, 97, 98, 112–13
Ibn Ṭūmart 24
Ijmā' 29, 52, 54–5, 68, 101
Ijtihād 6, 52, 53–6, 59, 62, 92, 100, 101, 127, 132
Ikhwān al-Muslimūn, al-, *see* Muslim Brotherhood
'Ilm, see Knowledge
Ilyās, Maulānā Muhammad 126, 132, 133
Imām 20, 95–7, 116, 120, 136, 138, 145
  see also Caliphate; Caliphs, qualifications and requirements of
Impeachment 108, 113–25
India 5, 94, 133
Injustice 20, 33, 42, 45, 109, 112, 153
  see also Justice
Instrumentalism 36
Iqbāl, Muhammad 7, 21, 28, 53, 55, 90, 101, 113, 116
Iran 30, 60, 94, 118–20, 126, 128–9, 132, 133, 136–8
Iraq 106
Isaak, Alan C. 18
Islāh, see Fundamentalism, Islamic
Islam
  Christianity and 9
  essence of the Ummah 66
  political theory of, defined 19–21, 31, 36, 85–90
  reason and 34, 53
  secularism and 1, 6–7, 25–7, 61
  universality 45, 66–7, 78, 81, 82, 85
Islamic Council of Europe 122–3
Islamic Development Bank 81
Islamic movements, 20th century, *see* Fundamentalism, Islamic
Israel 81, 137
Istiḥsān 54
Istiṣḥāb 54
Istislāḥ 42, 54

Jamā'at-e Islāmī 30, 126, 132, 135–6, 138
Jefferson, Thomas 2
Jews 64–6, 69
Jihād 21, 68, 69, 86, 129–30, 134, 135, 137, 139
Johnson, Andrew 108
Judiciary 14, 102–3, 117–18
Jurists, Muslim, *see* 'Ulamā'
Justice 42, 69, 87, 88, 97, 106, 109, 113, 114, 141
  see also Injustice

Kalam 34
Kashmir 36, 37
Kerr, Malcolm 27
Khallāf, 'Abd al-Wahhāb 50
Khan, Sayyid Ahmad 25
Khawārij 95, 97, 146
Khilāfah 28, 40, 41, 45, 47, 62, 68, 82, 86, 91, 146
  see also Caliphate
Khomeini, Ruḥ Allāh 30, 60, 119, 126, 129, 136–8
Khulafā', see Caliphs
Knowledge
  Islamic way of 35, 41–2, 45
  required of imam 97, 114
Kuffār, see Unbelievers
Kurdi, 'Abd al-Qādir 103, 117
Kuwait 106

Laski, Harold 107
Lasswell, Harold 18, 36
Law,
  Islamic 46–8
  Western concepts of 46–8, 60
Lawrence, Bruce 127
Leadership Council 118–20
Learning
  Islamic 43
  Western 10
Legislatures 13, 101–2, 107–8, 123
Legitimacy 115–16
  see also Authority
Liberalism 1–2

Macaulay, Thomas Babington 10
Machiavelli, Niccolō 83, 97
Madīnah 21, 29, 32, 43, 93, 95
  constitution 65–6, 72, 90–1
Mahdīyah 24, 131
Majlis al-shūrā 120–3
Makkah 72
Malik ibn Anas 55
Manẓoor, Parvez 58
Marx, Karl 3–5, 43, 83
Materialism 19, 132
Māturīdī 34
Māwardī 24, 36, 95–7, 98, 111, 112, 114, 117
Mawdūdī, Sayyid Abul A'la 20, 28, 29, 37, 59, 69, 79, 98–9, 102, 111, 113, 122, 126, 129–30, 135–6, 138
Mecca, *see* Makkah
Medina, *see* Madinah
Methodology, Islamic 32
Mill, John Stuart 2, 107
Model of an Islamic Constitution (document) 122–3, 169–85
Modernisation,
Modernism
  Christian 127
  Islamic 25–8
Monarchy 101
Morality
  political 17–18, 21, 36, 58, 88, 95
  social 33, 47

Movements, Islamic, 20th century
  anti-colonial 82, 132
  see also Fundamentalism, Islamic
Mu'ādh ibn Jabal 55, 110, 116
Mu'āwīyah ibn Abī Sufyān 93
Mughals 94
Muḥammad Aḥmad ibn 'Abd Allāh 131
Muḥammad ibn 'Abd al-Wahhāb 130
Muḥammad, Prophet
  caliphate as substitute for 24
  farewell sermon 72–4
  political leadership 21, 25–6, 43, 71–4, 88, 89, 90–1
  Sharī'ah and 49, 52–3, 62
  uswah ḥasanah 21, 53, 109
Mujaddid 130, 139
Mujibur Rahman 6
Muktafī li-Amr Allāh, al- 121
Murabiṭūn 24
Murad, Khurram 54
Muslim Brotherhood 30, 80, 131–2
Muslim countries 77, 95, 133
  economic conditions 14–15
Muslims,
  relations with unbelievers 64–6
  society, dual or hybrid 128
  society, organic 17, 38
  solidarity 19, 58, 74, 76; *see also* Ummah
  westernised 11–12, 27, 46, 138
Mu'tazilah 95–6
Muwahhidūn 24

Nahḍah, see Fundamentalism, Islamic
Naṣr, Seyyed Hossein 33, 39–40
Nationalism
  colonialism and 12
  Islam and 63, 77–81, 94, 132
Nation-states
  division of Muslims between 12, 95
  Western political theory 82, 86
Nehru, Jawaharlal 10–11
Neo-normativism, *see* Fundamentalism, Islamic

Nigeria 6, 10, 130–1
see also Sokoto
Nixon, Richard 108
Nizām al-Mulk 24, 112

Obedience, *see* Authority
Organization of Islamic Conference 81, 132
Ottoman caliphate 75, 81, 94, 120

Pahlavī, Muhammad Rizā 30, 129, 133, 137
Pakistan 30, 100, 103, 122, 126, 135–6
Palestine 37, 128–9
Patriotism 85
Perfect Man 43
Philosophers, Muslim 24, 27
Plato 17, 82–3
Political science
Islamic 36
values and, 39–40, 44, 98
see also Government, Islamic; Qur'ān, political teachings
Political system, Islamic, *see* Government, Islamic
Politics
defined 17–19, 36
shunned by Tablīghī Jamā'at 134
Positivism 32
Power
Islamic political theory 20–1, 70, 111–12
Western political theory 18–19, 36, 83–4
Prayer 19, 90, 106, 133–34
Press 2, 14
Public interest, *see* Istiṣlāh
Punishment 50–1, 59, 86

Qāḍi, see judiciary
Qāhir bi-Allāh, al- 21, 118
Qiyās 54–5
Qūr'ān
Arabic 80
enjoining good and forbidding evil 20, 37, 45, 71
family 38
jihād 21
knowledge 35
political teachings 86–90, 106
Prophet Muḥammad 21, 26, 88, 89
reason 34
Sharī'ah 49, 50, 51–3, 57, 59
Ummah 63, 64–5, 67, 68–70
Qurṭubī 49, 70
Quṭb, Sayyid 28, 43, 79, 98, 100, 102, 113

Rahman, Fazlur 28, 50, 122
Rashīd Riḍā, Muhammad 121, 122
Rationalism 33–4
Rāzī, Fakhr al-Din al- 37
Religion
liberalism and 2
Mardism and 4–5
organic 17, 33, 58
separation from temporal realm 17, 21, 33, 37–8, 106
see also Church and state
Resources, allocation of 18, 88
Revelation 35, 45, 53, 95, 129
Roberty, Eugene de 9
Rosenthal, Erwin 25, 27, 34, 65, 76, 82

Safāvids 94, 137
Ṣalāt, see Prayer
Samarqandi, Abū al-Layth al- 23
Saudi Arabia 60, 130
Schattschneider, E. E. 17
Science
Islamic 32, 34–5
modern 1–2, 33, 35, 44
Secularism
Christianity and 3, 8–9, 44
defined 1
Islam and 1, 6–7, 25–7, 61, 132
Islamic political theory 25–8
Marxist 3–5
Third World 5–6
Shāfi'i, Muhammad ibn Idris al- 23, 55
Shah, the, *see* Pahlavi, Muhammad Riza

Shahādah 65, 67, 69, 72, 113, 134, 150
Sharī'ah
  caliphs and 22, 29, 54, 59–60, 92, 94, 100, 110, 115
  defined 49–51
  divine origin 48, 57, 61–2
  individualism and collectivism in 68
  law and 46–8
  legislation 31, 85
  modern applications 60–1
  religious life of Muslims 24, 133
  sharī'ah and 48
  sources 51–5, 88
  temporal and spiritual in 21, 28, 29, 100
  unifying the Ummah 58, 76, 81
Sharī'atī,'Alī 138
Shī'ah 95, 118–20, 138, 150
Shūrā 52, 54, 68, 85, 87, 89–90, 91, 92, 93, 95, 100–6, 115, 120–3, 150
Smith, Donald E. 17
Smith, Wilfred, Cantwell 3, 25
Social science 32–4, 35
Sokoto 121–2, 130–1
Somalis 12
Soviet Union 5, 128
Spirituality 23
State
  Islamic political theory 85–6
  Islamic, *see* Government, Islamic
  secular 2, 13
  western political theory 17–19, 82–5
Stockholm Seminar on Knowledge and Values 40
Sudan 24, 77, 131
Sufism 23, 24, 41, 130
Sulaiman, Ibraheem 57
Shari'ah 51–3

Ṭabarī 50, 70
Tablīghī Jamā'at 132, 133–4, 138
Ṭāghūt 20
Tajdīd, see Fundamentalism, Islamic
Taqlīd 25, 56, 62, 132
Taqwā 89, 91
Tawḥīd 6–7, 20, 28, 40–1, 45, 62, 68, 78, 85, 87, 129, 151
Toleration, Religious 94
Totalitarianism 19
Tunisia 3
Turābī, Hasan al- 98, 101–3
Turkey
  Islamic parties 16
  Islamic reawakening 30
  legal system 60
  secularism 3, 77, 94

Uhud, Battle of 91
'Ulamā' 11, 23, 27, 43–4, 54, 62, 76, 81, 82, 95–98, 100, 111–13, 120, 133, 138
'Umar ibn 'Abd al-'Azīz 22
'Umar ibn al-Khaṭṭāb, 20, 36, 92, 97, 110, 115
Umayyads 22, 29, 60, 75, 93, 110, 117
Ummah
  defined 63–8
  organic unity 28, 38–9, 67–8, 72, 81, 129
  raison d'être 68–71
Unbelievers 64–6
United States of America 104, 108, 127, 137
'Urf 54, 152
'Uthmān dan Fodio 131
'Uthmān ibn 'Affān 22, 92, 97, 110
Utopianism 7, 43, 84

Values 39–40, 43, 98
Vilāyet-i faqīh 118–20, 137
Voll, John O. 127

Wahhabism 130
Waterhouse 8
Watt, William Montgomery 65
Weber, Max 33, 83–4
Westernisation 10–12, 27, 30, 60
Worship, *see 'Ibādah*

Yazid ibn Mu'āwīyah 93

Zakāh (or *zakāt*) 19, 70, 71, 77, 86, 90, 106, 153
Zamakhshari 109
Zia ul-Haq 30, 122, 136
Zia ur Rahman 6
Zionism 128
Ẓulm, *see* Injustice